GREAT WOMEN OF MACKINAC

1800–1950

GREAT WOMEN OF MACKINAC

1800–1950

Melissa Croghan

MICHIGAN STATE UNIVERSITY PRESS | *East Lansing*

Michigan State University Press
East Lansing, Michigan 48823-5245

Library of Congress Cataloging-in-Publication Data
Names: Croghan, Melissa, author.
Title: Great women of Mackinac, 1800–1950 / Melissa Croghan.
Description: East Lansing : Michigan State University Press, 2023. |
Includes bibliographical references and index.
Identifiers: LCCN 2022024422 | ISBN 9781611864533 (paperback) | ISBN
9781609177287 (PDF) | ISBN 9781628954968 (ePub) | ISBN 9781628964905 (Kindle)
Subjects: LCSH: Women—Michigan—Mackinac Island—History.
Classification: LCC HQ1438.M5 C76 2023 | DDC
305.4092/2774923—dc23/eng/20220602
LC record available at https://lccn.loc.gov/2022024422

Cover design by Erin Kirk.
Cover art: *Elizabeth Mitchell*, oil portrait by Melissa Croghan, 2019.

Visit Michigan State University Press at *www.msupress.org*

To Calla, Rafe, Luca, and Maddie

Contents

Part III. The Continuum: Into the Twentieth Century

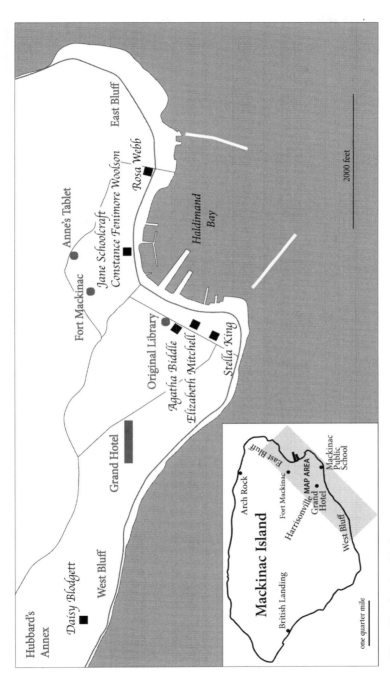

Hubbard's
Annex

Daisy Blodgett

West Bluff

Grand Hotel

Original Library

Agatha Biddle
Elizabeth Mitchell

Stella King

Fort Mackinac

Jane Schoolcraft
Constance Fenimore Woolson

Anne's Tablet

Rosa Webb

East Bluff

Haldimand
Bay

2000 feet

Mackinac Island

Arch Rock

British Landing

East Bluff

Fort Mackinac

Harrisonville MAP AREA

Grand
Hotel

West Bluff

Mackinac
Public
School

one quarter mile

1. Where They Lived on Mackinac.

MAP BY AUTHOR.

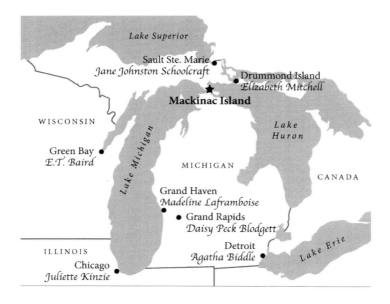

2. Their Movements to and from Mackinac.

MAP BY AUTHOR.

Introduction

Thirteen singular women were leaders on Mackinac Island in the nineteenth and early twentieth centuries. Their linked visions define this region of the western Great Lakes, with each woman emerging as a distinctive figure in American history. The part they played brings a new understanding to an island renowned for its natural beauty, picturesque forts, and unique horse culture. Missing from the postcard is the story of diversity and the women at the very heart of the Mackinac community.

Great Women of Mackinac, 1800–1950 is an attempt to recognize the overlooked women of Mackinac Island, Michigan, and the Great Lakes. More than half of these leaders were Anishinaabe. For instance, there was Jane Schoolcraft, an Ojibwe woman living on Mackinac in the 1830s. While she was writing her heart out about the losses her Native people endured, her husband, Indian agent Henry Schoolcraft, was crafting the treaty that robbed the Anishinaabe of sixteen million acres. Henry was not only working against her people, but unbeknownst to Schoolcraft, stealing her written words and claiming authorship. Right up the street from where Schoolcraft lived was another Native woman, Agatha Biddle. She and husband Edward, who was supportive of his wife and the Anishinaabe, were having meetings about the possibility of this same treaty in 1836 that would take three quarters of current-day Michigan from the Indigenous people. There is no record of Agatha Biddle and Jane Schoolcraft being friends, but surely they were acquaintances in this small community. It is intriguing to imagine the substance of their conversations. There was also the most famous fur trader of this age, Madeline Laframboise, and naturally she would have known both Jane and Agatha. Again, it was a small town, and the stories, and their cultural and political connections rippled across history.

A particular challenge in my project has been how few written records there are of women in the Western Great Lakes of the nineteenth century. In contrast, the East Coast saw a torrent of letters by those who rose in stature, whether it was Margaret Fuller or Harriet Beecher Stowe. Even there, the job of restoring the history of women has been tough; in the old Northwest it was truly daunting, for there is a paucity of source material on Mackinac Island residents who were women. Three of the women I have documented could not read or write, and others left few records behind.[1] Tragedies from a historian's perspective occurred as well. Though Daisy Blodgett was a prodigious letter writer, her communications had been stored in ten cooper barrels and then disposed of after her death. With this dearth of records pertaining to many of the women in this study, I did not have the lively discourse commonly available to biographers when writing about their subjects. This meant I had to go about my research in a different way. I often started with a couple of known facts. With Madeline Laframboise, for instance, I knew that her husband was murdered and that some years later she had become a well-known fur trader and humanitarian. Taking the interpolation of the two, I went forward and began digging for the truth and life that lay between.

There are three sets of women in this history, with the story of each presented chronologically. The first group connects the lives of five Native leaders: Elizabeth Mitchell, Madeline Laframboise, Therese Schindler, Agatha Biddle, and Elizabeth T. Baird. Part II examines a literature of witness as represented by writers Juliette Kinzie, Jane Schoolcraft, Anna Jameson, and Margaret Fuller. The third set of women, moving from the late nineteenth to the early twentieth century, includes Constance Fenimore Woolson, Rosa Truscott Webb, Daisy Blodgett, and Stella King. Beyond their success in commerce or the written word, the women of Mackinac were community caregivers and educators. How they were able to safeguard island life may be defined in a single word: *connection*. Whether Native or white, laws did not permit these women to hold positions in local government, and yet they banded together to serve the common good of Mackinac. How they supported and empowered one another forms the through line of this study.

Who They Were

The focus of my intergenerational biographies begins in the 1800s, though the enduring society of Mackinac began more than a thousand years beforehand with the Indigenous population. Following the Cherokee and the Navajo, the Anishinaabe of the Great Lakes and Canada were the most populous people in North America when the Euro-Americans arrived.[2] The Native Americans did not for the most part read and write in English or French, the languages commonly in use for written documents. Many of their stories have been forgotten, in particular those of the Native women.

Chapter 1 focuses on the first of these extraordinary leaders. Elizabeth Mitchell, who mentored the younger Madeline Laframboise, was a Mackinac farmer and fur trader. The townspeople respected her wisdom and guidance. This "Lady of Flowers," as her workers called her, also had a daring side that got her in trouble during the War of 1812. She suffered the threat of imprisonment for what she believed in, including the defense of her British loyalist husband.

Chapter 2 takes up the dynamic family of Laframboise, who leaned on her older sister, Therese Schindler. Therese's granddaughter, Elizabeth Therese Baird, looked up to all three women and she left a valuable record of Mackinac. Baird was an integral part of that dynamic family connection on Mackinac. As a child, she was the favorite of her great aunt Madeline Laframboise, and she grew up on the island. Her book, *O-De-Jit-Wa-Win-Ning; or Contes du Temps Passe: Reminiscences of Early Days on Mackinac*, was published in 1886–1887 and highlights her childhood years living on the island, 1800–1814.[3] The memoir includes close observations of Laframboise and Schindler, as well as the colorful and occasionally controversial Elizabeth Mitchell. As a Native woman herself, E. T. Baird writes with honesty about factions among the Anishinaabe of the Lake region, and trenchantly about the diversity and class system on Mackinac. She gives lively interpretations of weddings and daily interactions of residents in that sometimes contentious community.

Of this group of Native residents, Laframboise is the most well-known. Keeping her in contemporary thought is the physical evidence of the home she built on Mackinac and her influence on the construction of Ste. Anne's church. Both buildings are attractions today in a prominent part of the marina and downtown area. Largely neglected in history is her sister—comrade in arms, so to speak—Therese Schindler. The two lived side by side for many years between Main and Market Streets on Mackinac. Schindler's maple sugar business in the Great Lakes and her status as an entrepreneur in the fur trade were well-respected in her lifetime. Chapter 2 also explores the question of whether Madeline and Therese worked together or were rivals, and the substance of their impact on commerce and philanthropy.

A fourth Indigenous woman, Agatha Biddle, is the subject of chapter 3. She grew up on Mackinac with her Odawa mother and boisterous stepfather in the early tumultuous years of the nineteenth century. Agatha would surmount great difficulties and follow the example of the successful Marcot sisters, Madeline and Therese, as a businesswoman and humanitarian. Later when married, she juggled her steadfast work on behalf of Native women with the travail of a daughter whose path led to difficult life choices. Focused and courageous, Biddle would make a key impact on the Treaty of Detroit in 1855, when she stood as a witness for the Anishinaabe's hunting and fishing rights in Michigan.[4]

Chapter 4 follows the adventures of pioneer Juliette Kinzie, whose social history, *Wau-Bun*, looks back at her time on Mackinac and in Great Lakes country in 1830. In all likelihood Kinzie's husband, John, who had clerked for John Jacob Astor at the warehouse of the American Fur Company on the island, introduced her to Madeline Laframboise. Kinzie met and wrote about her connection with Laframboise.

Two Mackinac Anishinaabe have emerged as stellar literary figures. Along with Elizabeth Therese Baird, Jane Johnston Schoolcraft lived on Mackinac during a time when the island saw a mix of cultures unequaled today. Schoolcraft left behind a hidden trove of literature and song. She was a remarkable poet and author of Native stories. Her birth name, always used by her mother and siblings, was Bamewawage-zhikaquay, the translation of which is *The Sound the Stars Make Rushing through the Sky*. She and writer Anna Jameson figure in chapter 5. Jameson, who befriended Schoolcraft and stayed at her family homes, both on Mackinac and in Sault Ste. Marie, was an original thinker whose lively prose was published in an unforgettable travel history of the region.

The writings of Harriet Martineau, along with Anna Jameson's book about Schoolcraft and the Great Lakes in 1837 became the catalyst for author Margaret Fuller's journey to Mackinac. Chapter 6 highlights the powerhouse Fuller. She was also greatly inspired by "the poesy" of Native poet Jane Schoolcraft, and the former would acknowledge the loss of the Mackinac poet in *Summer on the Lakes*.[5]

Chapters 7 and 8 recognize two women who loved Mackinac and contributed to its growth in the late nineteenth century. The books and articles by Constance

Fenimore Woolson raised the profile of Mackinac as a tourist destination, while Rosa Truscott Webb's community action preserved the local and small-town identity of the island. Among her accomplishments, Webb is the founder of the Mackinac Island Public Library and the first community center on the island.

In an intriguing connection, Woolson lived in the same house Schoolcraft did thirty years earlier. Woolson's writerly talents brought her fame, but it is her connection to Mackinac and contribution to diversity in American literature that deserves attention. The island was the setting of her bestselling book, *Anne*.[6] The titular character of Woolson's novel is a white girl whose New Englander father marries a Native woman. Anne grows close to her Native siblings and stepmother. This history of the women of Mackinac calls attention to the mixed-race family as protagonists in that novel and examines its literary and historical value.

From the nineteenth to early twentieth centuries, the Mackinac women understood the benefit of teamwork. Chapter 9 examines the lives and contributions of Daisy Peck Blodgett and Stella King. Blodgett, born in Atlanta during the Civil War, married a Michigan lumber baron, Delos, who was already established on Mackinac. She and Delos lived on Mackinac during the summers, and in the 1930s she started a charity fundraiser for a desperately needed medical center. After several years of running the "Daisy Day" fundraiser, she asked Stella King, a nurse who lived in town, to join her in the effort. Despite a still-existing class system, the story of this pair working together is powerful.

New information late in my research suggests the strong possibility that Stella King was Anishinaabe. Learning of her Native identity tipped the balance of my thirteen women; I was no longer writing about seven white women and six Anishinaabe, but the reverse number. No matter whether white or Native, all subjects in this study fall under the larger umbrella of great women on Mackinac, with their specific struggles, their connection to one another, and mutual triumphs.

King had been the only healthcare provider living on the island for many years, and there are Native men and women today who count themselves among those whom Stella single-handedly delivered into this world.[7] The revelation of her background, along with her career as island nurse, fundraiser, and entrepreneur, deserves consideration.[8] King and Blodgett make up the final chapter, bringing the arc of Great Lakes women through World War I and II. Even under the lash of gender discrimination, each of these figures were innovative, courageous, and persevering.

The Island's Past and Present

Mackinac is situated between the Upper and Lower Peninsulas of Michigan in Lake Huron, one of the five Great Lakes in North America. Connecting Lake Michigan and Huron is the Straits of Mackinac, through which freighters travel from the St. Lawrence waterway to Duluth, Minnesota, or Detroit. Mackinac Island forms one of the boundaries of this shipping channel. On the island there are two bluffs that stand above a shapely harbor and town. On the east and west bluffs are a series of large Victorian cottages that are summer homes only. They can be viewed from the water and when touring the island on foot, bicycle, or horseback. Year-round residents live in town and in the village near the center of the island. There is also the picturesque Fort Mackinac and above it, at the highest point of the island, Fort Holmes. A ban on cars guarantees a pollution-free environment. With its wildflower- and cedar-clad trails and views atop the steep cliffs, Mackinac is a visual paradise. That 80 percent of the island is a Michigan State Park further ensures its pristine beauty.

The island is just eight miles in circumference, but this small size invites easy explorations of its beauty spots. Numerous cultural events occur in the summer season, though the winter population is also busy with library activities, concerts, winter festivals, and often an annual musical. There is a thriving public school, and the community center provides winter bingo and a host of other activities. In winter, a Christmas-tree trail across the ice marks safe passage to the mainland. Residents generally use snowmobiles to cross over, and in summer people travel by ferryboat.

The Anishinaabe first named Mackinac "Mishimiknaak" or "Great Turtle," because it resembled the profile of a turtle's long head and high rounded back. Artifacts pointing to a Native population date back more than seven hundred years before the first white explorers set foot on "The Great Turtle" in the seventeenth century. Many Native nations would come to worship the Great Spirit, or Gitchee Manitou, who is said to inhabit the island. Though greatly reduced in number, there are Native residents on Mackinac today.

The Straits region has a rich history, from its prominence as a meeting and trading place of Native people to a land of battle over resources and trade among the Anishinaabe and European powers. For nearly three hundred years, beginning in the sixteenth century, Europeans and Americans recruited Native people of North America as commercial partners and allies in their conflicts over control of the region. Many of the Native families were British loyalists and the warriors fought against the Americans in the American Revolution. Exploited mercilessly in war and trade by

Europeans and Americans, the Native people would in turn exploit Euro-Americans to advance their own positions of power.[9] They were strategists themselves and remained fluid in their allegiances.

Though the Jay Treaty in 1796 was a quiet transition that conferred the occupation of Fort Mackinac to the Americans, unrest would follow in the subsequent decades, resulting in the War of 1812 and British control of Mackinac until 1815.[10] The actions of Elizabeth Mitchell, Madeline Laframboise, and Agatha Biddle during these war years are set forth in their respective chronological chapters. Their disputes and diplomacy lend insight into the stance of residents during the turmoil. When Mackinac was deeded back to the Americans, the fort no longer had a role in defending or protecting the borders of American territory. Local residents on Mackinac went forward in commerce and in raising their families.

The fur trade was the primary commerce in the Great Lakes region during the earlier age of conflicts. Euro-American fishermen and other early settlers had worn deerskin coats since the seventeenth century, the time when the trade in furs got its start. Buying and selling animal furs became a lucrative business once Europeans began to covet beaver felt hats. In the Lake country, the Anishinaabe controlled the hunting and trapping of fur-bearing animals. While the men went after the larger animals such as beaver, Native women hunted small creatures such as martin.[11] The Native women cleaned and processed the pelts and in many instances became the ones who did business with the white traders. Elizabeth Mitchell along with Madeline Laframboise and Therese Schindler emerge as women who kept an eye on opportunity for resourceful trading with many different groups of Native people and the English, French, and Americans.[12]

With the arrival of John Jacob Astor's American Fur Company in 1815, Mackinac Island became the hub of fur trade in North America. Lake region trappers received payment in European goods such as kettles and tools, or whiskey and guns. The pelts were highly prized in the manufacturing of beaver hats and robes. The value of Mackinac traders such as Madeline Laframboise, Therese Schindler, and Elizabeth Mitchell is that they were trusted brokers in this complicated process. They spoke Native languages and were able to give Native trappers knowledgeable and honest information as to what their pelts were worth. The next step of the process saw these same women selling the furs to agents who sent them to European markets.

Traders such as Laframboise would live to see the industry wane by the 1830s. By mid-century, commerce on the island was dominated by commercial fishing and businesses supplying the needs of Fort Mackinac and its garrison. In the subsequent decades, lumbering and mining joined fishing as the mainstays of the economy in the rest of the Great Lakes region. In 1895, the Michigan State Legislature established Mackinac as a state park. The island was attracting more tourists than earlier in the century. Books written by Juliette Kinzie, Harriet Martineau, Margaret Fuller, and Constance Fenimore Woolson in the nineteenth century helped create a fascination among readers for Mackinac, which in turn encouraged the popular steamship and then rail travel to the region.

Their Importance to Mackinac

Each of the women who figure in this study wrote about or lived and worked on the island, and given the geographic reach of their livelihoods north and south on the lakes, they are rightly described as women of Mackinac and the Great Lakes. We might picture Laframboise in her longboat heaped with furs as she traveled the two hundred miles from Grand Haven, Michigan, to Mackinac; Mitchell paddling with provisions for those living on Drummond Island across waters still famous for their treacherous currents, or Jane Schoolcraft heading to the Upper Peninsula to see her mother, Ozhaguscodaywayquay.

Though Native women had long navigated the freshwater seas, it was not until the mid-nineteenth century that middle-class white women traveled without a chaperone. It was still considered a scandalous and daring act. Author Juliette Kinzie made her way to Mackinac and other parts of the Great Lakes by sailing schooner. Woolson would travel by steamer, but even that mode of transportation could be a dangerous proposition. Given ferocious lake storms and boiler explosions, one or the other could sink the ship. A journey by sailing vessel, canoe, or bateau (the flat-bottomed boat often used by fur traders) was even more fraught. Writers Jane Schoolcraft, Anna Jameson, and Margaret Fuller risked any number of dangers in their bateaux travels across Lakes Huron, Michigan, and Superior.

Some fifty years after Mitchell and Schoolcraft survived the War of 1812, Constance Fenimore Woolson would call attention to the Great Lakes fur trade in pieces that were published in *Putnam's*, a highly respected periodical published in New York.[13] Even in later life, as an expat traveling with her best friend, author Henry James, she wrote longingly of returning to that little island of entrancing beauty.[14] Woolson's colorful stories of the fur-trade era attracted Victorian and Edwardian visitors. Some of her readers, largely women, were interested in Mackinac as a summer respite. They became new residents of the island and would lay the groundwork for a thriving community in the twentieth century.

This community building was not an easy proposition; bold determination and careful tactics were required. Both white and Native women in the nineteenth and early twentieth centuries understood that because of their sex, they were born outsiders—excluded from the mainstream professions and lawmaking bodies in the land—and the Native women also experienced marginalization as American colonization undermined Anishinaabe power in their homelands. They recognized that they had to work hard to change society. The key to their success lay in working together and in not giving up. Whether it was Elizabeth Mitchell, threatened with prison for communicating with Native friends, or Laframboise and Schindler, who as widowed Native women found themselves excluded from the island's elite social gatherings, they persevered and were resourceful in their commerce on Mackinac. Poet and songwriter Jane Schoolcraft felt isolated, gawked at for being a Native woman during most of the nine years she spent on Mackinac. Thankfully for her future readers, she learned to turn her outsider status into art.

Social historian Margaret Fuller recognized that women of every race and creed were excluded from universities and from professions such as law, medicine, and government, all of which left women undeniably outside the mainstream of decision making in America. Her books called attention to this inequity. As for Daisy Peck Blodgett, she adopted an "I'll show you" attitude that led her to become president of an institution, the D. A. Blodgett Home for Children, and to start the first fundraiser for a medical center on Mackinac. Rosa Webb, activist on Mackinac in the early part of the twentieth century, felt the sting of being left out of decision making that could bring about important institutions like a community center and a library. She wrote beseechingly to a well-off male summer resident who sat on several island boards. She received support from him, but no others.[15] That was when she decided to band together with a number of women who would help her break through the "outsider" barriers and achieve goals for the good of the community.

Anishinaabe Women Leaders

Each group of women worked together. With few legal rights of their own, they found maverick ways to assert themselves and effect change. In the early nineteenth century on Mackinac, Elizabeth Mitchell, Madeline Marcot Laframboise, and her sister, Therese Marcot Schindler, stand out among the many Native women active in the fur trade in the Mackinac region.[16] The old Northwest benefited from its diverse population, and yet its people had the challenge of surviving a dangerous, ever-changing political landscape. Between the Battle of Mackinac that took place in the War of 1812 and the island's ascendency as a fur-trade center, it had gained a reputation as a wild and wooly place. Drama and ribald characters aside, it was also filled with racism, war, and misogyny. The kinships of Native women were advantageous to the white, male fur traders who married them in order to obtain the goodwill of the Native hunters and trappers in the business. However, the advantages did not always translate to the women. Many were treated as second-class citizens by the peers of their husbands. Scholar Karen Marrero writes of the manner in which French traders infantilized their Indigenous wives and sought to control their status.[17]

Nonetheless, these women were able to retain agency for several reasons. In her book about French Indigenous families of Detroit, Marrero points out the power these women had owing to a simple population equation. Men outnumbered women in the region, and the latter understood that they were in demand and ostensibly could make fair demands. This outsider status also conferred a certain freedom on some fortunate Indigenous women. It was a forced freedom, to be sure, one based on institutional racism. Yet they navigated "a multitude of gender norms of their nations" and were able to "defy the state that sought to hold them to European ideals of womanhood."[18] Additionally, it was not unusual for the husbands of Native women to perish or be away in travel for long periods. In these cases, women such as Mitchell, Laframboise, Schindler, and Biddle turned their fledgling fur-trading operations into wealth and became key businesspeople in the region.

Of the nineteenth-century Indigenous women in this study, only Jane School-craft and E. T. Baird could sign their own names. Though Madeline Laframboise most likely learned to read late in life, she signed all her trade documents and contracts, even her personal will, with an X mark, indicating that she did not write in the English language.[19] Rather than refer to these society-changing women as illiterate, a stance historians have often adopted, attention must be paid to the power of language held by Indigenous people. Their diverse manner of speech was little understood by Euro-Americans. While Europeans spoke two or three dozen languages when they became a print culture, the Native people of America spoke hundreds of languages from completely different linguistic families.[20] Like language, religion too was shared in an oral tradition and was highly complex. Numerous creation stories were markedly different from Judaism, Islam, and Christianity. Native people in North America did not have writing systems. They preserved crucial cultural stories by memory passed on from generation to generation. The Anishinaabe used celebration chants, condolence rituals, dance, and dream-sharing to preserve information. Valuable records were created and saved on shellwork belts, shields, and painted animal hides. As girls who stitched deer hides for their family, the two sisters Therese Schindler and Madeline Laframboise, for example, may well have painted or sewn symbols and dramatic events into the fabric, a language that was understood by their kin.

One more key question caused me concern at the outset of this book: does a historian have the right to document the lives of a race other than her own? Over hundreds of years, records by white men writing about people of color have not always served their subjects well. Where is the line between cultural appropriation and rendering a history of the diverse voices in one's study? Above all, it lies in the respect of the lives and culture one is writing about.

As a white woman writing about Indigenous people, I have illustrated the nuances of their experiences to the best of my best ability, and it is my hope that the acclaim they deserve translates to the reader.[21] Whether they are mixed-race or white, my overriding subject is the women who emerged as leaders of the well-known Mackinac community.

Regarding the specific names of my subjects, I often refer to the women by their last names, as might be expected. In order to avoid confusion when bringing their spouses into these biographies, I reference the men by their first names. To wit: I speak of Henry when alluding to Jane Schoolcraft's husband, an Indian agent on Mackinac, or Edward, who was married to Agatha Biddle.

Presenting another question is the discussion of proper terminology when referring to Native people. Anishinaabe is the Indigenous name for their people in Canada and northeastern America. The different nations of Anishinaabe include the People of the Fire: the Odawa, Ojibwe, and Potawatomi.

The Nineteenth Century and Women as Leaders

In nineteenth-century Mackinac and forward in time, the resilience of its townspeople stands out. This includes the Native population and its perseverance as a culture. What has been largely ignored in the many histories about the wars and the fur trade have been the stories of the women who created the unifying infrastructure of society beginning in the early nineteenth century. From the disparate threads of the Native,

Euro-American, French, British, and mixed-race ethnicities, island residents built a strong and adaptive community.

More than half of the movers and shakers in this study were Anishinaabe, and the rest range from Euro-American Michiganders to one transplanted Southerner and an Englishwoman. This study encompasses fur traders, healthcare workers, educators, literary and travel writers, philanthropists, and social historians. The body of work by writers that contributes significantly to a literature of witness includes E. T. Baird, Juliette Kinzie, Jane Schoolcraft, Margaret Fuller, and Constance Fenimore Woolson.

Margaret Fuller is one such woman who stood as a witness to the Indigenous and Euro-American culture on Mackinac. A brilliant and multitalented author, she was the first woman to be a war correspondent and was sent abroad by Horace Greeley of the *New York Tribune*, where she covered Italy's fight for a new republic. Fuller was most famous for a book on equal rights for women, *Woman in the Nineteenth Century*, in which she declared that her sex should not be stuck in the home doing domestic duty if they had other callings.[22] Her comment "Let them [women] be sea captains if they will" could have been a foreshadowing of her intrepid journey north of Mackinac by canoe in the freshwater seas of Michigan.[23] Her fine study of Mackinac in *Summer on the Lakes* was the result of that trip. Of her meeting with Madeline Laframboise, she noted that the fur trader and islander was renowned as "a shrewd woman of business."[24]

The success of the women of Mackinac requires a definition of leadership that diverges in some ways from that of the standards applied to male leaders. For some women, being a leader meant focusing on relationships, working together to improve education; for others it meant humanitarian outreach; and for still others, it was facing down discrimination.

Wars framed the lives of the thirteen women in these biographies. Mitchell and Laframboise expanded their businesses during the War of 1812. Jane Schoolcraft, while traumatized by that same war and its repercussions in Sault Ste. Marie, went on to become a memorable American writer. Daisy Blodgett was born in Atlanta during the Civil War, and Woolson lived through it in the North. Though affected by such conflicts, these women were not wholly defined by them. My research revealed several key patterns. The most intriguing was the intersection of ethnicity and class in postwar eras. That confluence brought together such women as Jane Schoolcraft and Anna Jameson, and later in history, Daisy Blodgett and Stella King. The chaos and new orders that arose from the war years—post 1812, World War I, and World War II—resulted in a mix of women from different backgrounds on Mackinac.

That freedom to interact with those of a background unlike their own encouraged a percolation of new ideas and forward action. While it is crucial to pay attention to the ways history labeled women in the eras represented on Mackinac—Daisy Blodgett, a society lady, or Stella King, a nurse from the working class—it is time to put to bed such signifiers and pay attention to the manner in which they were, above all, hardworking women who would not allow themselves to be stereotyped.

The social histories here cannot possibly represent all who contributed to civic society on Mackinac and in the Great Lakes, but the women in this study emerged as leaders in those postwar years. Not one of them worked in a vacuum, and their empowerment of one another changed society, whether through the written word or local action.

Men were as important as women in the equation of equality for all. David Mitchell, Edward Biddle, John Kinzie, and Delos Blodgett played supportive roles in the lives of their wives, Elizabeth, Agatha, Juliette, and Daisy. The domination of men over women in general was less of a problem than the confused roles assigned to them. This was particularly true for middle- and upper-class white women. They were adored as if they were dolls; they were put on a pedestal and yet not allowed to own property or to vote and take part in society as active, equal members. Women were not permitted to go out into the world and hold office that made the laws of the land. If beaten by their husbands, they could not go to court to plead for help; it was the man's right to inflict such abomination. It was no wonder many women felt they were essentially kept under lock and key in the domestic sphere. The confusion arose when men went off for long periods, whether to hunt, go to war, or even spend long months in Congress. These same women took charge in their absence. Women managed and ran the farm, delivered babies, and galloped on horseback. They kept the financial records of family businesses and did heavy work of all manner. Yet they were expected to retreat when the men came home. Women were raised to present the role of passivity, to hide their endurance, courage, ambitions, and life of action. These mixed messages came to a head in the nineteenth century when they recognized that regardless of sex, all humans deserve the same freedoms. Books such as those by Margaret Fuller raised awareness. The Civil War, followed by the two World Wars, afforded women work opportunities like never before. The intellectual and emotional climate surrounding these periods gave women courage to step up their involvement in the world and to speak out for their rights. As such, the rich and complicated lives of these women are what make up the individual and overlapping stories in these nine chapters.

Connections

The phenomenon of kindred souls and professional contacts emerged as I began exploring stories of the Great Lakes. I had been researching Jane Schoolcraft, a lost voice, a critical Ojibwe writer. On an overcast day in late December, I sat in the Library of Congress, following a lead regarding Schoolcraft's pen name, which was mentioned occasionally in the papers of her husband. Going over that information once again, my eyes and ears perked up at something new. It was an offhand allusion to a friendship Schoolcraft had on Mackinac Island, Michigan, with a woman named Anna Jameson. I followed the thread back to another study with a small number of references to Jameson, an English author who had emigrated to Canada in 1836. Before the week was over, I got hold of Anna Jameson's book *Winter Studies and Summer Rambles in Canada*, which includes her travels to the "Mackinaw region."[25] My fingers tingled as I turned over page after page of discoveries that Anna uncovered about Jane's personal tragedies and her remarkable contributions to American literature and culture. I saw that the connections between women such as Jameson and Schoolcraft mirrored those between Blodgett and King, or Mitchell, Schindler, Laframboise, and Biddle.

What surfaced in my ongoing research was that Schoolcraft's genius and eminence would have languished unappreciated after the appropriation of her work by her husband—if not for the records of her work brought to the public by the already famous Jameson.[26] When the two met they were in tough places, both as writers and women. Their friendship was what made the difference in their respective professional and emotional lives.

That discovery of the connection between Schoolcraft and Jameson gave me all the conviction I needed to continue digging for the history of these thirteen women. One generation mentored the next, effecting positive value for the people of Mackinac. The Native leaders in Part I of this book lived a stone's throw away from one another, and in Parts II and III, the women of Mackinac understood a support system that was crucial when the odds were stacked against their success outside of traditional roles. The histories here describe visionaries and action women whose stories deserve to see the light of day.

The Anishinaabe Connection

CHAPTER ONE

Elizabeth Bertrand Mitchell (1761–1827)

W henever people live in an interface of several different cultures, groundbreaking change can emerge. Elizabeth Mitchell, the earliest known Indigenous woman to leave a lasting mark on Mackinac Island, represents such change. She lived on the island as nationalities shifted and the Anishinaabe, French Canadians, British, and American residents cohabited. A complex person, Mitchell was a farmer, a fur trader, a daring adventurer in wartime, and a woman torn between loyalties. Her husband's anti-American stance, along with her relationship with the Anishinaabe on Mackinac who were British loyalists would lead her into personal danger. A survivor in the best sense of the word, Mitchell's character and career helped to define an age of colorful politics and business.

Mitchell was recognized as a leader in the town of Mackinac, even as she and other Native women were not included in many gatherings held by the local elite of American Fur Company families or the officers of the garrison. There was an occasion, however, when Elizabeth's guests of honor were a young Ojibwe woman and her beloved, an American military officer.

"On a soft summer day in the year, 1817, fur trader Elizabeth Mitchell waved the guests inside her fine home on Market Street. The single feather on her luxurious black beaver hat bobbed as she greeted friends and neighbors. She stepped into the center of the living room, hands folded over her ample waist covered in black silk." Elizabeth's dialect was a combination of French and a blend of several Ojibwe dialects. Some thought her speech peculiar, but those invited into the largest residence on Mackinac would have appreciated their welcoming host, who would have said something like

"We are here to witness the solemn oath of marriage between Captain Benjamin Pierce and Josette Laframboise, who is the daughter of my dear friend Madeline Laframboise. Above all, we are here to celebrate!"[1]

Islanders claimed they never saw Elizabeth Mitchell without her plumed beaver hat. In her memoir, the grandniece of Laframboise teased that perhaps Elizabeth even wore that hat to bed each night. Had the fur trader been asked directly, she might have laughed heartily, making clear that indeed her hat kept her warm at night. This was a practical woman and she felt no need to impress people with what she wore.

In addition to the striking hat, Elizabeth Mitchell's usual apparel was a long silk dress with deep pockets.[2] Was her costume unusual? If so, her deeds of bravery and presence on Mackinac matched her bold appearance. Those familiar with this island will not be surprised to learn that she was but one in a history of extraordinary women. Elizabeth's relationship to the Marcot sisters, Madeline Marcot Laframboise and Therese Marcot Schindler, was crucial to the younger women. Mitchell was about twenty years older than Madeline and Therese, who were both fur traders. These three women became independent traders and pillars of Mackinac society during the rocky years of war and rapidly changing society.

When Mackinac was ceded to the United States in 1815, Elizabeth's husband, David, who was a British loyalist, left the island for good while she stayed on another twelve years.[3] It was decided that although Elizabeth would visit him in his new home on Drummond Island, she needed to be on Mackinac to manage their farm and fur-trading business. In the male-dominated world of the nineteenth century, where a woman lost all personal property when she married, her vision and success were no mean feat. The politics of the age added to the uncertainty of life for Elizabeth.

An ebullient personality who spoke her mind, the young Elizabeth Bertrand had attracted the attentions of Scotsman Dr. David Mitchell,[4] and she was just shy of sixteen in 1776 when they wed. She would give birth a few months later. Elizabeth had grown up in the Odawa tribe in Arbre Croche, Michigan. Her father, who was French, deserted his family when Elizabeth was young. His name is unknown.[5] Elizabeth's Odawa mother married again, this time to a man from a neighboring tribe. As a result, Elizabeth grew up with two Native parents. That culture fueled her future success in business and community life.

We can only speculate how the fifteen-year-old Elizabeth felt about marriage to this British citizen eleven years her senior, a man whose Scottish background was alien to everything she had known. She mirrored both Madeline Laframboise, who was either thirteen or fourteen when she married a French Canadian, and Jane Schoolcraft's mother, Ozhaguscodaywayquay, who wed John Johnston at a young age in 1790, fled the marriage, and was forced to return. It was almost certainly an arranged marriage between Elizabeth and David. Many male Europeans and Americans in the eighteenth and nineteenth centuries sought the advantages that a union with Native people would lend to their fur-trading businesses.[6] The Odawa and other tribes were more knowledgeable than anyone as to the best hunting grounds, and they had provided pelt delivery to the Europeans for well over one hundred years. It is no surprise that once David married Elizabeth the couple began a fur-trading business.

Thankfully, all evidence points to an eventually happy union between Elizabeth and David. He was the only doctor in the Straits region, and two years before the couple entered the fur trade business, he became an assistant surgeon in the King's Eighth Regiment at Fort Michilimackinac.[7] Fearing that the Americans would attack, the British lieutenant governor, Patrick Sinclair, moved the families from within that mainland palisade to Mackinac Island in 1779. Once the Mitchells settled into island life, they never wanted to leave—not an uncommon affliction that strikes those who spend time on this island. Elizabeth in particular would have felt this connection. Mackinac has long been known to Indigenous people as sacred ground.

In 1780, Elizabeth and David faced the news that the British regiment was making plans to be transferred. The Mitchells dreaded the thought of moving. After careful consideration, they agreed that David would write his commanding officer for permission to resign from the regiment. The couple knew that they had to find a way to stay on Mackinac and were overjoyed when the request was accepted. When the regiment left in 1783, the Mitchells were evidently already prepared to remain on the island, for they had constructed a fine house with gambrel roof, a high attic, dormer windows, and two floors.[8] This large residence was built where the present-day Cindy's Riding Stable is located and is almost directly across from the Biddle House.

The Mitchell home had a large library, guest bedroom downstairs, and an inviting living room that became the center of social life for Elizabeth's Native kin and friends. The wedding ceremony of Josette, only daughter of Laframboise, that was held at the Mitchell homestead was a prestigious event. E. T. Baird wrote about this wedding, which took place in 1817, when her Odawa grandmother Therese Schindler attended the ceremony. Baird makes the point that it was an unusual occasion when Native people were in company with officers from the fort and their families. Further, she makes clear that this occurrence arose only because Josette was marrying Captain Benjamin Pierce. Baird is careful to tell us that though there had been other weddings held at Elizabeth Mitchell's home, "This wedding was a very aristocratic one, none but the officers and families of the garrison, and only two families of the town, being present."[9] Her commentary reinforces the status quo, the class and racial stigma of the time. This wedding ceremony was an exception to the usual hierarchy on Mackinac. Note that Baird states that there were only two families from town—or rather, two Métis families—present. The Métis were persons of a mixed-race background, generally Native and European.[10] Baird also refers twice to Josette as a half-breed girl, which again calls attention to the manner in which those who were neither white nor full Native found themselves with outsider status, as they were not fully accepted by either race. Yet during its heyday as the mecca of the fur trade, this small island became the setting for many ethnicities. That wedding day with its festivities stands as a testament to the lifeblood of Mackinac.

The appearance of most of the guests at the wedding held in Mitchell's home that day would have been colorful in a way that is not seen today. The soldiers in attendance were smartly dressed. Like Agatha Biddle, an Indigenous woman who also married on Mackinac, Josette's wedding dress honored her Native American roots. Ribbons and beads would have adorned her double broadcloth skirt. A blanket edged with elaborate beadwork was often worn around the shoulders. The other Native women in the party, including Laframboise and Schindler, wore "full Indian costume," colorful dresses and leggings, some with beads around the neck and down the front of the bodice. Silver brooches too, for those who could afford it. Fuller skirts were often worn, loose-fitting at the waist, and of calico—unless you were Elizabeth Mitchell, who was always in silk.[11] As for the groom, he was in dress military uniform. An oil portrait of Captain Pierce from the time when he married reveals a young man with laughing eyes. He had short hair with a steep part and a sudden wave of curls rising from his forehead.

Captain Pierce would also achieve fame as brother of the future U.S. president Franklin Pierce. Despite their auspicious beginning together as a couple, two years later tragedy occurred. In 1821, Josette died in childbirth. Afterwards, Elizabeth Mitchell was there for her friend, Madeline Laframboise, who had lived through the violent death of her husband and now the loss of her only daughter.

Elizabeth gave birth to twelve children. She certainly knew what it was like to lose children and had an especially difficult recovery in 1809 after she lost her son,

David Jr. Being an emotional support for her friends was but one of the gifts Elizabeth gave to the world. While raising a large family, she also fulfilled the kind of ambition and largess not often associated with women of her era.

Despite his loyalty to the British, David took on the position of physician for the American garrison on the island. He was paid eight shillings a day to care for the Canadians and Native Americans who were building Fort Mackinac. He and Elizabeth were also involved in the lucrative business of fur trading. Their ace in the hole was Elizabeth and her wide connections with the Ojibwe who did the hunting and trapping of beaver pelts in the region. She used her tribal network to set up the business and soon the couple was trading profitably. Circumstances saw David moving to Drummond Island, but under Elizabeth's able hand, their fur trade on Mackinac throve. By 1823, David had lived off-island for eight years. During that time, Elizabeth worked hard to expand the family business, and the Mitchells became the third largest taxpayers on Mackinac.[12]

Mitchell was also a superb farmer and gardener. Over time she gained a reputation for her contribution to the Mackinac economy. She and David had obtained a sizable property on the island for farming. She also had a large plot of land outside of town under the East Bluff, near the government garden. This vegetable and flower garden was enclosed in a five-foot-tall, whitewashed picket fence.[13] Between her farm and garden, she became a busy harvester of potatoes, corn, and oats. The fruit-bearing bushes were less successful, but there was a modest yield of plums and cherries. While David contributed with fishing, especially for trout and whitefish for islanders, Elizabeth discovered that her "Mackinac potatoes" were a prized item.

She also grew an abundance of flowers, and her Native friends and workers dubbed her "Queen of Flowers." E. T. Baird, in her reminiscences, describes her as always dressing in black, wearing a beaver hat with a single feather, and a kerchief tied around her neck.[14] She was a tall and, by then, stout woman, and we may picture her as she stood proclaiming—often with hands thrust deep in her pockets, according to Baird.

Then as now, hay was in short supply on the island and usually had to be imported from the mainland. Yet Elizabeth's farm produced a good volume of it, and this was a valuable crop on an island that had cows, sheep, and other livestock to feed. There were horses too and Elizabeth owned one. She could be seen daily driving her own two-wheeled carriage, a calash.[15] Not for her to have a hired groom. She wanted to handle the lines herself.

E. T. Baird speaks of Mitchell's charisma and speculates that she must have been beautiful as a young woman. Baird tells us that wherever Elizabeth Mitchell went, whether at a party or on the street, people would gather around this raconteur. She demanded respect as well. When tying up her horse at the farm, her workers greeted her as "My lady."[16]

Owing to her mixed dialect, there were some who did not immediately understand Mitchell's speech, and yet her meaning was said to be clear. She made great use of expressive hand signals. On an island where there were both French- and English-speaking people, along with any number of tribal languages, the ability to use body language would come in handy. She supervised a large staff at her house and ran a successful retail store, as well as her farm and prosperous fur trade.

The little that has been written about Elizabeth focuses on her husband or her own "knack" in various areas. Thankfully, the memoirist E. T. Baird emphasizes her strong business skills and remembers that "Mrs. Mitchell owned" a large hay farm on the island, and that "this hay farm was of great profit to the owner." E. T. Baird speaks of Elizabeth as a highly intelligent person with "exceptional business faculties, though entirely without book-learning. Her skill in reading character was considerable."[17]

Meetings were held at the Mitchell house, along with social activities ranging from whist to dance parties. Elizabeth was a great fan of both and was generous with her invitations to islanders, new and old. Into the fold came the Reverend David Bacon and his young wife, Alice. This was 1802 and the pair formed the first Protestant mission for the Native American population on the island. Elizabeth was friendly to the Bacons, encouraging them in their desire to learn the languages of various tribes. She made polite noises in response to the couple's attempt to convert her. The Bacons felt certain the Mitchells would come around to their way of religious devotion. But Elizabeth's first loyalty was to family and business. She had no time for religious indoctrination, much to the reverend's chagrin.

Between ribald voyageurs, soldiers, and lively businesswomen, Mackinac was not a decorous society in the early 1800s. Alice, the reverend's wife, wrote to her friend Jerusha in Connecticut in 1803: "What a place this must be! Could you be transported hither and hear the awful language which I daily hear, methinks you would be filled with horror, and imagine that this is the place where infernals rave."[18]

Elizabeth was no writer, and it would be up to others, such as E. T. Baird, Juliette Kinzie, and Anna Jameson, to draw attention to Mackinac's positive features. Though there were dances and card parties in the Mitchell homestead, she was not interested in the details of these social activities. Elizabeth left it to Josette Pierce, daughter of Laframboise, to make all arrangements. Her son Daniel, a great friend of Josette's, assisted her and organized the whist gatherings.[19] So refreshingly undomesticated was Elizabeth, especially given the pressure on women to be so in that era, that "It was said she knew not the use of a needle."[20] That refusal to sew may well have been deliberate on the part of a woman who saw her own worth measured in other ways.

———————————

After he left the King's Eighth Regiment, David Mitchell remained a staunch loyalist to the British crown.[21] In 1811 he decided to formally rejoin British forces and took an appointment as hospital mate at Fort St. Joseph on St. Joseph Island. The War of 1812 erupted when the British landed on the back shores of Mackinac in the middle of the night on July 17. David assisted the British in hauling cannons up to the highest point on the island. American commandant Porter Hanks, along with his fifty-seven men, surrendered. During the attack, Elizabeth hid out in a distillery. Afterwards, she resumed full management of the family's expansive hay farm, fishing, and fur-trading businesses.[22] It would not, however, be an easy transition to that former life on Mackinac, especially given the turbulence and temper of those years.

By 1814, American ships of war were threatening the region. They drifted near Mackinac, and the Americans had attacked both St. Joseph and Sault Ste. Marie. Coming on the heels of Commodore Perry's victories in 1813, those in favor of British rule were extremely nervous. David remained intensely anti-American.[23] The Ojibwe had been loyal to the British for years, and it was not unexpected that Elizabeth and her kin spoke of taking up arms against the "long knives," or white Americans. When the Americans lost the Battle of Mackinac, it was Elizabeth's peers this time around, the Ojibwe and Odawa, who waylaid the Yankees and defeated them.

It was a time of shifting alliances in young America. Perhaps nowhere more so than in the wilds of the old Northwest, where Scotsmen along with the Irish, Native American, English, and French jockeyed for cultural and political position. The ruling government on Mackinac changed dramatically in a fifty-year span. After the Treaty of Ghent in 1814, English citizens were no longer allowed to be merchants or traders with Native people on American territory. Even so, the British kept their various businesses going with the Anishinaabe on Drummond Island, presumably with the aid of Dr. David Mitchell, until 1828.[24]

When the Treaty of Ghent conferred rule over Mackinac to the Americans, David made up his mind once and for all to pack up and leave his longtime home on Market Street. He and Elizabeth did not separate as a couple, at least emotionally, and it was a tough decision on her part to stay on the island. But someone had to manage and grow their jointly owned businesses, and Elizabeth knew she could do so. Two sons went with David to go live on Drummond Island, where the British military had moved. Along with her other children, her son William remained behind, ostensibly as chief assistant to Elizabeth. The drawback was that the Protestant evangelicals on the island had converted the young man, and he believed that it was unethical to use liquor in trade with the Ojibwe. He stood his ground, and thereafter he refused to participate in the fur trade.[25] It was left to Elizabeth's practical mind to assume all duties in the family business.

Trouble was brewing elsewhere for the intrepid Mitchell. After the war, a contentious spirit reigned on Mackinac. The Native people had never been overly fond of the Americans, and the new "Indian agent," one Henry Putthuf, had taken a special dislike to Elizabeth Mitchell. He was angry at what he viewed as the impertinence of her son, who walked downtown in his British red coat. Putthuf took a jaundiced view of her friendship with the Odawa on the island. He believed she would influence them, and on September 9, 1815, he put up a public notice on the door of a church that stated Mitchell was not permitted to hold meetings with any Native people on Mackinac.[26]

Strident letters between the British and American military caused David Mitchell to draw comparisons between the unrest in Algiers and Mackinac. He claimed there was more "true liberty" in Algiers than at present on Michilimackinac.[27] The irony hit home with Elizabeth and her family, for at this time Algiers was the home port of pirates who were the captors of American seamen.

When Putthuf threatened her with arrest, referring to Elizabeth and her kin as "those unfortunate deluded People," she felt she had no recourse but to escape in the dead of night. She took off in a small canoe and made the journey to safety on Drummond Island. It was a challenging time for David and her. The Drummond post had little food and many of the inhabitants were scurvy-ridden. Eventually the mood between Americans and British improved. Both sides calmed down, and in later months Elizabeth applied her diplomatic skills to return home, where she regained the successful commercial farming business she had started years earlier. Once she was home on Mackinac, the Ojibwe thanked Mitchell heartily for her support in wartime and honored her with a deed to land on Round Island, their burial ground.[28]

Over the next decade, Elizabeth visited David as often as her businesses permitted. There are tales too of smuggling activity between Drummond and Mackinac in these years.[29] Perhaps as the fur trade began to falter, the Mitchells sought other avenues of revenue. This speculation may have been idle gossip as there are no documents to support the notion. At this time, David was described as being "built large and bony, with broad, rugged features, crowned with tangled masses of grizzled hair."[30] The pair of them, David with his wild gray hair and Elizabeth with her substantial figure, kerchief, and beaver hat, form an interesting portrait of two decidedly rugged individuals of the old Northwest. Through many trials and tribulations, Elizabeth emerged as a town leader. She was a strong personality, one who stood at the center of community life, ready to guide, offer support, and provide goods whenever needed.

During a visit to Drummond to be with David and her son Andrew in 1827, Elizabeth fell sick. It is not known what illness struck her down, but she was not to return to her beloved Mackinac again. She was sixty-six when she died in late February.[31] She had lived on Mackinac fifty-odd years. Her wish was to be buried on Mackinac, and when the ice melted that spring, Andrew traveled with her body in an open Mackinaw boat, taking her safely home.

CHAPTER TWO

A Dynamic Family
on Mackinac

Therese Marcot Schindler (1775–1855), Madeline Marcot Laframboise (1780–1846),
and Elizabeth Therese Baird (1810–1890)

T hey were linked by blood, culture, and even professions. Madeline
Marcot Laframboise and Therese Marcot Schindler were sisters, and
the latter was the grandmother of E. T. Baird. They lived on Mackinac,
and of the three, Laframboise was the most famous fur trader in the
Great Lakes region in the early part of the nineteenth century. Laframboise became
widowed with children after her husband was murdered, yet she went forward to
unprecedented achievement as an independent trader. Known as a brilliant yet fair
negotiator, Madame Laframboise was not the only stellar trader on Mackinac. Indeed,
her sister, Therese Marcot Schindler, appears to have been a teammate in their joint
success in the man's world of rough-and-tumble trading in the nineteenth century. The
two dazzled customers and visitors alike with their fluency in French, English, and
multiple Native languages. Both rose to astonishing heights in a cutthroat business
that had high risks. While Laframboise spent winters in Grand Haven during the
bulk of her career, Schindler was the sister who lived on Mackinac year-round. She
had a lucrative fur-trade connection in Arbre Croche, Michigan, and was able to
make short trips there in the winter months.[1] Deserted by her first husband, and
with the second one in failing health, Schindler found a way to stay strong and to
succeed in dual careers.

Beyond trading, Therese Schindler owned a maple sugar business on nearby Bois
Blanc Island. While she managed her sugar camp, with Mackinac residents traveling
there to work, Madeline started a school in her home for young Native girls.[2] Both
sisters were renowned for their outreach to others—taking in those without a roof
over their heads as well as donating money and food to the needy. The third woman
in this remarkable family was Elizabeth Therese Baird. Though her contributions as

a writer have been overlooked, her memoir is an indispensable social history of Great Lakes people and their struggles and triumphs in the early nineteenth century. She gave particular attention to the lives of her grandmother, Therese Schindler, and her godmother and great aunt, Madeline Laframboise.[3]

Living next door to one another on Mackinac for many years, the Marcot sisters, Therese and Madeline, shared community commitments, daycare of their children, and their personal drive to succeed. When John Jacob Astor brought his American Fur Company to the island in 1815, it is likely the two women exchanged information about the competition. Gurdon Hubbard, later a successful businessman from Chicago, was a frequent visitor at the homes of Schindler and Laframboise, and credits them with generously sharing their knowledge of the trade.[4]

It was no wonder he paid attention to this pair—Laframboise cleared $5,000–$10,000 annually and Therese $8,000–$10,000.[5] Astonishing figures for that era when your average trader was doing well if he could net $1,000 a year. Schindler would join forces with the American Fur Company, but did business with other independent traders as well, including Michael Dousman and Joseph Bailly. Though Schindler and Laframboise became well-known, many other Native women who doubled the number of trades made by their male peers remain anonymous. In Bruce White's study of Ojibwe fur-trade patterns, he observed that despite their accomplishments, the low status of women made their names too unimportant to record.[6]

There were a number of key features that fueled the particular achievements of Laframboise and Schindler. Their connection to one another on an island that became the mecca of fur trade in the old Northwest figures largely. Given that they were sisters, the question arises as to whether a sibling rivalry existed between them, and if so, did it serve as a spur to their respective businesses? Or perhaps they worked together as a team. As will be explored in this chapter, another key to their success may be traced to their shared childhood in the fur trade. Together these features along with their connection to Elizabeth Therese Baird reveal a fascinating family dynamic on Mackinac.

When distinguished personalities came to Mackinac in the nineteenth century, they wished to meet or consult with Laframboise and Schindler. No doubt writerly curiosity also played a part when Alexis de Tocqueville, Margaret Fuller, and Juliette Kinzie made a point of meeting Laframboise, with the latter proclaiming Madeline's "dignified deportment," prodigious energy, and work ethic.[7] Madeline and Therese possessed expertise in a range of subjects. Regarding the history of the Straits region, they were consulted as to their view of the conspiracy of Pontiac during the attack on Michilimackinac in 1763.[8] Therese was interviewed by Indian agent Henry Schoolcraft, and Madeline by historian Francis Parkman. As eminent businesspeople and community builders, the perspectives of these women mattered.

Between 1800 and 1840, thousands of Native people came in the summer months when the commerce of fur trading took place. Only one home belonging to the Anishinaabe was a structure other than a lodge or wigwam.[9] This imposing house on a rise of land with a close view of Lake Huron belonged to Madeline Laframboise. Of the two sisters' homes on Mackinac only Laframboise's is standing today. Though we know they lived next door to one another between Main and Market Streets before Laframboise built her later house,[10] there is no extant document of precisely where those early structures were. The later home of Laframboise is now the Harbor View Inn, and adding to her presence on the island today is Ste. Anne's Church. As one of Michigan's great early philanthropists, she donated prime land near the harbor on Mackinac for the building of this hallmark edifice.[11]

It was all the more remarkable that Laframboise and Schindler were business leaders in an era of ruthless dealings between French Canadian voyageurs, British and American soldiers, along with the factions among the Anishinaabe. Throughout the chaos, they kept their moral ground and were known as a steadying influence on others. With such stellar accomplishments, are we to assume that these two had well-off husbands or a father who left them a fortune, something that explained their extraordinary success? Hardly. Madeline and Therese had role models. They grew up in a society where hard labor was required and at dawn each day in their village it was the women who hauled the water, gathered the fuel, and started the fire.[12] The youthful Marcot sisters witnessed them as community builders who also manufactured canoes and the lodges they lived in. When young, the two sisters saw the older females in their village take charge of bartering for the beaver pelts with traders.[13]

Chief among those who influenced Therese and Madeline was their mother, Marie Neskitch, a single parent raising her family among her Odawa kin. Madeline would count both her mother and her sister Therese as her closest allies. When Laframboise later moved to Mackinac, Elizabeth Mitchell mentored her and offered support in times of need.[14] No doubt, Mitchell's success as a woman who expanded her trading and ran two retail stores on her own gave Madeline and Therese courage to stick with their trading professions. Agatha Biddle cannot be left out of this group.

Laframboise mentored Biddle, and though she was seventeen years older than her student, they became fast friends. Surely the eminent fur trader took heart in Agatha's deep commitment to their shared Native heritage.

It is common knowledge that European and American women endured the pejorative of "weaker sex" well into the 1970s. For years, they were shut out of education and voting rights, and it was a challenge for them to land a professional job. The language was different in Native homes, and while women certainly endured discrimination, they also assumed positions of authority. Voyageur Michel Curot noted that Native women were the chief business managers in fur-trading transactions in Canada, and Samuel Hearnes of the Hudson's Bay Company recorded that in order to protect the men from being laden during travel for the fur trade across Canada, "No persons in this country are so proper for this work as the women, because they are inured to carry and haul heavy loads from their childhood and to do all manner of drudgery."[15]

There are two ways to view the above statement. Historian Richard Perry takes the perspective that the overwhelming difficulty for these women suggests that "the Chipewyan women did not voluntarily submit to this regime," and that they "had a low status."[16] Conversely, Bruce M. White notes the crucial positions of power women possessed. He observes that men in Ojibwe villages "only wanted alcohol in exchange for furs while women demanded a wide variety of European goods in exchange for rice," and further, that they were generally "in charge of the furs their menfolk had collected, making women into important players in the fur trade."[17]

Laframboise's and Schindler's rise in the fur-trading world of the old Northwest stands out. Their business models for women and men in the young nation are relevant today. The manner in which they worked both independently and with a corporation—the American Fur Company—was admirable. This pair also modeled a form of cross-pollination in working with several cultures at once. Both were canny and prudent in their dealings with Indigenous trappers and with French, British, and American merchants on Mackinac. Incredibly driven and organized, they stood at the center of what was in many ways the great emporium of the old Northwest.

The background of Laframboise and Schindler was the catalyst for their success. Therese was born in 1775, and Madeline in 1780. Their mother was an Odawa woman, and their father, Jean Baptiste Marcot, a French Canadian. The two sisters along with their siblings grew up conversing in several mother tongues. Both girls would become highly respected linguists and traders in the Great Lakes region. Their ambition and demonstration of success, one to the other, spurred each woman forward. Not an unheard of scenario between sisters, and it makes sense in this case as the two were close and in the same business. When Therese married the fur trader George Schindler in 1804, the couple lived on Mackinac and were independent traders. Two years later Madeline would be widowed and carry forward her own trade successfully. Therese would also continue her work and prosperity as a trader after George died. While women worked as a team with their husbands, it was unusual for single women such as the Marcot sisters to outstrip the men in the field. These sisters had each other to look to for strength in their given profession and civic life. Their connection to each other would extend to other ambitious women in the community, creating a strong base for civic society on Mackinac.

Madeline Marcot Laframboise

Her first name has been referenced variously as Marguerite, Magdelaine, and Madeline. The Michigan Women's Hall of Fame records Madame Laframboise as Madeline Laframboise, as do several scholarly studies. The Odawa who bequeathed her land also refer to Laframboise as Madeline, as does the fur trader's own last will and testament. For this study and the sake of consistency, that is how she will be known.[18]

Despite some confusion surrounding her first name, everything we know about Laframboise indicates that there was no doubt in her mind as to who she was: her identity as Anishinaabe was strong. She wore Native dress every day of her life and would open her own home as a school for Native children. Though she became a greatly admired figure in the community of Mackinac, she never forgot her background and the Indigenous people with whom she had daily commerce. They were kin, friends, and customers in her fur-trading business. While remaining a true friend to her mother's people in Grand Haven and a philanthropist on Mackinac, Laframboise is also recorded as having been a scrupulous trader who paid attention to rules and regulations in the marketplace. Every year she obtained a license from the American government, and records show her being "engaged at Mackinac" and "employed at Grand River" in the fur-trading market.[19]

Their association with the island came early. Madeline and Therese were brought to Mackinac at ages six and eleven, at which time they were baptized.[20] In all likelihood, the two had further introduction to the island as young girls.[21] Regarded as a holy place by the Native population, Mackinac would have been a desirable destination for her mother, Marie, and her brood to visit. While missionaries were intent on converting Indigenous people, it was not as if they were filling a religious vacuum in their lives. Native people had a complete set of beliefs when the Europeans arrived. A good number of Indigenous "converts" paid lip service only and held fast to their original spiritual life, but there were also staunch believers in the Christian faith. Certainly, Madeline was one. Many Native women incorporated the new faith into their already existing set of beliefs and cultural life. The two easily coexisted.

In an age of great disparity between the sexes, young girls, often no older than twelve, thirteen, or fourteen, were offered up in arranged marriages in the fur-trading world. Madeline became Madame Laframboise in 1794, at age fourteen, though a record of Madeline's legal marriage on the island was entered in 1804.[22] After the death of her husband, Joseph Laframboise, in 1806, she lived on Mackinac for the full summer season. The island became her second headquarters for work and a place of refuge for the next forty years. In the summers, she sold a harvest of furs that had been trapped and prepared during the long northern winters along the Grand River in Grand Haven, Michigan.

> Madame Laframboise would return in June to Mackinac with her furs. The servants whom she left in care of her home there, would have it in readiness upon her arrival and then she would keep house for about three months and then go back to her work.[23]

After Madeline Laframboise retired from the fur trade in the early 1820s and built her grand home near today's marina, she lived year-round on the island.[24] If Madeline worked hard during the winter months when in Grand Haven, she also experienced the calm of quiet industry in that off-season away from the frantic summer trading. In a conversation with Regina Gasco-Bentley, chairperson of the Little Traverse Bay Bands of Odawa Indians, I learned that the Anishinaabe continue to uphold positive values during winter on the Great Lakes of northern Michigan. She discussed "the creator's blanket of snow designed to give us rest and calm," with people still maintaining work responsibilities. Between the executive and tribal council departments, Regina and her teams fight for education, vaccinations (and all manner of healthcare), housing, and jobs for the Odawa.[25]

Long before Mackinac became her home, Madeline and Therese Marcot scampered along the Grand River, which flows into Lake Michigan. Travel by canoe—presaging their later busy life canoeing with pelts to Mackinac—was a familiar mode of transportation to the sisters. In life with her mother's clan, the majesty and power of the waterways was not lost on Laframboise. Later as a young widow, it appears as if Madeline discovered that work and movement on the river and lakes gave back meaning to her life. After Joseph's murder, she took his body for burial to Grand Haven and immediately returned to work. With great purpose and determination, she took up the fledgling fur-trade business she and Joseph had begun.[26]

Madeline's life as a carefree girl may have been short-lived. Before the age of ten, she and sister, Therese, were expected to go to work sorting beads and learning the mysteries of quillwork, an occupation of tribes for generations before the arrival of the French in the Great Lakes region. The porcupine quills had to be soaked, trimmed, and dyed before use. As a preteen she was in all likelihood schooled in basket weaving, sewing moccasins, and making birchbark boxes, all skills that the two would incorporate into their annual sales on Mackinac.[27]

We can envision that the year Joseph took Madeline as a common-law wife we can envision the fourteen year old girl already an expert in the handiwork of making porcupine boxes. She would also be cleaning beaver pelts, familiar with the melting softness of their undercoat and rougher topcoat in colors that varied from deep russet to subtle mixes of brown and black. All the while, Laframboise might have dwelt on the larger picture, projecting a way to success, utilizing Native skills and those she was learning with Joseph, and his experience as a trader.

In their childhood years, not only did she and Therese witness the women of their village conducting business transactions for the pelts, but also overseeing the cooking: the rice and maple sugar and also the pemmican that formed a staple the traders and Native people depended on for fuel. Pemmican was a high-energy meal of tallow (suet), dried meat, and berries. In short, the two Marcot girls were surrounded by competent, involved women in the trade. Yet no amount of idealism can cover over the hard existence for most of them. In her extended visit to Mackinac in 1837, Anna Jameson observed numerous examples of women toiling on the shores. She describes young fishermen who loll on the bank as the women carry out the canoes and the trappings for a fishing expedition. The women paddle industriously and the male sits with spear at the ready. After procuring the fish, the women bring him back "to rest" where he "lounged away without troubling himself farther."[28] They drag the canoe to shore and begin the work of cleaning the fish, kindling the fire, and cooking the catch.

A Native woman's work was "never done," quite literally. Jameson points out that an Ojibwe woman's very burial points up the differences in daily labor of women and men. The vision of heaven for Native people was outwardly a lovely one, very much an extension of earth, only set in perfect weather, and in field and forest that were teeming with game. While a Native man was to travel beyond the grave simply with his tobacco and bow and arrow buried at his side, the women were "laid to rest" with carrying belts and paddles to take with them to the afterlife. These carrying belts were stocked with utensils, including axes, snowshoes, kettles, and other tools to do the required cleaning, cooking, and other work in the next life.[29] Not exactly a rest after great toil in this world.

Nonetheless, cultures the world over assign workloads to men and women in different ways. As a middle-class white woman, it is possible Jameson misunderstood what constituted acceptable gender roles for the Ojibwe and was not aware of the nuances of their power relationships. Additionally, Regina Gasco-Bentley at the Little Traverse Bay Bands remarks that today treatment of women by Native men varies greatly in different bands and even bands within regions.[30]

Madeline's father, Jean Baptiste Marcot, died when she was three years old, the details of which are unknown. He left Marie a widow with seven children, all of whom would grow up inured to hard work, whether tending to crops, cooking, curing pelts, or making and selling birchbark boxes called *mocock*. Jean Baptiste had been a "factor," or fur-trading agent of some standing, in the North West Company. Though his children were young when he died, his influence in the fur trade would have been felt. Though the Marcots lived at Fort St. Joseph in Niles, Michigan, his interest in Mackinac is evidenced by his signed agreement to assist in construction of buildings on the island.[31] After his death, Marie took her children to live in her Native village along the Grand River, also in Michigan.

Madeline's and Therese's maternal grandfather, Chief Kewinoquot, or "Returning Cloud," is remembered as "one of the most powerful chiefs of the [Odawa] tribe," and Laframboise's mother has been described as having "royal blood."[32] Madeline understood that her father had been a trader, and perhaps this knowledge along with her mother's standing in the clan lent self-confidence to the girl. Even so, her future success alongside the likes of Robert Stuart of the American Fur Company was a phenomenon. After the death of her husband, it would have been all too easy for Laframboise to seek out a quiet life with her mother's people. There was a fire in the young woman that drove her towards a more ambitious future.

Fur trading was in Madeline's and Therese's blood. They grew up with the knowledge of their father's employer, the North West Company, which emerged after the British takeover of New France.[33] Well before they were born, extensive networks of the trading business had formed. Begun in the 1600s in Canada, these networks and the trappers and traders gradually migrated south to the Great Lakes region. The Native people hunted, trapped, and readied their pelts to bring to trading centers in exchange for goods. Laframboise and Schindler acted the part of intermediary agents, receiving the furs and selling them to a European market hungry for the furs of beaver, muskrat, and mink for hats, coats, and luxury clothing.

The community life in Madeline's Odawa village at Grand Haven was strong, and from her mother, aunts, and grandmother, she gleaned a core belief in the support system of family and clan. The older siblings in the Marcot home had been sent to boarding schools in Montreal, but after the death of Jean Baptiste there was in all probability not enough money to send off the two youngest, Therese and Madeline. Growing up, these were the only siblings in their family who were not given a formal education. Clearly, neither Madeline nor Therese let this stop them.

With her skill set and kinship network, Madeline joined hands with Joseph in the fur-trade business. They established outposts along the Grand River and in Fallsburg, Michigan. A year into their relationship, Laframboise gave birth to a daughter, Josette. A son, also named Joseph, was born in 1805. Only a year later, tragedy struck when Laframboise's husband was shot dead.[34]

It was in the autumn of 1806 that a Winnebago named White Ox approached Joseph one evening, demanding liquor in return for the furs he had delivered.[35] Joseph felt that the fellow had already been paid in full and hardly needed more alcohol. He refused the request and paid with his life. Laframboise would never forget the circumstances under which her husband died. In bereavement, she carried on bravely, and eventually expanded her fur trade exponentially. Interestingly, Robert Stuart, who ran the American Fur Company along with John Jacob Astor and Ramsay Crooks, saw fit to avoid any payment in liquor to Native workers in the fur trade. A teetotaler himself, he was convinced that alcohol was not a good business mix. Surely Laframboise knew of his approach, but there is no record of her following suit in her thirty years of trading.[36] Perhaps fearing a reprise of the tragic death of her husband, she thought it best to pay her workers in liquor when they so requested.

Madeline first operated her business in the years when the French Canadians, Anishinaabe, and British controlled the fur-trade business, and later when the American Fur Company came to town. Gurdon Hubbard, who would eventually establish the first community of summer cottages on Mackinac, wrote about his gratefulness to Laframboise, Schindler, and Mitchell, stating that from them, he "received much good advice, as well as instruction in the method of conducting trade with the Indians, which was of much benefit to me in my after life as a trader."[37]

Laframboise was instrumental in the development of the fur trade that centered in the Great Lakes region.[38] She and her sister, Therese, were easily the most successful independent traders in that era, among both men and women. Laframboise worked on her own for a decade before John Jacob Astor brought the American Fur Company to Mackinac.[39] She then began to trade for them, and yet maintained her own separate business. Laframboise has been described as "a formidable trader, whose competition was feared."[40] That rival traders bowed out of the market under pressure from the better capitalized American Fur Company while she stood her ground, speaks volumes.

There is an interesting twist to this story. Throughout her business career, Laframboise could not read or write.[41] Apparently, others were not concerned by her lack of schooling. After all, she could speak French, English, Odawa, Ojibwe, and several other tribal languages. These linguistic talents served her well in the fur-trade business. She was a sharp business tactician who knew how to compensate for the liability of illiteracy. She signed all her trade agreements with a single mark, X. It is likely that her own struggles gave rise to a desire to help others and to give children a leg up in the world. After retiring from the fur-trade business, Laframboise gave herself to philanthropic work, beginning with a school for the young on Mackinac. Approached by the Presbyterian missionaries William and Amanda Ferry about a facility for such an endeavor, she offered up rooms in her house to become classrooms.[42]

That Laframboise also looked at her own illiteracy and did something about it is further evidence of her dedication to education. Between age forty and fifty, she may have learned to read, though not to write. No one person has been given credit for teaching Laframboise, but it is tantalizing to consider that it might well have been poet Jane Johnston Schoolcraft. Schoolcraft, who was well educated, translated English for Native women in her home at the same time Laframboise was desirous of learning to read.[43]

Laframboise was the one many people turned to for aid on Mackinac. Henry Schoolcraft noted in his memoirs: "A poor decrepit Indian woman, who was abandoned on the beach by her relatives some ten days ago, applied for relief. It is found that she has been indebted for food in the interim to the benevolence of Mrs. Laframboise."[44] She was a major force in the life of Agatha Biddle, who would also become a humanitarian. After helping the Reverend William and Amanda Ferry with their classrooms for students, Laframboise opened a school for Catholic children on the island, with twenty-six boys and girls enrolled.[45] Madeline would also take in Sophia Bailly, Agatha

Biddle's stepsister, in a time of need. As a result of her tutelage in the Laframboise school, Sophia would become a fine teacher in St. Ignace.[46] The connections between the Anishinaabe on Mackinac were in full evidence.

In 1815, Madeline's daughter Josette met Captain Benjamin K. Pierce. When the pair became engaged, Laframboise prevailed upon her good friend Elizabeth Mitchell to host the ceremony at her spacious home on Market Street. This wedding took place in the summer of 1817. Despite her auspicious marriage, Josette would die in childbirth four years later. After the death of her daughter, Madeline closed up most of her business. She built a home for herself on Mackinac and began to live on the island full-time, perhaps feeling a need for the island community in that time of sorrow.[47]

As for Laframboise's son, Joseph, he was educated in Montreal. When still young, Joseph Jr. and Laframboise set off on the long canoe trip over water to his new school. Under the care of her nephew, Alexis Laframboise, Joseph went to a French school in the city. The love between mother and son has been documented by Alexis, who wrote of how Madeline was "such a good mother who does everything in order to procure his happiness."[48]

In taking full measure of Madame Laframboise, it is crucial to acknowledge her courage in dealing with life as an outsider, as both a Native person and a single woman in business. Though distinguished visitors to the island made sure they called on her, it is likely that Laframboise was fully cognizant of her outsider status, especially where islanders of the upper crust were concerned. With a Native heritage, she was excluded from most gatherings among the elite. Fort officers and their families, the Stuarts at the American Fur Company, and other Americans would not as a rule invite her to gatherings: "their skating and hunting parties, concerts or holiday festivities."[49] She was excluded for being a single woman, as well—in contrast to the way single officers were included as a matter of course in many island parties.

She did not have the social status her daughter achieved by marrying Captain Pierce. Laframboise "lacked the tie to a prominent American male—a requirement if she had hoped to be fully accepted."[50] Even Madeline's good friend Elizabeth Mitchell would have fared better in terms of receiving invitations to teas or dinner parties by Euro-Americans. Marrying a Scotsman gave her instant cachet, at least until the War of 1812, when his strong British loyalties caused him trouble on the island.

When meeting Laframboise, New England author Margaret Fuller, who spent time on Mackinac in 1843, discussed the fur trader's reputation as an astute businessperson. She also noted that Madeline "spoke French fluently and was very ladylike in her manners. She is a great character among them." These descriptors add up to a range of qualities indicating Laframboise's multiple habits and strengths. She had good manners, exhibited enviable business expertise, and possessed a colorful personality. Worth mentioning is that middle- and upper-class white women of the nineteenth century were supposed to be ladylike and passive, negating the chance for them to have the kind of "character" that Laframboise admirably possessed. Fuller boarded at Laframboise's home in her visit to Mackinac and had the opportunity to witness how people "were all the time coming to pay her homage, or to get her aid and advice."[51]

Eventually both Laframboise and her sister, Therese, retired from the fur trade. Over time the population of mammals whose luxurious furs fed the market for traders had diminished. While the slaughter of these mammals appears deplorable today, at the time in which these women lived there was no consciousness of the finite number of species in the vast Michigan forests. Many people assumed there was an unlimited supply.

When Laframboise sold her business to John Jacob Astor, the Odawa chiefs of her Native lands gifted her with property along the Grand River.[52] This was their way of recognizing all she had done for them and for the way she had remained loyal to her Native roots. This kinship network also calls attention to the spiritual life of many Indigenous people, their ties to nature and to the land.[53] In her study "Mediating Mackinac: Métis Women's Cultural Persistence in the Upper Great Lakes," Bethany Fleming writes that in the 1800s, "the French Canadian, Métis and Indian peoples" had a "predominant faith [that] was a pastiche of beliefs, blending Roman Catholicism with Native religious belief."[54] Laframboise adhered to the tenets of the Catholic faith, and yet it is clear that this most famous fur trader also embraced the culture and spirit of her birth mother and grandfather. When author Margaret Fuller stayed in the home of Laframboise, she noted the fur trader was "Indian by birth, and wearing the dress of her country."[55] We may easily picture the trader sitting with Agatha Biddle, making *mocock* and listening to her speak of meetings with Native bands. Laframboise's place in history cannot be defined entirely by her prowess in the world of commerce, for she was also a pillar of the Mackinac community.

Therese Marcot Schindler and Elizabeth Therese Baird

Therese would spend forty-eight years living on Mackinac, and approximately two-thirds of that time she was an active trader.[56] She had grown up in a large family that was connected to the fur trade. Three out of the seven children in her family became traders: her older sister Catherine Cadotte in the Sault Ste. Marie region, and both Madeline Laframboise and Therese emerging as leaders in the trade on Mackinac. As Susan Sleeper-Smith notes:

> In fact, some women gained enough power that they faced opposition from other traders, who objected to their control over trading practices. Some, such as [Madeline] Magdalaine Marcot la Framboise and her sister Therese Marcot LaSaliere Schindler, became so powerful that they were able to set themselves up as independent fur traders.[57]

There is debate as to whether Indigenous women benefited overall from their interdependency with white male traders. Mary C. Wright analyzes the way they did not receive the merit due them.[58] Schindler and Laframboise stand out, for they garnered a rare high profile in the trade. Still, they struggled to achieve that status.

At age fourteen Therese was married to Canadian voyageur Pierre LaSaliere, with whom she had a daughter, Marianne. When her husband left the union soon after she gave birth, Therese began to spend time on Mackinac. After marrying again, this time to George Schindler, the couple moved permanently to the island in 1805 and established their fur-trading enterprise. At this time, the village had a year-round population of 250, with nearly 4,000 in the summer season when trading was at its height.[59] George Schindler was a Protestant, Therese a baptized Catholic, while also holding to her Native beliefs, and her daughter Marianne became an island teacher and held both Protestant and Native beliefs.[60] Historian John Jackson writes of the "fur families" that included "displaced women who lived near forts and formed networks among themselves." Regarding marriages between Native women and white traders, "Catholics tried their best to validate these unions through marriages. But missionaries and priests often had trouble categorizing the women, especially when establishing tribal identity."[61]

Karen Marrero addresses the travesty of Indigenous women whose cultural identity was stripped in multiple ways. She discusses the narrow cataloging of Catholic marriages and how it reveals a limited genealogy of women. She emphasizes the far larger number of women and marriages outside the patriarchal Church.[62] Theresa Weller, an Indigenous author, adds to the subject, having written extensively about reintegrating the genealogy of Native women into history.[63] Regina Gasco-Bentley, chairperson of the Little Traverse Bay Bands of Odawa Indians, weighs in on the question of those whose identity has been stripped and how hard it was in the past to speak up on their behalf. With her own severe experience as a student at the Holy Childhood boarding school in Harbor Springs, Michigan, and the witnessing of a young girl who was beaten daily, she states that it is important to finally speak up about the wrongdoing of forced cultural and physical assimilation in America. The school, which was on the Great Lakes and thirty-four miles south of Mackinac, did not close its doors until 1983.[64]

Though it was a rocky path finding her way to a professional and social position on Mackinac, Therese was determined. After George died, she found that having her sister Madeline living nearby was especially important. Both had just one daughter and would support one another when their beloved girls died. Not only did the two commiserate as widows, grieving mothers, and Native businesswomen in the fur trade, but Schindler's only grandchild, Elizabeth Therese Fisher, bounced back and forth between the homes of her grandmother, Therese, and her great-aunt, Madeline. Laframboise was also the child's godmother. As E. T. Baird proudly tells us in her memoir, she was also a great favorite of her aunt.[65] As there are several "Elizabeths" in this study, the author and granddaughter of Therese will be referred to as E. T. Baird, her published name.

Beyond sharing nineteenth-century daycare duties, it is conceivable that Schindler and Laframboise worked together. As children they grew up with their father and their grandfather, Chief Kewinoquot, in the fur trade. The two girls had shared duties in this environment, whether it was sewing deer hides or sorting and cleaning beaver pelts. As youngsters, Therese and Madeline may well have played at being traders, just as girls everywhere today enact inventive career games when small. While girls in the recent past—those in the 1950s, '60s, and even '70s had few role models for this kind of positive envisioning of a career, Therese and Madeline Marcot were raised in a climate that may have favored their ability to see themselves as successful businesspeople.

When the British attacked Mackinac in 1812, Therese, Madeline, and their families escaped to the Dousman distillery on the far side of the island. Both sisters returned to their commercial fur trade after the conflict, a mark of their extraordinary perseverance, diplomacy, and encouragement of each other. In addition to forging similar businesses, their social and familial bond further cemented their connection. E. T. Baird writes of both Therese and Madeline dressed in Native wear and attending the same festive occasions.[66] It is likely that the two women worked as a team in preserving their livelihood, perhaps sharing privately with each other the ways in which to compete with the arrival of the American Fur Company in 1825. Laframboise and Schindler were in the commerce of furs for survival, at least for a large part of their career.

The American Fur Company was a powerful corporation that wanted to dominate the market by being the only ones to buy furs. It is to Madeline's and Therese's credit that they managed to stay solvent after the advent of John Jacob Astor and company. During the years that the Marcot sisters were both independent traders, they may have been friendly rivals, yet this did not affect their overall affection for one another. They understood their respective positions of power. Most of the Native people and Euro-Americans felt a willingness to trust them, and it was this trustworthiness that gave them an edge in commerce.

Schindler had found contentment with George, but when he "lost health and property" she took over their jointly owned fur trade. While George could no longer be active in the business, he pursued his more scholarly inclinations and started a school for boys on the island.[67] In the years when he was in ill health, Schindler went forward as both a trader and maple sugar manufacturer. After her husband's death, she continued to live on Mackinac and prospered as an entrepreneur.[68] Her support system included her daughter, Marianne Saliere Fisher; granddaughter, E. T. Baird; and Laframboise and her children. Therese was rightly proud of Marianne, who became a lead teacher at the island school. She was hired by Robert Stuart, manager of the American Fur Company and great supporter of Amanda and Reverend William Ferry's mission school.[69] Baird makes the point that her mother, Marianne Fisher, a Native person herself, was keenly interested in teaching the mixed-race girls on the island.[70] It is likely it was the Ferrys' mission school where Marianne taught. The Stuarts were closely affiliated with the Ferrys, socially and in religious beliefs. Robert grew up in Scotland, a largely Presbyterian country, and in 1813, he and Elizabeth married in a Presbyterian church. Historian John McDowell points out that Marianne taught at a boarding school on Mackinac, and the chief (and perhaps only) boarding school with female students was the mission school. The Mission Church on Mackinac was constructed in 1829 and stands today on the far east side of town.

Marianne had married an "excitable" man, Henry Monroe Fisher, and the two became parents of Elizabeth Therese Fisher in 1810.[71] Henry was employed as a trader at the Hudson's Bay Company. He was not on Mackinac when the British attacked. His wife and young daughter took refuge in the distillery with Therese and Madeline. Therese's son-in-law was a British Loyalist who had escaped to Prairie du Chien, Wisconsin, during the War of 1812. He would not rejoin his wife Marianne or their daughter Elizabeth at any point after the war. Marianne stayed on Mackinac making a name for herself as a teacher. Though Laframboise would also start a school, Marianne stands out as one of the island's strong teachers, a single mother who provided for herself and gave girls in the community the chance to be educated.

The Schindlers were also closely connected with the David and Elizabeth Mitchell family on Market Street. Therese, Madeline, and their friends Agatha and Edward Biddle congregated at various social events held at the Mitchell household, including dances and card parties. When ice-bound in the winter, these groups delighted in dogsledding across the straits and traveling from one island to another. On occasion, young Elizabeth Fisher (the future E. T. Baird) accompanied her grandmother Therese when she attended to her maple sugar manufacturing on Bois Blanc Island.

> My grandmother [Therese Schindler] had one sugar camp on Bois Blanc Island, about five miles east of Mackinac. About the first of March, nearly half of the inhabitants of our town, as well as many from the garrison, would move to Bois Blanc to prepare for the work. Would that I could describe the lovely spot![72]

The distance across the water from Mackinac to Bois Blanc is thirteen miles, not five, and speaking wryly, we might surmise that E. T. Baird so enjoyed her visits to her grandmother's camps that the travel seemed less than half its actual distance. When Baird was too small to travel to the sugar camps, Therese would send a miniature barrel of maple sugar back to Mackinac for her granddaughter.[73]

Organizing and doing the labor of the syrup business was an area of expertise that was familiar to many Native women. However, Schindler stands out as one who expanded her business to an unusual degree. Her operation gave jobs to Great Lakes inhabitants, especially those on Mackinac, and the syrup was an energy source for the residents in the region. In contemporary times, maple syrup is primarily considered a condiment, but in an earlier day it was a major food source when added to rice or corn. Long before Europeans came to America, the First Nation people tapped maple trees, referred to as sugar bushes. The sap they collected was boiled down in a process using hot stones from a fire. Therese and her crew would tap the trees as early as March, with men and women carrying the buckets of sap on yokes to an open fire. After two boilings at different heats, the liquid maple sugar was poured into decorative molds in the shape of bears, beaver, and crosses and then placed into the birchbark *mocock*.

There were many festive hours at the sugar camp, and Baird recalls sitting down to dinners of "partridge roasted on sticks before the fire; rabbit and stuffed squirrel cooked French fashion; and finally [we] had as many crepes as we desired." These they served swimming in maple sugar syrup. The thin pancakes or crepes were made on the bottom side of frying pans and much laughter ensued during contests to see if the men and women could "try their skill" at flipping the crepes—with the highest thrown cake the winner. Often they missed their mark, causing "great glee of the party." It was during one of these crepe contests that Therese's granddaughter met Henry Samuel Baird. Henry had become greatly attached to the Mackinac region, where he often visited. A relationship between the two followed and Elizabeth Therese Fisher married Henry in 1824. Of this union she wrote that "the wife (was) but fourteen." E. T. Baird would always refer to herself in her memoir in third person.[74]

She moved with her new husband to Green Bay, Wisconsin, on Lake Michigan's west shore where Henry had established himself as an attorney. He was the first practicing lawyer and the first attorney general of the Wisconsin Territory. Like many a young bride in a settlement that is far from home, she was lonely. With her signature humor and touching voice, Baird remarks that after her husband mounted his horse and was gone all day at work, she shed many tears, and her only friend was the cow, whom she talked to and "coaxed her to remain by the kitchen door by feeding her."[75] In discussing her "solitary" life after moving to Green Bay, she tells us that her closest neighbors spoke English, and she, only French, reminding us that in the early 1800s on Mackinac, French was the primary spoken language.

E. T. and her husband were able to put her French to good use in this Lake Michigan town in Wisconsin:

> As soon as my husband could give me the necessary instruction in the routine of his business I became his translator. His clients being entirely French, and he not understanding the language it became necessary for him to resort to this method

in order to conduct business at all. I was gratified indeed to assume the duties as it enabled me to learn the English language.[76]

She kept the "office of Interpreter" until one Alexander Grignon filled the position. Baird tells us that after he moved on, she took over the job again and would do so as needed throughout her marriage. We see how essential a partner she was in this successful marriage and business. Yet Baird's fame stems from her fascinating memoir with its very title drawing attention to her mixed-blood heritage: *O-De-Jit-Wa-Win-Ning; or Contes du Temps Passe.* "Tales of Times Past" is the English translation of her book, which was published more than twenty years after she left Mackinac permanently. Though Baird was surrounded by mostly English-speaking people in the last thirty years of her life, she chose a title and text that honored the French and Indigenous people in Lake country.

Baird published her vibrant cultural document of the people and movements of the Western Great Lakes in 1886–1887, first in serial newspaper articles, and later in book form. Set in the early part of the century, *O-De-Jit-Wa-Win-Ning* explores her childhood memories of the first fourteen years of her life on Mackinac, 1800–1814.[77] The memoir is not a study in nostalgia but a revealing look at the mixed culture and people of the early nineteenth century. She is intrigued by the traders Elizabeth Mitchell and her own grandmother, Therese Schindler, along with Madeline Laframboise. Baird's observations include those of Agatha Biddle and family, and she does not spare them the controversies of the time. Her analysis of the ways in which Sophia Biddle, Agatha's eldest, was drawn into a tug of war between Presbyterians and Catholics, with each denomination claiming Sophia as their own, points up the cultural battle over the souls of Native people, who undoubtedly would have preferred to make up their own minds as to their religious preferences.[78]

There are places in Baird's nonlinear memoir with fewer available dates than the historian would like to see, yet the narrative crackles with life as it brings into view many individuals in the Lakes region in the early part of that century. There is no other record of its kind written from the Native perspective. At her death in 1890, E. T. had witnessed a time when much of the Wisconsin territory was still owned by the Indigenous population. To visit with her mother and grandmother on Mackinac, she traveled by canoe or horseback, and in sleighs and wagon on scarcely existing roads. No matter the challenge, Baird believed in maintaining connection with others. With honesty and insight, and perhaps not a little courage for a document written by a mixed-race woman in this era, she addresses head-on the factions among her Native kin and her reservations and sometimes real fear of, Euro-Americans.

After 1824, when the first circuit court was held in Green Bay, Baird was witness to two Native men who committed murder. She tells us they were large men sitting near her with painted faces while waiting to go into court, but she was not afraid of them in the least. E. T. claims at first that her fearlessness may be attributed to youthful nerves, and adds: "Yet I think I should have been afraid of *white* murderers."[79] Of the complex nature of her own heritage, she writes on page one of her memoir:

> To live among the Indians and not fear them would scarcely seem possible to many
> a reader, this was true of the writer, whose childhood was passed among them. To
> know we had Indian blood in our veins was in one respect a safeguard, in another
> a great risk.[80]

She speaks of "tribal clannishness" and of each tribe "always at enmity with the others."[81] It follows that the rivalries between bands were exacerbated by the advance of the white culture taking over Indigenous land. To see one's own patch threatened can lead to defensiveness.

Presumably Baird sent letters to Mackinac, where her mother and grandmother continued to live, but only Marianne in this family group could read and write. E. T. Baird was not about to let her connection to Grandmother Schindler falter, and the writer made sure she traveled home often, spending many summers on the island. She relished her trips back to Mackinac, once arriving in a splendid flotilla of boats, guided by a family friend, Joseph Rolette.[82] Baird's wide subject matter is noteworthy, and her contribution as a memoirist of the Great Lakes and Mackinac culture is invaluable.

Possibly Therese Schindler's strangest and most heartbreaking connection is one that reveals the fault lines of assimilation and racism. That narrative recorded by Baird takes a hard look at Schindler's long acquaintance with John Tanner and his family. When still a young woman, Schindler met one James Tanner, a white man in search of his brother who had been abducted as a child by a band of Odawa. Baird does not give the exact year, but given Schindler's relative youth when the incident occurred it may have been about 1800.

> Madame T. Schindler became very much interested in the case; her sympathy was
> greatly aroused and this she imparted to her Indian relations and friends, telling to

them the story of the stolen boy and describing his appearance as told to her by his brother.[83]

Schindler's kin looked for the boy, but he did not turn up. She was surprised to learn of his appearance as a grown man in 1819. At that time, he was discovered living in a tipi in the Selkirk Settlement of Manitoba; after several months John Tanner was persuaded to grudgingly return to white civilization.[84] The young man was a hunter and content in his life in the village with his Native family. He was married to Therese Akwemikons, an Odawa woman, most likely from Arbre Croche, Michigan.[85] Tanner and his wife and children, Martha and Lucy, moved to Mackinac at the recommendation of his brother, who never forgot Therese Schindler's offer to help find John. Schindler's granddaughter writes that once the Tanner family was on the island, "They pitched their wigwam on the beach opposite the home of Madame T. Schindler."[86] She befriended them, yet John's wife wanted to leave Mackinac and return to her kinspeople and village. Altercations between husband and wife followed, and an early-day custody battle blew up. John Tanner, uncomfortable and often laughed at in the white man's clothes his brother forced upon him, had grown bitter. He took the children from their mother, leaving her with Therese. In months to come he returned the little ones, and Schindler and her daughter, Marianne Fisher, became a crucial part of the extended family, raising the children, in particular the baby, Lucy. The children were baptized, and Therese found their mother work as a housekeeper. Over time young Lucy became a great favorite of Madame Schindler's, and E. T. Baird displays self-referential humor, saying that the only grandchild of Schindler (referring to herself in third person) was incredibly spoiled and it was a good thing that baby Lucy came along to put a stop to the coddling.[87]

Lucy was an able student in the boarding school where Marianne taught. Fisher was a scholar as well as a teacher. After teaching on Mackinac, she entered a mission at Grand Haven, where she translated excerpts from the Bible into Native language. Therese's daughter immersed herself in the work of translation only a few years after Jane Schoolcraft began translating her own poetry into Native language.

Lucy Tanner was not the only child whom Therese would take in and care for. Among the other children she raised, there was the son of a slave, one François LaCroix. He was one of a small number of African Americans present on Mackinac at that time. As for Martha, Lucy's older sister, her story encapsulates what many a brilliant woman, whether Indigenous or white, experienced when attempting a professional career with an honorable goal. As a mixed-blood person, Martha endured a double whammy when trying to establish a school for Anishinaabe children. She was promised a building for the children in St. Ignace, Michigan, but ran afoul of a local priest who refused her bid to give instruction in her Native culture. He insisted she teach catechism, and when she resisted, he denied her the use of the building. Author Theresa Weller reveals letters exchanged between Martha and Mackinac Indian agent A. M. Fitch, and she further documents the situation: "After the priest discovered Martha had no intention of renovating the Catholic school, he told the Native community they were "strictly forbidden to send their children to her school."[88] To E. T. Baird, Martha later wrote of how "suffering such impositions and injustices from Priest and Bishop made my life and employment an insupportable burden."[89]

The Tanners, especially Martha and her father, John, whom Schindler took in, stand out as a family caught between cultures and the tragedy of assimilation. Martha was left infuriated and bereft when she was refused her dream of educating Native children. Her father was never the same after being persuaded to join the white world of his brother. On Mackinac and north to the Hudson Bay he became increasingly pugnacious. He left the island and wherever he traveled he chose not to live inside a house if he could help it. In the Hudson Bay area, he was charged but not convicted of murder. Eventually he disappeared and his family did not hear from him again. Referring to Tanner, Baird, a Native woman, tells us: "The father never learned to talk like a white man. . . . Though he could not speak English, he talked Chippewa as well as any Indian of the tribe."[90] Though Tanner was white, he suffered the wrath of many Euro-Americans because he chose the Anishinaabe way of life. He stands as an example of racism directed towards Native culture, regardless of one's ethnicity.

Beyond her professions as a fur trader and proprietor of a lucrative maple sugar camp, Schindler was a person sought out for her knowledge of historical record. In October 1836, Henry Schoolcraft, the United States Indian agent on Mackinac, invited her to his office for an extensive interview. It is helpful to know what these agents did, and to understand Therese's probable wariness. Beginning in 1793, the U.S. federal government hired men to "handle" Indigenous tribes. These Indian agents were instructed to settle conflicts between whites and Native people. They also pushed for assimilation of the Anishinaabe, a U.S. government policy that attempted to strip them of their culture. Most of the Native men and women interviewed by Henry were left unnamed, but Therese, as a pillar of the community, was dignified with a date and name. Historian Edwin O. Wood observed that Schindler was of interest to the Indian agent because she had "lived through a historical era of much interest on the Island."[91] Indeed, Therese, age sixty-three, offered him details on the post of Fort Michilimackinac. She remembered the British commanding officers well, including Doyle, Robinson, and Sinclair. She spoke of an Indian interpreter, Hans, from that period, and of Langlade, the interpreter during the time of Chief Pontiac's war on the fort.[92] Along with sister Madeline Laframboise and Therese's granddaughter, E. T. Baird, these three women contributed to the history of culture and of wartime, with their testaments to both.

Therese Schindler outlived her younger sister, Madeline, by nine years. She had her photograph taken late in life, and this document is valuable. Not only does it give us an image of her handsome face, but given the nature of family resemblance, it offers a suggestion of what Laframboise may have looked like as well. There were no photographs or paintings of Laframboise in her lifetime.

In her last will and testament, Madeline left money for the poor, and for family and friends. She had requested that she be interred under the altar of Ste. Anne's church next to Josette and her grandson.[93] For years after her death in 1846, her body languished outdoors in a courtyard area next to the church. In 2013, her bones were moved indoors to a museum in the basement of the church. Perhaps this last action is a sign we are moving closer to an honest appreciation of the greatness of Madeline Laframboise. The same may be said of Madame Schindler. In 1853, several years after the death of her daughter, Marianne, Therese left Mackinac and went to live with her granddaughter, E. T. Baird, in Wisconsin. On the last day of October 1855, Schindler died in Green Bay at age eighty. In accordance with her wishes she is buried on Mackinac next to her daughter, Marianne. Therese had a wide circle of family and colleagues, and was a leader in community and commerce on Mackinac in the nineteenth century.

As the proprietor of two strong commercial ventures, she emerges as the unsung sister of Laframboise on Mackinac. Like Madeline, Therese was capable of moving successfully in several directions. Laframboise and Schindler were uncommon historical figures and key players in Big Lake country commerce. No two women on Mackinac before or after achieved their visionary reach in the fur trade. Yet the story of the women of this family did not end there, as demonstrated by the record of the succeeding generations on Mackinac, including Marianne Fisher and E. T. Baird. Baird in particular, with her lively and revealing social history, brings the family ties of this group full circle.

CHAPTER THREE

Agatha Biddle
(1797–1873)

The life of Agatha Biddle, a 2018 inductee into the Michigan Women's Hall of Fame, illuminates the early development of civil society in the Great Lakes region. An Odawa who faithfully served Native people in Michigan through care, support, and mediation, Biddle represents an influential figure who stood at the edge of the Métis and American cultures. The intertwined community of women on Mackinac Island supported and galvanized her. Fur trader Madeline Laframboise's generous spirit and masterly negotiating skills in commerce made a great impression on Agatha. While Biddle was Métis, she is said to have identified as Odawa.[1]

She did not achieve her strong voice overnight. Yet with persistence, Biddle surprised the American community on Mackinac. Eric Hemenway, of the Little Traverse Bay Bands of Odawa Indians, discusses her role as a witness to the Treaty of Washington in 1836, when 16 million acres of Native land was ceded to the U.S. government. Initially, the government permitted many tribes to stay on small reservations and maintain their rights to the natural resources. Years later, Agatha was a spokesperson at the Treaty of Detroit in 1855 when she helped to secure the fishing and hunting rights of the Native people in the Straits area. Deeply involved in the Indigenous community, Agatha met for years with an Odawa band on the island.[2] She donated medicines and even contributed coffins and performed burial services for the Native people who died on the island.[3]

She was renowned for her aid to those suffering starvation, poverty, and illness. There are records of Agatha giving prodigious quantities of flour, fish, corn, wood, tea, sugar, and coffee to her Native relatives and friends who came to Mackinac. Many resided at the Biddle house, which was often full to bursting with guests. Public notary Samuel Abbott confirms this with reports of seeing Agatha's kitchen "crowded with Indians, receiving shelter and food."[4]

In 1819, Agatha married Edward Biddle, a Protestant American from Philadelphia. The majority of Native women who married Euro-Americans formed a union with French Canadian men. While the French traders and voyageurs absorbed much of the Native culture, this was less true of the Americans, who strove for the mantle of dominant culture. Once they were married, Agatha and Edward must have experienced mutual culture shock. Agatha had grown up in a small village with two Native parents, her mother and stepfather, and her education included birchbark basketry, quill work, and immersion in a hunting and trapping milieu—while Edward Biddle was raised in the primarily white city culture of Philadelphia. Adding to the confusion of cultures for the pair, the Great Lakes region was a new experience for him when he arrived soon after the War of 1812.[5] Further, the language barrier added to their challenges. Edward spoke English, while the primary language for most Métis on Mackinac at this time, including Agatha, was French.[6]

Born Agatha de la Vigne, she was young when her family moved to Mackinac. According to E. T. Baird, Agatha and her mother, Marie Le Fevre, were certainly on Mackinac by the time the girl was around seven.[7] This was 1804, a time of shifting alliances in politics, religion, and culture. In order to make her way in the world Agatha became a sharp observer, and it appears that after her marriage to Edward, she brought a degree of diplomacy that would help the relationship to thrive. Biddle was accepted into Mackinac society in ways that were denied to Madeline Laframboise and many Native residents who were socially "excluded by the Americans."[8] Socializing with Americans was not remotely easy for Agatha; the pressure to assimilate would have been great.

E. T. Baird, who knew her, states that Agatha was "one of Laframboise's converts" to the Catholic faith, and Keith Widder discusses the "folk Catholicism" of many of the Métis.[9] Agatha and her band on Mackinac still adhered to Native culture and beliefs as well, and often adopted tenets of the Christian faith to a moderate degree or in order to placate the elite white culture. Even the Biddle wedding held cultural and spiritual components of both Native and white beliefs. The ceremony included Edward's American officer friends along with Agatha's Native family.[10] Yet this kind of event was an anomaly. The Anishinaabe had enormous difficulty being accepted as equals by white America.[11]

Earlier in American records, an analogy may be seen in the feast of Thanksgiving between Indigenous and Euro-Americans in seventeenth-century New England. Revisionist history recognizes how rare an event that was, one not repeated afterwards. Despite a fine meal shared by the Pokanokets and Governor William Bradford and his settlement—deer and birds turned on wooden spits and pottages with corn, squash, beans, and barley—there was great division of cultures, and the Native people were not often welcome.[12] So it was with American society on Mackinac. The mixed-blood people were referred to often by others in their era as "half-breeds." In his study of the challenges the Métis faced, Darren R. Préfontaine writes: "The children of these often-illicit unions lived precariously near or at various Great Lakes fur trading and military posts, or with their mothers' bands."[13]

Agatha Biddle was described as having a fair complexion, black eyes, and long dark hair.[14] As discussed in my study of Madeline Laframboise, Elizabeth Mitchell, and Elizabeth Therese Baird, those who were neither fully Native nor white were vulnerable to exclusion from either group, and certainly the "Euro-American society had mixed feelings about Agathe's [sic] status among them."[15] Nonetheless, their mixed-race status may have given some women in the Great Lakes region a certain freedom, and perhaps courage to enter business in ways not available to others of their sex.

The American and British women were tethered to laws of inequality and culturally ingrained notions of them as "the inferior sex." Women lived their lives largely according to housebound rules and roles established for generations. Naturally, Native women had their respective strictures as well, but the frisson arising from mixed marriages engendered change. Added to this was the political and social upheaval in the years following the War of 1812. Under such circumstances anything could happen, including the higher profile of women fur traders or social activists like Agatha Biddle. In part, the very chaos of wartime conferred a new kind of freedom and authenticity on women in the fur trade and other arenas. No doubt this was a double-edged sword. If the Métis women were accorded greater freedom than their Euro-American sisters, it was equally true that they endured hardship and discrimination.

Agatha is one of many Métis people who populated the Straits region. They formed what author Richard White calls a middle-ground society in the Mackinac of the early 1800s.[16] According to White, this mixed-race society all but disappeared with the advent of the "Americanization of the island." Bethany Fleming puts forward the theory that indeed the "middle ground" did not disappear after 1815, as proposed by White. Both Fleming and Susan Sleeper-Smith posit that owing to the Native women's determination to preserve their way of life, the Métis culture was maintained.[17] Resisting acculturation was not easy, and in all likelihood Agatha's social position was often uncomfortable. Mixed-race people were viewed as a group separate from the "Indians" and Euro-Americans, and as such were at "the bottom of the social hierarchy at Mackinac."[18] As a result, and despite Native women such as Biddle and Schindler or Laframboise succeeding in fur trading and other professions on Mackinac, they assumed a distinct *outsider* status.

There is no evidence Agatha had her own winter outpost and was ferrying furs in her bateau, as did Mackinac trader Madeline Laframboise. Nonetheless, she, too, would have had struggles in the male-centric world of the nineteenth century. It took extraordinary courage to assert herself, whether trying to be taken seriously in her transactions at the American Fur Company or in encounters with the trappers, voyageurs, and soldiers. Though rarely spoken of, violence to women was common in the old Northwest, and fear of dangerous encounters was never far from a woman's mind.[19] Relevant similarities between the past and present exist. Regina Gasco-Bentley speaks of the hotlines to call for women today in the Little Traverse Bay Bands of Odawa. She has attended conferences on Mackinac for "Violence Against Native Women."[20]

Marriages between Native women and Euro-Americans were either a locked door or a gateway for them to carry forward their heritage. Both Elizabeth Mitchell and Agatha Biddle had husbands who supported their wives in their Native culture. Madeline Laframboise was widowed at an early age, and we do not know the extent to which her French Canadian husband would have held up Madeline's beliefs during her long life. The life on Mackinac of Ojibwe poet Jane Schoolcraft has not been explored before, but will be taken up in a close study in this book. Her marriage to the Indian agent Henry, and consequently her freedom to carry forward her Native poetry, song, and stories became a great personal challenge.[21]

It was not easy for the Anishinaabe to hold fast to their traditions in an era when they were expected to negate their former heritage and adhere culturally to Euro-American ideas of language, religion, education, dress, and business. The very tone of letters written on Mackinac by Euro-Americans in the early nineteenth century reveals a presumption of cultural superiority. This is apparent in letters, whether written by Alice Bacon from Connecticut speaking of the "raving infernals" on Mackinac, or when Myra Peters Mason comments disapprovingly that the island is a halfway world existing somewhere between "civilization and barbarism."[22] Such stances reinforced the reality of exclusion of people from the majority of Euro-American social events. Even Agatha Biddle, married to a Philadelphian, would have felt the sting of condescension to one whose heritage had been the dominant culture in North America for thousands of years.

Most of the Métis who made up the "middle ground" on Mackinac lived modestly. Islander Augustin Cadotte and Marie, his Ojibwe wife, lived in "one shell of a house" and had a very "small garden without fence."[23] For the most part, the Métis socialized with their Native American friends and relatives, and had their own cultural traditions. While the soldiers at Fort Mackinac had fellow Americans to gatherings in the holiday season, the Métis would read services until midnight on Christmas Eve. On New Year's Eve, the elderly fishermen would visit all the Native houses attired in "grotesque dress," meaning ugly or comically distorted garb. They sang boisterously to the daughters of each household, threatening to take the girls away and causing a great fright among them.[24] Given the early age at which young Native girls were married off, the very idea of such a proposition—even in fun—may have been alarming.

Families like the Cadottes dug potatoes for baker William McGulpin, hauled firewood, and sold whitefish to soldiers and merchants alike. Elizabeth Mitchell, although achieving a certain degree of wealth, did not have the pedigree Agatha Biddle gained from marrying a member of the East Coast upper crust. Well-off though she was, Elizabeth was nearly always hard at work. She would have delivered hay and garden harvest to the Biddles. Meanwhile, it is likely that other Native families such as the Cadottes delivered fish and wood to Agatha and her husband, Edward. In return, the Biddles, as businesspeople, sold nutmeg, whiskey, candles, and other prized goods to the Cadottes, and to numerous other Native trappers. The Métis and French Canadians labored in the harsh winters of the north country, and they ventured out into the stormy lake to ferry merchants, traders, clerks, and families to their destination on Mackinac. The mixed-race citizens played an indispensable part in this island community.

From an economic vantage point, Agatha fared better than most Native women in the western Great Lakes region. That she made it her business to reach out to many in need is noteworthy. She could have chosen a relatively insular life with Edward Biddle. This she did not do. Her outreach was widespread. Public notary Samuel

Abbott stated that "the number thereof who were participants of Mrs. Biddle's charity, independent of those who have entertained on account of trade or business, were annually great." Abbott was an acquaintance of Edward and Agatha.[25]

It is not known what year Agatha's father died or disappeared from her life. The girl's first stepfather was an Odawa medicine man, named Kougowma but often called Le Vigne.[26] The girl lived with her Native mother, Marie Le Fevre, and Kougowma in Arbre Croche, Michigan. Those formative years cemented Agatha's connection to her heritage. There is no record of another sibling when Marie brought her daughter to live on Mackinac. The girl's second stepfather, Joseph Bailly, was a boisterous fur trader from Montreal. He and Marie were not married right away and he brought several children from his prior marriage to the relationship.

Agatha's mother was known as "a good woman" and a gifted storyteller who could regale friends with tales that were as entertaining as *The Arabian Nights*. The Indigenous writer Elizabeth T. Baird describes Marie as "an Indian of unalloyed blood and had been very little among the white people." Both mother and her daughter, "the Indian girl," wore Native dress. Agatha's mother was a role model whose strong traits held the daughter in good stead during difficult times. One such challenge occurred on Mackinac when her stepfather, Bailly, sent his biological daughters away for a formal education, yet did not extend this opportunity to Agatha. If she felt deprived, Agatha's integrity guided her forward.[27]

Overall, Bailly was said to be a kind, if vain and noisy, man. Owing to his vociferous presence, islanders said they easily knew his whereabouts anywhere on Mackinac.[28] Living with Bailly and her mother—whose stories people never tired of listening to—the girl grew up in a lively atmosphere. Added to this was the upswing of the fur-trade industry with its bustle and myriad colorful characters. In its midst, a portrait of Agatha Biddle emerges. Here is a perceptive, ambitious, and diplomatic young woman. Here is a woman with a quiet determination to effect change.

It is useful to revisit the Native mentors in Agatha's life, those who shaped her character. Older women surviving the uncertain years after the Ojibwe and Sauk attack on Michilimackinac and leading up to the War of 1812 include Madeline Laframboise and Elizabeth Mitchell.[29] Agatha would have been in awe of the formidable Mitchell, her close neighbor with the outsized personality and talents as a fur trader and farmer.

Agatha could not have missed the sight of Elizabeth in her carriage, lines in hand, guiding her horse through town. Whether driving her calash first to her garden and then onward to work on the Mitchell farm, the older woman's independent personality was on display. It is possible that particularly in her teen years, Agatha may have had conflicted thoughts about Elizabeth Mitchell. Certainly E. T. Baird, memoirist, had moments when she hardly knew what to make of Mitchell's strong character.[30] There was her largess in opening her home and hosting the wedding of Agatha's friend Josette Laframboise, but look again and several years later here was this same hospitable woman getting herself in trouble with the Americans. In the small community of Mackinac, surely there were murmurings about David and Elizabeth's loyalty to the Crown. Surely Agatha's family knew that David had to leave the island after the American takeover, and it would have been all the news that Elizabeth was consorting with her Native kin and friends who were loyal to the British. Even worse, the public notice threatening her arrest had been tacked up on the front of an island church. The message to Agatha would be to maintain a politically neutral position for several reasons: for her own safety, and also to proceed unhampered with her business and outreach interests.

This politically neutral position was further reinforced by her awareness of another pair of strong women. The Ojibwe poet Jane Johnston Schoolcraft moved to Mackinac in 1833. She grew up in Sault Ste. Marie with an Irish father who had pronounced British loyalties. Her unpublished poetry reveals private concerns regarding her childhood culture, yet her public face on Mackinac hid her fealty to the Canadian region that she called home.[31] Schoolcraft's husband, Henry, was the Indian agent on the island for nine years, and his reputation for stealing and exaggerating Native history disturbed Edward Biddle and, most likely, Agatha. Edward made clear to author Francis Parkman that he thought the Indian agent had "mangled" and "fabricated" Native history.[32] While both Agatha and Jane Schoolcraft were married to Americans, there is no record of them being friends, which makes sense given the Indian agent's position and actions in the Mackinac community. It is clear, however, that both women strove to maintain politically neutral demeanors.

Madeline Laframboise was a dynamic presence in the life of young Agatha. In teaching classes in catechism to her, Laframboise was giving the girl an opportunity to attend the island school the older fur trader had started. Separately, Laframboise was a living example of the business success to be had in remaining neutral during the back-and-forth years of British versus American possession of Mackinac. Agatha would later become a significant negotiator in her own right.

Biddle was not only a witness in the signing on Mackinac of the "Treaty of 1836" but also remembered for her later participation with the People of the Three Fires in the Great Lakes region, and with the signing of the Treaty of 1855.[33] Though she would not live to see the Odawa regain many of the rights they had lost, this treaty was the foundation for future voices to speak up on behalf of Native people in the Straits region.

Society and sisterhood were intertwined on the island. At a time when the female population could not own property and they were indeed considered the property of their husbands, these women needed one another in order to survive. Like Laframboise, Agatha looked out for the welfare of Native people and others on the island. In addition to caring for her immediate family, she took in the sick and the starving, the elderly and young orphans. One such family were the Moconamas, who came under Agatha's wing for two years. Another young woman, Cornelia Fonda, the daughter of a Native woman and an African American man, lived with Agatha and Edward for six years, until she was taken under the wing of the missionaries Amanda and William Ferry.[34] There was also Keshawa, an orphan Native girl whom Agatha educated and included as one of her own in the 1820s and 1830s. Keshawa would reside with the Biddles for sixteen years.[35]

At her wedding on Mackinac in 1819, Biddle wore a traditional Odawa dress, as did her mother and Madeline Laframboise and Therese Schindler, also in attendance. The mixed-race women dressed in layers of silk and broadcloth, embellished with colorful ribbons and beads. At the civil service performed by Samuel Abbott, Agatha was attired beautifully, from long braids tied up "making a double *quett*," to her black skirt, blanket, scarlet leggings, and moccasins. The ceremony took place in Joseph and Agnes Bailly's home, he boasting about the match between his stepdaughter and the groom from a fine East Coast family.[36]

Eventually, Agatha and Edward Biddle moved into what is now a historic landmark on Market Street and one of the oldest houses on Mackinac. Edward put a down payment of $100 towards the house in 1822. The deed to the home came in 1827, but it is possible the couple moved in a few years earlier. The Biddle family owned the house for two generations. Several owners later, there was a fire that burnt down the homestead in 1910. Eventually what remained was dismantled and rebuilt with some of the original lumber. This historic reconstruction took place in 1959–1960 and was instigated by the Women's Architectural League of Detroit, along with the Michigan Society of Architects and building industries.[37] It is worth noting how many historic buildings across America have been saved and preserved by women's groups, from the Daughters of the American Revolution (DAR) to historical societies of all stripes.

In Agatha and Edward's era, the house would have looked a good deal more rustic than it does today with its fresh coats of paint. It is an outstanding example of Quebec rural architecture. Inside, the front hall led to the good-sized main room where immediate family, relatives, and friends gathered. Perched in a prominent space was the spinning wheel, an indispensable tool to spin wool into thread that Agatha used to make clothing and blankets for her family and others.[38] Upstairs there were bedrooms for Agatha, Edward, and their children. On the main floor there was another bedroom for guests and those whom Agatha took in. They included seasonal workers, perhaps fur-trading parents leaving off children when they went for supplies, or the ill and disabled coming to the island. The kitchen was ever a busy place. The historic interpreters at the Biddle House in the twentieth and twenty-first centuries cooked in much the same manner as Agatha would have, the savory smell of soups, fish, and fowl inviting tourists to visit Agatha's home. When cooking squash, carrots, and mashed potatoes, the Mackinac State Park interpreters availed themselves of herbs from the house garden similar to the one Agatha had. Lard was used for baking, as this was an age before refrigeration. For decades before the summer of 2020, the Biddle House history guides greeted visitors in period dress and faithfully re-created the living quarters of Agatha and Edward. Today the interpreter is intact, but the interior home has become a Native American museum.

The Biddles ran a moderately successful fur-trading business, with Agatha managing the inventory and accounts. The American Fur Company records show Agatha Biddle in commerce with the Company store just a few doors down from the Biddle home. The account books from the retail store on Mackinac reveal payment of bills with moccasins and birchbark containers.[39] Bethany Fleming writes that "Archaeological evidence from the outhouse site used by the Biddle family in the 1820s and 30s reveals numerous pieces of birch bark and quill work, suggesting Agatha's every day work life, making such items as mococks."[40] Further evidence of regular attendance to business accounts by Agatha is reflected in her purchases. One record shows that she bought cambric linen "at 89 cents a yard." This was an expensive and durable material that was used to make undergarments and blouses. Her business accounts also point to a degree of prosperity.

The oldest of seven children, Sophia was born to Agatha in 1820. She was expected to straddle the dual cultures of Native and American heritage. More troubling, religious challenges sprang up as the Native population became the focus of proselytizing groups. Missionaries, both Presbyterian and Catholic, eyed the mixed-race people of Mackinac for conversion to their respective dogmas. This is not to say that all missionaries were dogmatic, but in the 1800s there was a heated contest for "saving souls" by quashing the Native American beliefs in a nature-based spirituality.

Sent away to Philadelphia to be educated, Sophia returned home to the island with fine manners and an elegance to match. She had lived at the home of her father's first cousin, Nicholas Biddle, president of the United States Bank, and this family saw to it she was given a formal education.[41] Counted among her many admirers was Lieutenant Pemberton, later a lieutenant-general in the Confederate Army. As has been pointed out, Mackinac was nothing if not diverse. In the early to mid-nineteenth century, there were at different times French, English, Scots, Irish, French Canadians, Métis, Native Americans, and African Americans who lived on the island.

When Sophia was growing up on the island, she experienced the atmosphere of what had been a "religious war," as E. T. Baird described it.[42] The strained atmosphere was felt by all. Agatha's daughter became caught up in the struggle and was drawn to the example set years earlier by the Ferrys. With friends on either side of the ferment, Sophia was torn after returning from boarding school off-island. According to Baird, she felt "persecuted and unhappy. . . . ashamed of her [Native] blood." We can only imagine Agatha's deep unhappiness, for Sophia refused to walk with her mother to Catholic service. Eventually, Madame Laframboise intervened once again. She is said to have "worked hard to win her [Sophia] back" into the Catholic fold. This she did, and there was peace once again between mother and daughter.[43]

A happy outcome was not in the cards for Sophia Biddle. She became consumptive—most likely pulmonary tuberculosis—and died in 1848 at age twenty-eight. The Biddles also lost their youngest, Mary, when she fell through the ice crossing between Mackinac and St. Ignace. This child's grave is the oldest known marker in Ste. Anne's Cemetery. Having lost children herself, perhaps Agatha sensed that helping others in need might provide a salve to her own bereavement.

Her participation with a group of Native women on Mackinac indicates that in 1870 she was chief of the "Mackinac Band, the Chippewa affiliated group" that was based on the island.[44] Edward learned from Agatha about the virtue of aiding the Native population on Mackinac, and she convinced him to "respect the customs of her people." Over time, the couple fed many Native people, baking bread annually for hundreds of hungry souls. Eventually, and as a result of Agatha's claims to the Bureau of Indian Affairs in Washington, DC, the couple was awarded restitution by the U.S. government. As testament to the assistance, the documents were signed by numerous chiefs, including Pawiss, Machecawishis, Chawnese, and Shawmsgheshick of the Odawa tribes.[45]

The Biddles were a strong presence on Mackinac, and though Agatha lost Edward in 1859, she remained fully engaged in the island community for years to come.

Through her actions she fought against racial and gender stereotypes. When Agatha was seventy-two, Susan B. Anthony and Elizabeth Cady Stanton would organize the National Woman Suffrage Association. Interestingly, future summer residents Delos and Daisy Blodgett were strong supporters of Susan B. Anthony and the fight to give women the vote. Agatha would likely have appreciated that pair and their belief in a voice for all people.

Agatha lived for forty years in the Biddle House on Market Street. She died in her home on Mackinac in 1873. Her humanitarian outreach was remarkable, and she stands as an example of one who struggled to embrace the diversity of her age. She fought against such labels as "half-breed," and as an outsider she succeeded because of the supportive network of Native women in her life who modeled strength of character. Biddle straddled multiple cultures and emerged as a highly esteemed diplomatic figure and community leader.

PART II

Saving History

A Literature of Witness

We remember history because of preserved documents. Over thousands of years the known records have been published mostly by men. Yet there are significant, lesser-known historical records by Juliette Kinzie, Jane Schoolcraft, Anna Jameson, and Margaret Fuller. These authors wrote about Mackinac and chronicled the plight and the strengths of the Native American and the culture of the westward-striving United States and Canada.

The second wave of extraordinary women in this study gave us a crucial history of the Anishinaabe women on Mackinac: Elizabeth Mitchell, Madeline Laframboise, Therese Schindler, and Agatha Biddle, none of whom left behind diaries or autobiographies.

CHAPTER FOUR

Juliette Magill Kinzie (1806–1870)

T he following encounter between Kinzie and Laframboise gives an imagined personal look at the connection between two key figures in the Great Lakes, and imparts a felt sense of life on Mackinac in the year 1830. It is based on Kinzie's own observations after meeting the well-known fur trader.[1]

Despite the humidity, a blue sky brightened the spirits of the islanders. Juliette Magill Kinzie walked briskly beside Madeline Laframboise, to whom she had been introduced only hours earlier. As a young woman not yet famous for her history of people and pioneer life in the Midwest, Kinzie felt honored to be invited to join the busy fur trader on her way from Market Street down to her home on the shore road.

Laframboise was said to wear Native dress every day. Two rows of neatly stitched colored beads on her bodice glinted brightly on this summer afternoon in the high season of Mackinac. Kinzie pushed to keep astride of the tall, older woman, the floppy lace collar on her sturdy broadcloth dress flapping up in her face from a sudden breeze. She was a small woman with large inquiring eyes. Oblivious to her own beauty, Juliette was ever intent on those around her, pulling her bonnet close about her face as if to discount her own physical presence.

She could not suppress a sharp intake of breath at the sight of the vibrant life on the shore near town. Many more wigwams had sprung up since yesterday when she had arrived with her husband, John, a former clerk for the American Fur Company. It was noon, and both smoke and the smell of delicious whitefish on the fires filled the air. One woman dexterously filleted a fish with one eye, and with the other, watched her children venture towards the edge of the shore. In deerskin and beaded moccasins, one little boy and girl leapt up and down, calling out to a canoe advancing to the beach. Heaped with pelts, it was very possibly the children's father's boat with goods to trade. Kinzie saw that Laframboise took note of the canoe, and it seemed to the younger woman that the famous trader had done a quick tally of the furs before turning to smile at a friend passing by.

As they walked along, many greeted her warmly, and Madeline had a thoughtful response to each individual they passed; a marked decorum when she spoke to Robert Stuart of the American Fur Company and Amanda and William Ferry, the couple who were Presbyterian missionaries. Warmth and humor flowed when Madeline spoke to the voyageurs and Native people, some of them her relatives.[2] She stopped for extended conversation with Agatha Biddle, who was eager to fill her in on a meeting she had organized with their band of sister Ojibwe. A minute later and the two friends, Agatha somewhere near the age of Kinzie herself, began talking about storehouse supplies at the warehouse on Market Street. At one point in the conversation, Agatha turned to Juliette, saying, "Madame Laframboise was my teacher, you know."[3]

On parting, Laframboise extended a maternal hand and patted Agatha's thin shoulder. Kinzie and Laframboise walked on towards the east end of town where the older woman lived. Not breaking her stride, she inclined her head to Juliette: "Your husband John seems a fine fellow. My kin respect him." Kinzie beamed, thinking of John and his hard-working ways. Before becoming an Indian agent, he had lived on Mackinac and worked in the fur trade.

Madeline spoke again: "I pray you will have him by your side for many years to come." Juliette glanced quickly at her new friend, expecting a doleful face. Should she extend a word of sympathy to the fur trader? She knew that Madeline had lost her husband years ago in a violent encounter. It took but a moment for Kinzie to realize that the trader had spoken these words in a matter-of-fact way; she did not expect pity.

Juliette had in no way experienced the sorrows of Madame Laframboise, but the recently married easterner could feel in her bones that the loneliness and fears that accompanied life on the frontier would soon be upon her. A little while later she bid Madeline goodbye in front of the trader's large and charming home. Kinzie watched her move gracefully up the walk, Laframboise's regal bearing evident even at a distance. The younger woman thought about another kind of distance traveled, that of the trader's early hardships and the path she had followed to this moment in her life. Juliette caught herself before speaking aloud: "Madeline Laframboise, you have been my teacher, too."[4]

Edwin O. Wood, editor of *Historic Mackinac*, writes that Juliette Kinzie is "one of the best known writers associated with early Mackinac."[5] In 1856, she published *Wau-Bun: The Early Day in the Northwest*.[6] The title, as translated from Ojibwe vocabulary, means the dawn, the break of day. Elsewhere Kinzie describes the early days of pioneer settlement in many parts of the Lake region and the cultural connection with the First Nation people, the Anishinaabe. With sharp observations of Mackinac in 1830, *Wau-Bun* stands the test of time as both a cultural and sociological study of frontier life and of the people in the old Northwest. That twenty-six years later she was compelled to publish her record of connections, most especially with Native women, indicates the deep impression they made on her.

In lively prose, Kinzie wrote about meeting Madame Laframboise, who was "of a tall and commanding figure and most dignified deportment." We are told about the early death of Madeline Laframboise's husband at the hands of a "Winnebago named White Ox," and of how Laframboise went on to enlarge the fur-trading business she and Joseph had begun. Madeline regularly visited all her trading posts, superintending the clerks and doing everything possible to make her trade profitable. Laframboise was a living example of one who did not let self-pity sneak into her life and ruin it. As a frontier woman who had already endured hardship herself, Kinzie must have felt a certain kinship with the great fur trader.[7]

She writes with aplomb about the period after the War of 1812: "These were the palmy days of Mackinac" when the Anishinaabe came to the island with peltries of "beaver, otter, marten, mink, silver-gray and red fox, wolf, bear. . . . along with smoked deerskins" and maple sugar to trade. She comments on the Native peoples' "toy-models of Indian cradles, snow shoes, canoes, &c., &c."[8] Kinzie is impressed with the Indigenous people who are doing everything possible to survive. With the gift of hindsight in 1856, Kinzie writes:

> Little did the noble souls at this day rejoicing in the success of their labors at Mackinac, anticipate that in less than a quarter of a century there would remain of all these numerous tribes but a few scattered bands. . . . their lands cajoled or wrested from them—the graves of their fathers turned up by the ploughshare—themselves

chased farther and farther towards the setting sun, until they were literally grudged a resting place on the face of the earth![9]

Born in 1806 in Middletown, Connecticut, Juliette Augusta Magill was a brilliant girl who absorbed books and life with equal intensity. On her mother's side she was descended from Roger Wolcott, governor of the state in colonial times, and her forebears helped to establish Windsor, Connecticut. Her family was a strong force in her life, and Juliette had an exceptional education for a girl of her time. She went to boarding school in New Haven where she was taught Latin and modern languages. After that, she attended an established girl's school in Troy, New York.[10]

Her uncle, Alexander Wolcott, introduced Juliette to her future husband, Major John H. Kinzie, during the latter's visit to Boston. Wolcott, who became a medical doctor in the Chicago area, had sent letters home to New England that fired Juliette's imagination about the Midwest.[11] Keen for adventure, she found John a colorful character. Earlier in his life, he "had charge of the American Fur Company's retail store" on Mackinac selling "buckskin coats, moccasins, flannel shirts, and gaudy neckbands" during the lively and sometimes dangerous period of 1818–1823. Dr. Jesse S. Myers has written an informative account of this era with descriptions of the street fights with "brigade bullies," and of a frightening incident. John Kinzie was in charge of the retail store at the corner of Fort Hill Street when a rifle was discharged, striking Canadian voyageur Alexis St. Martin and resulting in "a cavity the size of a man's fist" in his stomach. St. Martin was taken inside the store, where Dr. William Beaumont, the Fort Mackinac army surgeon, subsequently performed multiple investigative operations on the man's open stomach while he was conscious.[12]

In addition to running the retail store, John had apprenticed for Robert Stuart at the American Fur Company on Mackinac. In 1818, Gurdon S. Hubbard came to work for John in "the assorting-warehouse," where his job was to "count and record the number and kinds of furs received from the various trading-posts." Gurdon, and we may assume, John, worked long hours from 5:00 A.M. to 7:00 P.M. Hubbard formed a strong friendship with fur traders Therese Schindler and Madeline Laframboise. The collegial friendship Gurdon Hubbard had with John Kinzie, Therese Schindler, and Madeline Laframboise represents the connection between women and men who contributed to the Mackinac community. Also underscoring the close ties among Mackinac women was E. T. Baird's friendship with John Kinzie's parents. Juliette would come to know this couple and document their extraordinary pioneer experiences later in her life.[13]

By the time Juliette met John, he was an Indian agent stationed at Fort Winnebago, then part of Michigan Territory. As a representative in an appointment by President John Quincy Adams, the job of an agent was to closely observe the lives of the Anishinaabe and to make reports to the government that invariably favored whites. These agents possessed huge power, and while some were honorable, there were many others who were anything but ambassadors serving the Anishinaabe. Their duties included keeping peace between whites and Native people and making sure the latter received their annual annuities from the U.S. government. Unfortunately, some lined their own pockets with monies rightfully belonging to tribal bands.

John Kinzie was one of the honorable agents, and Juliette must have sensed this. He also possessed a charisma that attracted her. His good looks and stories of life in the west were an antidote to the staid fellows she knew in the east. As editor Louise P. Kellogg writes in her introduction to *Wau-Bun*: "He [John H. Kinzie] bore about him that breath of romance from that frontier region where wild men lived and wild deeds were common. . . . Now the west stood embodied in youth who fulfilled all her dreams of adventure."[14]

This was Juliette's picture of a dashing frontiersman before she married him. Little did she guess at the hardships in store for her. How she met these trials is a study in faith and courage. After they wed and traveled to Mackinac, the pair moved to Fort Winnebago near the portage between the Fox and Wisconsin Rivers.[15] By all appearances, their marriage was strong, and in their life together she was able to fulfill her destiny as a historian.

On arrival in 1830, Juliette notes the way John is greeted by the Anishinaabe on the island. She writes with both amusement and delight: "A shout of welcome was sent forth, as they recognized Shaw-nee-aw-kee, who from a seven years' residence among them, was well known to each individual."[16] The translation of Shaw-nee-aw-kee was "Silver Man," in reference to John's father, who had been a silversmith, making and repairing much jewelry for the Native people where John's family lived in southwest Michigan. As a tribute, they gave this name to members of the Kinzie family. Juliette writes that the Indigenous residents on Mackinac kept up their warm salutations and she was happy to accept "all the good wishes showered upon "Madame John."[17]

Though her husband was known to be one of the humane Indian agents, Juliette understood what a complex relationship there was between the Native population and those, like John, who were tasked with making sure they were given the payments that were due them. Agents also had to mediate between tribal factions and address the whites' ongoing conflict with them. Yet Kinzie's observations of how Anishinaabe land was "wrested" from them draws attention to the U.S. government's overarching plan for their not-so-gradual displacement, the ploughs that overturned graves so that "they [the Indigenous nations] were literally grudged a resting place on the face of the earth!"[18]

Kinzie's first publication was a 34-page pamphlet published anonymously and assumed to be the work of her husband. *The Narrative of the Massacre of Chicago, August 15, 1812, and of Some Preceding Events* was well received. Once she saw its positive reception she admitted to authorship. In this narrative based on the Black Hawk War, Kinzie included documents of the Native Americans who were exiled by her husband's family. Such a perspective reveals her sensitivity to the plight of the Anishinaabe, unusual for a white woman of that time. Kinzie looked at all sides of the culture clash, including the journals of her relative Thomas Forsyth and his belief that the Americans rather than the Sauks were responsible for the bloodshed. *Narrative of the Massacre* would have twenty-three reprintings over the course of the nineteenth and twentieth centuries.[19]

Her book, *Wau-Bun*, includes the attack on the Chicago territory, but is also a chronological journey narrative that covers three years, 1830–1833. She examines the territory between Fort Winnebago and Chicago, including Mackinac. This is no strict history of battles and the lives of soldiers. Though it is a first-person account, she avoids the conventions of male discourse and that of the narrow memoirist.[20] She scarcely mentions the lives of her children, or that three of the seven died in childbirth. Instead, Juliette keeps an eye trained on the intersection of cultures that she encounters.

Both Kinzie and poet Jane Schoolcraft were married to Indian agents. Jane would arrive on Mackinac two years after Kinzie. Of the two men (Henry Schoolcraft married Jane), John Kinzie was the more sympathetic to the Anishinaabe. Unlike Henry Schoolcraft, he had grown up with Native people as an everyday part of his life. John's father was a fur trader at a time when many traders coexisted with the Ojibwe and had an interdependent relationship. Juliette's John became fluent in several Native languages in his childhood. Though Kinzie's caring attitude towards Native people is obvious in her writing, she and John were Euro-Americans, part of the ethnic group that would displace many Native Americans. Juliette's compassionate look at their lives suggests that regarding her position of white privilege, she was more perceptive than many. One of many examples will suffice.

During her journey through dark waters and deep snow to Mackinac, she experiences an emotional tailspin and states that "I am not ashamed to confess my weakness [and] for the first time on my journey I shed tears."²¹ While sinking into the slough of despond, Kinzie notices an Ojibwe girl staring at her in curiosity. With acute awareness, she writes: "Probably she was speculating in her own mind what a person who rode so fine a horse, and wore so comfortable a broadcloth dress, could have to cry about."²² In one fell swoop, Kinzie employs humor (directed towards self) and empathy for another human being, in this case, one who does not have the same creature comforts that Euro-Americans possessed. Though it is equally possible that the girl was merely curious even as she was content in her own life, the point is that Kinzie stayed aware of people from other cultures and knew how to pull herself out of a teary freefall.

Coming to Mackinac in 1830, Kinzie and her husband rode the steamer the *Henry Clay*, from Detroit, and experienced a frightening storm on the way. However, Juliette does not dwell on the danger of traversing the turbulent waters at Thunder Bay. She simply marks the fact of a challenging journey. This fortitude and upbeat attitude towards her difficult life as a frontier woman make an impression on the reader. At one point in her journey, she discusses a conversation with one Mrs. Lawton, a sister pioneer in Illinois, who "complained bitterly of the loneliness of her condition, and having been brought out there into the woods, which was a thing she had not expected, when she came from the east."²³ Kinzie cannot help but wonder why this woman had not weighed and taken into consideration all that was at stake in choosing to move to the old Northwest.

Kinzie was an accomplished watercolorist. Music, too, was important in her life. She describes the great lengths to which she went in bringing her upright piano from Connecticut to the Great Lakes region. When she at last published *Wau-Bun*, the book was a beautifully bound edition that included many of Kinzie's paintings. The author understood the significance of art as a key medium in preserving history.

It is apparent that she uses her writing, music, and art to express an interior and exterior view of the world. In Kinzie's writing, we see a woman using her tools of trade to summon courage in the face of adversity. She did not live in a safe environment. Skirmishes and a treacherous attack had occurred just miles from her home in Illinois. Her husband had to travel often in his capacity as an Indian agent, and in his absence, Juliette was said to keep two loaded pistols near her pillow at night. In *Wau-Bun*, she details her mother-in-law's years of captivity by the Seneca after the attack at Fort Dearborn in 1812.²⁴

Her social history takes a look at the Anishinaabe's connection to the fur trade on Mackinac and their yearly annuities in 1830. Kinzie may not have realized that by the time of her trip the commerce of fur trading was in steep decline. Nonetheless, her descriptions reveal its glory days:

> It was no unusual thing, at this period, to see a hundred or more canoes of Indians at once approaching the Island, laden with their articles of traffic, and if to these we add the squadrons of large Mackinaw boats. . . . some idea may be formed of the extensive operations and important position of the American Fur Company, as well as of the vast circle of human beings either immediately or remotely connected with it.[25]

After a safe arrival on Mackinac, she and John were ushered into "the mansion" owned by Robert and Elizabeth Stuart of John Jacob Astor and Stuart Fur Company fame. Robert was both an old friend and a former employer of John's. He was married to Elizabeth, a philanthropist and avid supporter of the Presbyterian Mission House, which served as a school and was located on the east side of the island. Elizabeth was set on taking Juliette immediately to see this "object of especial interest to Mr. and Mrs. Stuart. . . . through the zeal and good management of Mr. and Mrs. Ferry, and the fostering encouragement, the school was in great repute."[26] Kinzie's observation contributed to the recognition of education at an early island school on Mackinac.

Though Kinzie writes of its "flourishing conditions" and the prospects that gladdened the "philanthropic hearts" of the Stuarts, the Mission Church would not flourish beyond 1836.[27] The editor of *Historic Mackinac* discusses the religious revival under Amanda and William Ferry's ministry that Kinzie witnessed. Most telling is editor Wood's comment that the Presbyterian church and connected school began to fail owing to its declining number of Native students. He remarks: "The Indians of this part of the country were being deported to reservations in the far West, . . . and it became difficult to secure pupils."[28]

Though impressed with the church and its education outreach—the school had 150 students on the island at its height—Kinzie was momentarily shaken by one visitor at the Mission who lectured her: "Do you not realize very strongly the entire deprivation of religious privileges you will be obliged to suffer in your distant home?" These words might have frightened someone with less grit; however Kinzie, who knew she was bound for Fort Winnebago, a new trading post in Michigan territory, took a moment to recover and then responded with vigor: "I shall have my Prayer-Book, and though destitute of a church, we need not be without a mode of worship."[29] In later years she would become an active participant in the civic growth of a young

Chicago, in both education and religion. She founded the first Episcopal church in the city, St. James, which is today the cathedral for the Diocese of Chicago.

On Mackinac, she evinced little interest in the attempts by the Presbyterians and Catholics to convert the Odawa and other tribes. Rather, as always, she paid attention to the subtle cultural interface of the different races, and their struggles to live in accord.[30] She notes that despite the U.S. government's best effort to gain the allegiance of the Native people they maintained a loyalty to the British Crown: "nor did our government [the U.S.] succeed in winning or purchasing their friendship. Great Britain, it is true, bid high to retain them."[31]

Nonetheless, the Americans fought competitively in commerce, and the store-houses at the Fur Company on Market Street provided the Anishinaabe with ammunition and liquor. Quite opposite, Kinzie notes, were their British friends who "commendably omitted to furnish them" with guns and alcohol. She is duly impressed, however, by the storehouses of the American Fur Company with their sale of such commodities as "blankets, broadcloths or strouding, calicoes, guns, kettles . . . looking glasses," and the singular *mocock*, small boxes made of birch bark and porcupine quills. Her account offers a useful and concrete list of items at the John Jacob Astor warehouse towards the end of the fur trade on Mackinac.[32]

Several times in *Wau-Bun*, Kinzie mentions her visit with the Mitchells of Mackinac.[33] By the time she was on the island in 1830, Elizabeth had been dead three years, and David living off-island for many years. We may assume that the Kinzies were socializing with one of the Mitchell sons who had stayed on the island to assist with his mother's businesses. Juliette experienced the joy of spending time with his wife, a captivating personality who was part French and Sioux. Through this friendship between the younger Mrs. Mitchell and Juliette, the intertwining spirit of the women of Mackinac is carried forward.

Beyond her connection with the Mitchells, Juliette clearly delights in the company of Madame Laframboise. Her first mention of the philanthropist and fur trader makes clear that her reputation preceded her. After walking "leisurely over the white gravelly road" she comes upon "the dwelling of Madame Laframboise, an Odawa woman." Later Madeline Laframboise will impress Kinzie with her intelligence, and Juliette learns that she uses "the knowledge she had acquired for the instruction and improvement of the youth among her own people."[34] Kinzie mentions that the fur trader's "husband had taught her to read and write," yet this observation is not corroborated by other historical accounts of Laframboise's literacy. She may well have learned to read, but there is no evidence that she learned to write, and she would always sign documents with an X.[35]

We learn from Juliette that Laframboise "was a woman of a vast deal of energy and enterprise."[36] Perhaps Kinzie, who would later be instrumental in helping to found the Historical Society and St. Luke's Hospital in Chicago, was inspired by this Odawa woman who took care of others and, as Juliette witnessed, received a "a class of young pupils daily at her house, that she might give them lessons."[37]

Though men play a part in *Wau-Bun*, it is primarily the women who are the storytellers and cultural firebrands. On Mackinac, Kinzie is struck by the "musical intonation" of the Métis women, whose voices combine "the French and native blood." As a female and a writer, she accomplishes an effective balance of homey interior concerns with the drama of the wilderness—and those who peopled it, both Euro-Americans and the Anishinaabe.[38] *Wau-Bun* is a noteworthy early history of American women and cultural history of the Chicago and Mackinac region. Kinzie worried when first publishing the book in 1857 that as a woman she would be judged for having written in first person, instead of "more modestly put forth in the name of a third person."[39] *Wau-Bun*'s enthusiastic acceptance by the public over the next hundred years and its many reprintings prove that she had nothing to fear.

Kinzie's own voice is not unlike the "pure, clear, living waters" of Mackinac that she describes.[40] She is ever "ready for fresh adventures" and her gift to us is a sharply drawn social history of the still "plummy" years of a fur-trading milieu, a world that was fast vanishing.

CHAPTER FIVE

Literary Leaders

Jane Johnston Schoolcraft (1800–1842) and Anna Brownell Jameson (1794–1860)

J ane Johnston Schoolcraft and Anna Brownell Jameson were writers who led by original thinking that effected change in the way the Great Lakes region and its people were perceived. Unlike Jane's husband, the Indian agent Henry Schoolcraft, who hid his wife's words away, Anna Jameson shared the poet's work in *Winter Studies and Summer Rambles in Canada.*[1]

Jane Schoolcraft, a Native American who lived on Mackinac for nearly a decade in the 1830s, was the first American poet to translate Anishinaabe songs and stories. She spoke French, English, and Ojibwe and chronicled stories and poems in both Ojibwe and English. Schoolcraft was the earliest recorded poet to write down her poems in a Native American language. She was inclusive in her cultural work and saved and passed on the authentic tales and songs of her Anishinaabe heritage. Her friend, Jameson, spent over two months with Jane and her Native family, recording the stories, songs, poems, and observations of the writer.[2] Jameson gives an unsurpassed eyewitness account of this reclusive poet, and she emerges as a key figure in assisting scholars and readers to realize Schoolcraft's significance as a transformative writer in young America. As for Jameson's own contribution, her down-to-earth observations and refreshing focus on women in the region offer a study of Mackinac and the Great Lakes like no other.

Anna Brownell Jameson

Anna wrote as if in conversation with the reader, which garnered immediate attention and resulted in a wide readership of *Winter Studies and Summer Rambles.* First published in 1838, this record contributed a vital social history of the western Great Lakes, including a long section on Jane Schoolcraft and her Native family. *Winter Studies* was reprinted in an abridged version in 1852. A restored unabridged edition followed in 1923, including Jameson's revealing footnotes and all of her original illustrations.[3] The editor noted that "Mrs. Jameson had the rare faculty, among travelers of seeing with the eyes of others." He also had this to say:

> She [Jameson] brought to the writing of these sketches, wide reading and a practiced pen. She had begun her literary career with a book of Italian travels, and before she came to Canada she had published a number of volumes, historical and critical, including *Characteristics of Women*, which is still widely read under the fresh title, *Shakespeare's Heroines*. She later became distinguished in the field of art criticism, and is now best remembered for her *Sacred and Legendary Art*.[4]

Jameson was well ahead of her time and stands out as an original thinker among both women and men. She wrote and was well published until her death in 1860. Late in *Winter Studies*, she discourses on some of the dubious advances of civilization and then catches herself:

> God forbid that I should think to disparage the blessing of civilization! I am a woman, and to the progress of civilization alone can we women look for release from many pains and penalties and liabilities, which now lie heavily upon us.[5]

It was rare to publish such words in 1837. Jameson wrote that women needed laws to act and to protect themselves, and that the sacrifice of one sex (female) to the other "is no general good, but a general curse,—a very ulcer in the bosom of society."[6] It rattled some of the male critics of her day, one claiming that if a woman such as Jameson was an intellectual then surely she must be an "eccentric."[7] Not to be deterred, Anna employs her intelligent voice, slipping it between the cracks of male authority. Speaking honestly about "the progress of civilization" must have lent courage to women reading her popular book.

Born in Dublin in the spring of 1794, Jameson came from creative stock. Her father was an outspoken patriot and a portrait painter who left Ireland in a hurry when his political views got him in trouble during the Irish Rebellion in the fin de siècle. In 1798, he and his family went to live in England, where for a time he was a successful miniaturist. Eventually his career took a nosedive and it was left to Anna to school her younger siblings in literature, science, math, and art. Ambitious and well-read, she realized she could also educate children in other families. With no money of her own, Jameson, at age sixteen, began to eke out a living as a governess.[8] Her first publication grew out of her experience tutoring the children of the Marquis of Winchester. In her subsequent trips as a governess to countries on the Continent, including Italy, she witnessed an eruption at Mt. Vesuvius and expanded her interest in art history with museum visits wherever her employers traveled. In short, she had discovered the pleasures of foreign travel as a stimulant for her writing and drawing.

Older than most women of her day when she married in 1825, Anna and Robert Jameson lived in England until he took a government post in Dominica, in the West Indies. Anna remained in Britain, writing her first travel book, *A Lady's Diary*. Published anonymously at first, its popularity galvanized Anna to use her own name. The book she wrote about Shakespeare's heroines was published in 1832 and brought her high praise. By this time, Jameson could announce all of her work as her own. Critics marveled at her careful attention to powerful female characters in the fabled Shakespearean dramas. Before Jameson, no writer had analyzed their strengths and overall contributions to his plays. Later she would write influential art history, introducing a novel way for reader participation with the great artists under discussion. Though she is remembered as the first British art historian, Jameson's contribution to Great Lakes history has been overlooked.

Where marriage was concerned, Jameson was not successful. There was serious incompatibility between Anna and Robert Jameson. The exact nature of their discord is not known. Still, one can draw certain conclusions. For starters, the pair were unlike in their most basic makeup. Anna was an intellect, an artist and social historian who married a bureaucrat. It is likely that it was a disturbing notion to Robert Jameson to find himself living with an unconventional woman. In turn, Anna felt constricted by him, and it appears as though she and Robert were seldom in the same house in the first ten years of their marriage. They limped along, living mostly apart until he was appointed attorney general of Upper Canada in Toronto. Robert then made it clear that he needed his wife present if he was to achieve his goal of becoming a vice-chancellor of the Court of Chancery. Dutifully, Anna traveled to Canada in 1836.[9]

On her way to Toronto she visited New York, where she expected to be met by her husband—as this was her first trip to the New World. He did not show up, but

Anna made the best of things and was surprised at her reception by New Yorkers. She was much feted for her success as a well-respected author. After being supported by literary circles, she then traveled to Toronto to join Robert. Her new surroundings were a shock to the system:

> At present its appearance to me, a stranger, is most strangely mean and melancholy. A little ill-built town, on low land, at the bottom of a frozen bay, with one very ugly church without tower or steeple; some government offices, built of staring red brick, in the most tasteless, vulgar style imaginable.[10]

She tells us that she had not expected much from Toronto, but was hardly prepared for her time there. When living through the winter months in that city, she wrote: "So slow the unprofitable moments roll / That lock up all the functions of my soul, / That keep me from myself." Thankfully, Jameson realizes that what she needs is change and travel. Soon enough she devises a trip to Niagara and the Great Lakes, and finds herself in a sleigh "absolutely buried in furs; a blanket netted for me by the kindest hands . . . buffalo and bear skins heaped over all." Her humor is everywhere in her writing, and we smile at her note that she must duck under cover "before my nose was absolutely taken off by the ice-blast."[11]

Her journey began with that sleigh ride to Niagara. She was a natural explorer, and once she set off on a trip, her curiosity and enthusiasm took over. From Niagara, in the spring, she traveled by steamship to the Great Lakes, where she would stay with Jane and Henry Schoolcraft on Mackinac. Contrast that earlier description of Toronto with one on the island some months later. Standing on the porch of the Schoolcraft home, she tells us that she is looking down

> upon the scene I have endeavored to—how inadequately!—to describe to you: the little crescent bay; the village of Mackinaw; the beach thickly studded with Indian lodges; canoes fishing, or darting hither and thither, light and buoyant as sea birds; a tall, graceful schooner swinging at anchor. . . . The exceeding beauty of this little paradise of an island.[12]

With prescience, she continues to extol "the salubrity of its summer climate" and "the facility of communication lately afforded by the lake steamers," concluding that soon Mackinac will become "a sort of watering place for the Michigan and Wisconsin fashionables." It was good guesswork on her part, and she sensed too how lucky she was to be there. Little could she guess at the twenty-first-century Mackinac with its many shops, hotels, and throngs of tourists. Of the commercialization of the island that she predicted, Jameson wrote: "I am only glad it has not yet taken place, and that I have beheld this lovely island in all its wild beauty."[13]

No longer stuck in Toronto, her gloom lifts. She is transformed by the lifeblood of Mackinac, and by her introduction to Jane Schoolcraft. Upon leaving the island, she travels with the poet and her children by canoe to Sault Ste. Marie. At one point, she accompanies Jane's Ojibwe brother, George Johnston, and daringly shoots the rapids of St. Mary's River, the first white woman to do so, according to George.[14] Jameson's journey is tantamount to a spiritual pilgrimage. By the end of her weeks on Mackinac and her five to six weeks in the Sault, her life is pointed in a new direction. She decides not to live in the prescribed box so many Englishwomen were caught in. No more unhappy societal marriage for her. As for leaving behind her new friends from Mackinac and Sault Ste. Marie, she states: "I am sorry to leave these kind, excellent people, but most I regret Mrs. Schoolcraft."[15] Perhaps she also regretted not being able to help Jane out of her most particular "box"—far more complicated in some ways than Anna's.

On her return to Toronto, Anna and Robert procured a formal separation. Jameson let him know she was returning to England, although like many a dutiful woman she promised to stay until she set up a pleasant home for him. Her rumblings of unhappiness before her journey with Jane and her Ojibwe family were unmistakable, as was her changed positive demeanor after this remarkable time of inward and outward adventure in the Great Lakes region. Here is a woman who would spend the last twenty years of her life (she lived until age sixty-six) writing and publishing Christian devotional books, and yet she was open-minded enough to write about those who questioned her religion of choice. She marvels at the elderly Ojibwe chief Wangoman, who tells her that he does not see the sense in getting converted. He calmly explains that he and his brethren in North America have worshiped the Great Spirit and animal spirits for thousands of years, and he has never heard of, much less seen, any indication of God falling down to earth and dying.[16] The sensitive Jameson accepts his beliefs as valid while keeping intact her own.

Though her husband "was displeased" with the success of *Winter Studies and Summer Rambles*, she persevered with her writing, guided by determination and courage. By nature, Jameson was fascinated by other people's lives and their imprint on society. This social historian wrote it all down, leaving an indelible record of the colonial period in the Great Lakes area and in parts of Canada in the mid-century.

Jane Schoolcraft on Mackinac

Jane Johnston Schoolcraft moved to Mackinac in 1833 and lived there for eight years. She was one of the brilliant Métis women on the island at this time. When still a teen, she would have met Madeline Laframboise during a visit with her father to Mackinac. On that trip in 1818, Jane sewed linen shirts with Josette, the daughter of Laframboise who married Captain Benjamin Pierce. The role Jane's father, John Johnston, played in the War of 1812 is part of her story that will be addressed. Of their visit to the island at this time, Johnston wrote to Jane's brother, George: "Have been on a visit to Capt. and Mrs. Pierce. The kind friendly and hospitable reception we had from them . . . could not be surpassed anywhere."[17]

An auspicious beginning for Jane's connection to other Métis women on Mackinac, but not one that was easy to pursue once she married Henry Schoolcraft five years later. His position as superintendent of Indian Affairs in the Mackinac and wider Michigan region contributed to this hardship. He was known to be a difficult man and most of his friendships fell apart quickly. Additionally, the wariness the Anishinaabe—whether Agatha Biddle, Elizabeth Mitchell, or Madame Laframboise—felt towards a man with the job of keeping "the Indians under control" did not help Jane Schoolcraft's connection with these strong town leaders. Even Edward Biddle, of the prestigious Biddle family in Philadelphia, who married Agatha, found Henry an unscrupulous man.[18] Small community that it was, Henry would have met Mitchell, Laframboise, and the Biddles in his trips to Mackinac before he became the resident Indian agent. Jane Schoolcraft may have met the unforgettable Elizabeth Mitchell when she came to the island as a teen, but of the three community leaders, Elizabeth had died by the time Schoolcraft lived on the island with Henry.

Despite living there for nearly a decade, the poet's own reserve and solitary writing habits encouraged her partial isolation on Mackinac. She deeply missed her homeland and Ojibwe relatives in Sault Ste. Marie, also known commonly as "the Soo." Henry's determination to keep his wife's literary works under wraps would not have contributed to her sense of well-being. One of her poems was appropriated by Henry and then handed off to Longfellow. Believing the source material to be written by the "Indian agent," the famous American poet went forward to use it (uncredited to Jane) in his wildly popular "Hiawatha."[19]

Some of her work showed up in a magazine jointly published by Henry and herself in 1826–1827. The *Literary Voyager* or *Muzzeniegen* was praised among the Schoolcrafts' small circle of friends, though Jane's poems appeared under the pen names of Rosa and Leelinau.[20] Women often used a male pen name, as a man's work was more likely to be read than a woman's, but in this case a female pseudonym was chosen for publication. It is possible that Henry did not want the name Jane Schoolcraft highlighted as that would call attention to her original work, some of which he was claiming as his own. Obscured in history for nearly two hundred years, she is at long last being given her due. A good part of the credit for shining a light on Schoolcraft goes to Anna Jameson, whose crucial connection to Schoolcraft is evaluated for the first time in this study.

It was unusual for a Native and white woman to form such a bond. Nowhere in Michigan history of the nineteenth century do we have two such women who viewed each other as friends and complete equals—an empowering friendship that fostered lasting documents of society in the Great Lakes region. Their connection was important to each of them during a difficult time in their lives.

Schoolcraft's stories and songs would have been all but lost if not for Jameson sharing and elevating them in her popular book *Winter Studies*. Also overlooked is Jameson's extraordinary attention to language. Her female voice brings an intellect and emotional immediacy not seen in male observers of language in the 1830s. Of one Chippewa song that she hears, Jameson relates: "I have been myself wound up to painful excitement, or melted to tears." Further down the page, she snaps into analytic mode, speaking of Schoolcraft's "mourning recitative" and how "This song is in a measure, ten and eight syllables alternately."[21] Her critical faculties are a boon to cultural history, whether she is homing in on the semantics and musicality of the Indigenous people she meets or the translations of song and story by Jane Schoolcraft.

Jane Johnston Schoolcraft grew up in Sault Ste. Marie and was a precocious and physically lovely child.[22] In an age when women scarcely garnered a footnote in histories (much less girls), a prestigious Canadian volume of "great men" saw fit to say a few words about her. In his biography of John Johnston, the editor of the *Canadian Monthly and National Review* writes that John and Ozhaguscodaywayquay, who was also known as Susan, took their "eldest daughter, Jane, a young girl of surpassing beauty, and of great sweetness of disposition, then twelve years of age" to England.

While there is no mention in other sources of Ozhaguscodaywayquay having traveled to Britain, Jane and her father did make the trip. In England, the Duke and Duchess of Northumberland were so charmed by her that they wanted to adopt the girl and make her an heir. This brief biography of Johnston's life also speaks of Jane in her later years as "a woman of culture, some of her fugitive poems being of a high order."[23] The "fugitive" description is an intriguing detail that describes the poet's work that had been largely hidden from view.[24]

The attention to the poet's physical appearance would only increase as she grew older. Two years before Jane's death, Eliza R. Steele writes about meeting her on Mackinac. Steele was visiting the commanding officer of the fort and his family. After passing through a copse of maple and birch outside the fort, she enters a tent that has been set up as a fete in honor of several guests, herself included. Unfortunately, the second she spots Schoolcraft, Eliza Steele indulges in exoticism, a spectatorship of Native people.

> The grace and beauty of Mrs. S—t [Jane Schoolcraft] made great impression upon us. To me she was peculiarly [sic] interesting from the fact of her being descended from the Native lords of the forest. . . . From the accent, the deep brunette of her smooth skin, and her dark hair and eyes, I should have taken her for a Spanish lady.[25]

No one wants to be gawked at, and over the years Schoolcraft was oppressed by many such situations. In contrast to the focus on her appearance as an Indian, it is noteworthy that author Anna Jameson would instead focus on the poet's singular character, pensive qualities, and above all, her literary gifts. Schoolcraft must have appreciated that Jameson immediately saw connections that overrode any racial differences.

In recent years, Jane's songs, tales, and fifty odd poems have begun to be published, and there is some biographical detail of her movement and a critical study of much of her work.[26] Nonetheless, little attention has been paid to the manner in which Jameson captures Schoolcraft's daily existence, warmth, and intellect, particularly on Mackinac and in her life in the Sault after marriage. Additionally, the English author examines the powerful language in Schoolcraft's work, such as when she describes the poet's "emphatic" song that is achieved through "continual repetition of the same phrase or idea."[27] It is my aim to reveal the breadth of this connection between the two women and how this illuminates both writers' contributions to history and literature.

O How Passing Lovely It Was! How Beautiful and Strange

This was Anna Jameson's reaction as she approached Mackinac Island. When she arrived on Mackinac in 1836, the most she knew about Jane Schoolcraft was that she was married to the Indian agent of Mackinac and was sister to Charlotte MacMurray, a woman she spoke to briefly in a chance meeting before boarding a steamer in Niagara. That agent, Henry Schoolcraft, was supposed to be Anna's contact for her trip to Mackinac and Sault Ste. Marie. Charlotte, or Ogenebugoquay, whom Jameson had spoken to in Niagara, indicated she would get in touch with the Schoolcrafts about lodgings for the writer on Mackinac.

Jameson, a published author of several books, an art historian, and artist, had planned an exploration that would be the basis of a travel history of the Great Lakes region, Niagara, and parts of Canada, but as she approached Mackinac she grew nervous. During her travel towards the Great Lakes, Anna wonders if indeed Henry Schoolcraft has received communication about her plan to spend time on Mackinac. After arriving at the island, she worries about having no letter of introduction to hand to the Indian agent. As she stands on the boat dock watching her large steamer disappear, Anna is seized with "alarm to find myself so far from any human being who took the least interest about my fate."[28]

It was not easy to be a woman traveling alone in the old Northwest. Hardly reassuring in the year 1836 was Mackinac's reputation as a war- and religion-torn island, still surrounded by wilderness. Reverberations of the rambunctious fur-trade era continued to be felt. The War of 1812 with nations jockeying for power, which resulted in Mackinac once again becoming American property, made for an air of unpredictability even in the 1830s. Additionally, the ongoing strife between Catholic and Presbyterian faiths who angled for control of souls on the island was in strong evidence.[29]

Many people in a place far from home have been assailed by panic or loneliness. One of Anna's strengths as a writer is that she presents such feelings honestly, and readers identify with her. She soon learns there are no rooms available in the one boarding house she stops into on the island. Anna is informed she'd have to turn out the visiting bishop of Michigan in order to get a bed to sleep in. Such a thought is inconceivable to her. In order to cope with the unknown future, Anna has the wisdom to stay positive.

She decides to focus on her delight at first sighting Mackinac an hour earlier when the steamer approached the harbor: "O how passing lovely it was! How beautiful and strange!" She proclaims "a sense of enjoyment keen and unanticipative as that of a child" and states that "looking neither before nor after—I soon abandoned myself to the present."[30]

This mindset of staying in the here and now pays off. Having arrived at daybreak, she writes, sketches, and explores, waiting until a civilized hour to venture to the Schoolcrafts' residence, which is near the Indian Dormitory. It is 10:00 A.M. when she knocks at the door. Henry sticks his head out with an unwelcoming expression, and it is not clear to Anna that he and Jane are expecting her. With a grave face, he tells her that his wife is indisposed and has not left her room for days. Anna is horrified at the thought of imposing and considers the many wigwams she's eyed on the beach. Perhaps one of the Native families will let her stay with them.

She apologizes for bothering him, a fear of being "de trop." It is only then that Henry explains that he and Jane are expecting her visit after all. All is well, or will be once Jameson meets "Mrs. Schoolcraft."

In the weeks to come, she will connect not only with Schoolcraft, but with Jane's Ojibwe family in Sault St. Marie. Anna discovers that she and her new acquaintance share literary tastes, not to mention the same curiosity about culture and life. Both are warm, quirky women. Jameson notes Schoolcraft's "soft, plaintive voice." Also that "her countenance, told too plainly of resigned and habitual suffering."[31]

No doubt she wondered what afflicted Jane Schoolcraft. As a literary person, Jameson zeroes in on the poet's speech, and with her natural compassion she soon elaborates on the possible great friendship in the offing:

> Her accent is slightly foreign—her choice of language pure and remarkably elegant. In the course of an hour's talk, all my sympathies were enlisted in her behalf, and I thought that she, on her part, was inclined to return these benignant feelings. . . . there are a thousand quiet ways in which woman may be kind and useful to her sister woman.[32]

Henry tells Anna that his wife is not a strong woman, and yet a marvelous transformation occurs in the coming weeks. Jameson's very presence seems to lift Jane Schoolcraft out of her malaise, suggesting that her reclusiveness and outward weakness is more a mental state, and as will be apparent, greatly connected to her selfhood as an Ojibwe woman in a compromised situation.

Schoolcraft's birth name was Bamewawagezhikaquay. Since Ojibwe was the language spoken in her home growing up and that which she used with her own children after marriage, it is likely she was called Bamewawagezhikaquay on a regular basis in her life. Yet she signs her communications as Jane Schoolcraft, and that is how I most often refer to her in this study. Whenever she could manage it, Jane visited her mother in Sault Ste. Marie, with whom she always spoke Ojibwe. Eventually Schoolcraft would undertake an extended trip to the Sault with her children and Jameson. As the weeks passed, both on Mackinac and in the Upper Peninsula, Jane and her Native family grew closer to Anna. The English author saw firsthand the kinship and nurturing between family members, in particular that of Jane and her mother: "Mrs. Schoolcraft, who looked all animation and happiness, acting as interpreter. Mrs. Johnston speaks no English. . . . but in her own language she is eloquent."[33]

In *Winter Studies and Summer Rambles*, Anna Jameson describes getting to know the singular poet Jane Schoolcraft. It happens in a most natural way. The author makes the reader feel as if she is right there, comfortably ensconced inside the Schoolcrafts' home on Mackinac, or standing at the garden gate where Jane shaded her eyes as she spoke to Anna, the two of them contemplating the wigwams lining the shore. Surprising revelations regarding the fate of her Native people sometimes emerged. Other times, the English author observed the poet as she spun around inside the house, tenderly caring for her children. Two out of four had survived early childhood illness.

Jane might well have referenced Ovid or Homer when she and Anna leapt into conversation. Both women had classical educations, and Schoolcraft had grown up in a home where the walls in the main hall were lined with books. Anna Jameson describes Jane as having a "pensive intelligence," and the adjective is repeated in the poet's own work. It is remarkable to think how history has missed the contributions of this Native American woman. At age twenty, Jane penned this poem.[34]

The sun had sunk like a glowing ball,
As lonely I sat in my father's hall;
I walk'd to the window, and musing awhile,
The still, pensive moments I sought to beguile:
Just by me, ran smoothly the dark deep stream,
And bright silvery rays on its breast did beam;—
And as with mild luster the vestal orb rose,
All nature betokened a holy repose,
Save the Sound of St. Mary's—that softly and clear
Still fell in sweet murmurs upon my pleas'd ear

Like the murmur of voices we know to be kind,
Or war's silken banners unfurled to the wind,
Now rising, like shouts of the proud daring foe,
Now falling, like whispers congenial and low.

The above piece, aptly titled "Pensive Hours," is a reflection on life in her home some years earlier. The peaceful life along St. Mary's River would not last for Jane. Tragically, the library, the hall, and indeed her entire house went up in flames when she was fourteen years old. Given the approximate dates of her earliest poetry, this is the time frame that Jane began writing poetry. Like any highly sensitive boy or girl, Jane was devastated, her world destroyed. It was the War of 1812 that had signaled the fate of her once secure home life. During the conflict, the garrison at Michilimackinac appealed to her father for assistance. As a British loyalist, he agreed to help, and conveyed men and supplies to the island. When the United States discovered John Johnston's actions, they retaliated. The North West Company's fur-trade warehouses on St. Mary's River were torched, along with the Johnston homestead. When Jane's house was raided, the family fled. They hid out in a nearby forest as her home burnt to the ground.[35]

Jane's poetry often addresses the theme of loss, whether it is about the death of her children, a resounding fear for the future of the Anishinaabe, or a lament for her grandfather, a war chief. She also finds ample ground to write about pride in her ancestors and the Ojibwe reverence for nature.

Schoolcraft's poetic voice was little recognized in her own time, and a large reason for such silence resides in the particulars of her marriage to Henry. The poet worked on her own, but she also edited side by side with her husband, Henry. Although it was Henry who had an office in the Indian Dormitory in Marquette Park on Mackinac, it is likely Jane was there almost daily. Edwin O. Wood, the editor of the comprehensive two-volume *Historic Mackinac*, opens his chapter on Henry Schoolcraft with remarks that highlight the linguistic talents of Jane Schoolcraft:

In 1823 he married Miss Jane Johnston, a young woman of education and culture, a grand-daughter of the Ojibway chief Wabo-jeeg. Her father was Mr. John Johnston, an Irish fur-trader of wealth and social distinction. Jane had been sent in early life to Europe for her education, in care of Mr. Johnston's relatives. Schoolcraft's marriage to a woman equally well versed in English and Algonquin was a great aid to his research, which he carried on with her intelligent assistance at the Sault and at Mackinac. She accompanied him to his new scene of labour at Mackinac in 1833.[36]

"A great aid" indeed. Quite the understatement. It is revealing that the editor of these two histories of Mackinac chose to legitimize the Indian agent with an immediate description of his able partner, Jane Johnston, and the manner in which she enabled her husband to achieve the lion's share of a reputation based on "his" Indian legends. Henry's prodigious output depended in large part on what Indigenous tales and poems she wrote and shared with him. To add to Schoolcraft's difficulties, nothing was black and white in her relationship with Henry. Though he plagiarized Jane's written word, publishing much of it under his own name, he kept a sizable lot of her original work, which can be found buried in his voluminous papers housed at the Library of Congress, including his "Indian History" tome, *Algic Researches, Comprising Inquiries Respecting the Mental Characteristics of the North American Indians.*[37]

He edited her poems with an eye to presenting the form he decided white colonists should read. For instance, in Jane's "Invocation" ("To my Maternal Grand-father on hearing his descent from Chippewa ancestors misrepresented"), Henry's edited version reads:

When the false Outagami, leagued fast with our foes,
And panic and dread spread around, til you rose
Like a Star in the West, and with weapons in hand,
Drove dauntless and reckless the foe from the land.

He changes her words to magnify a fearful presence where there is none. Jane's original depiction of her maternal grandfather, Waujobeeg—warrior that he was—does not emphasize, or indeed mention, a weapon in hand.

Can the warrior forget how sublimely you rose?
Like a star in the west,
When the sun's sunk to rest,
    That shines in bright splendor to dazzle our foes?[38]

In contrast to his changes to the above poem, Henry tends to soften and sentimentalize her words in other verse. Regarding Jane's original version of what became "Hiawatha," it would seem that Henry simply assumed he could take her work and hand it off to Longfellow. It appears that Henry stole the story of Hiawatha and many other tales, songs, and poems from his wife, not out of malice, but entitlement and twisted ego. The original text of "The Corn Story" or "The Origin of Corn" is found in Henry's papers in the Library of Congress.[39] That story along with others by Jane would become "The Song of Hiawatha." In a letter dated January 15, 1838, Jane writes Henry: "I wrote out the corn story, and got Francis to copy it for me, which I send you and hope it will please you better than it did him." Francis W. Sherman, who was a nephew of Henry, also writes him: "I have just finished copying for Mrs. S. the corn story, and I have copied it verbatim from hers. The story is a good one."[40] Apparently, the draft of the future "Hiawatha" pleased Francis more than Jane Schoolcraft realized. Clearly Henry thought so too and acted on it. In contrast to Henry's covert methods, Jameson is delighted to share Schoolcraft's stories and songs in *Winter Studies*. Jameson writes that Schoolcraft offers untold "new sources of information" regarding her Ojibwe people. "She takes an enthusiastic and enlightened interest in her people."[41]

Henry's ambitions were huge, and he largely realized them with his many publications. His entitlement did not stop with the poet Jane Schoolcraft. It extended well beyond his wife to virtually hundreds of tales he garnered from the Ojibwe, who trusted him and sat in his office while he hungrily took down their stories. No matter that he knew their full names; rarely did he credit them in his books. Apparently, the plagiarism "pattern extends across Henry's career," including travel books and other published work.[42]

Jane Schoolcraft was close to her mother, Ozhaguscodaywayquay, who was full Ojibwe. In the course of Jane's adult years, she and Susan had a significant literary collaboration. It was Anna Jameson who witnessed and wrote about the amazing connection of this mother-daughter team. Jane would get out her pen and paper and interpret the stories her mother told her, adding and creating many of her own.[43] This team incorporated the oral history of Ozhaguscodaywayquay and enlarged on that body of work with Jane's own remarkable poetry and song of the Ojibwe people. Their relationship made for a historical harvest.

Ozhaguscodaywayquay inherited some of her father's dual strengths. He was both a former war chief and a community leader. Waubojeeg's leadership was recognized among his own people and in regions extending beyond northern Wisconsin where he lived. It made sense to Jane's father, John Johnston, whose ambition was to become a successful fur trader, to marry into this influential Ojibwe family. "Kinship and ties of affinity proved more than merely useful to the traders. They were both a source of power and a necessity if one was to achieve success in the trade."[44]

Though we may consider that he and Susan eventually had a mutually beneficial union, it hardly began that way.[45] As Jane Schoolcraft explained to Anna Jameson, her mother (Susan/Ozhaguscodaywayquay) ran away from her new husband after being married ten days. She sought shelter at the house of her father. On her arrival, Waubojeeg beat her and threatened to cut off her ears if she did not return to John.[46] Such is the complex family history of Jane Schoolcraft.

She revered her grandfather, but is honest about his less-than-humane side as well. She was nurtured by clan culture and by the library her father built. Jane was the eldest girl in the Johnston family, and easily their most literary child. Her own father's literary penchant is evident in the catalogue of books in Johnston's library in his home in Sault Ste. Marie, along with his determined education of his children in the classics, especially Jane.[47]

Emigrating from Belfast, John left behind a prominent family in Ireland. His maternal uncle was attorney general of Ireland, and his father a civil engineer who constructed Belfast Water Works. Johnston himself had been deeded land near the Giant's Causeway in Antrim County. Yet Schoolcraft's father was an adventurer eager to make a fortune in the New World. He arrived in Canada with letters of introduction to Lord Dorchester, governor of the colony. Johnston discovered an educated and wealthy set of colonists who had formed the North West Company fur-trading business in 1787, with agents, clerks, guides, and voyageurs.[48] Johnston became a business partner, and understood that he needed the allegiance of the Anishinaabe in the region in order to succeed. In time, John used his own inheritance to set up a business, and with Susan, to purchase extensive land in Sault Ste. Marie.

In the cultured setting she grew up in, Jane was conversant in the language of Shakespeare, reading his plays and quoting from *The Merchant of Venice* (whose heroine, the lawyer Portia, was a strong female character). At the same time, she was steeped in the rich language and lore of her mother's Native family. Despite the challenges of frontier life, Jane would have known the security of a stable family life and community when she was young. There was wide acceptance of her kin in the Sault, a fluidity of cultures, and trading across the borders of what would eventually become permanent American soil.

Jane was not in contact with white women in her growing-up years.[49] This study notes that even when she moved to Mackinac as a married person, she made no friends with Euro-Americans until she met Anna Jameson, who stands out as Schoolcraft's closest white female friend in her lifetime. Their literary connection was strong. It came naturally to Jameson to include historical and literary allusions in her work; her writing is full of telling quotes that range from Elizabeth and Robert Browning to George Eliot, Mrs. Gaskell, and Harriet Martineau. Of that group of luminaries, the Brownings and Martineau would become Jameson's friends after she returned to England. If Schoolcraft was impressed with her new friend, then certainly the reverse was true. Schoolcraft was not only fluent in her mother's Ojibwe language but equally so in English and American literature. She read voraciously in her father's library, which included Goldsmith, Johnson, Irving, and Cooper.[50]

Grave financial woes visited the Johnstons after the arson of the family home in 1814.[51] They would rebuild the homestead, but it was a devastating blow to their business when the United States burnt down the North West trade warehouses. Eventually, Jane's mother would valiantly petition for reparations of this wrong, and her action remains a telling document of the destruction wrought and her own abiding strength throughout. In those unsettled years of war, the overall culture of Sault Ste. Marie began to change drastically. The Americans, now in control, were suspicious of the mixed society of the region, making it difficult for Ozhaguscodaywayquay and Bamewawagezhikaquay, along with John Johnston and his cohorts. Gone was the easy camaraderie among different nations and people, including the Ojibwe, French, Métis, English, and Canadian. Eventually, Jane's father found a way to recover some prosperity and would become a commissioner to mediate the competition between the Hudson's Bay and the North West Companies.

No doubt, his part in creating the merger between the two made an impression on Schoolcraft. In her future life in America, living for nearly a decade on Mackinac, Schoolcraft was markedly quiet about her father's roots in the British Isles. Yet, it may be said that she simply took care not to espouse American, British, or Canadian loyalties, and the ability to withhold political judgment is a trait of the diplomat. Moreover, it may be said that she was a literary diplomat. The translations she made of her Ojibwe poems into English—while keeping intact the Native version—had never been done before. She was sharing the stories of the Anishinaabe with Euro-Americans, connecting one cultural group to the other. Where language was concerned, Schoolcraft greatly advanced the cause of multiculturalism. As for Anna Jameson, her book *Winter Studies* revealed Jane's stories to a wide audience who were able to begin thinking about Schoolcraft's legacy.

Jane and Henry

Just as Jane's father had married a Native person to further his career, so Henry Schoolcraft married the daughter of a prominent Ojibwe family with an ambition to advance his studies of "the red man." Like one who has stumbled upon a treasure chest, he writes almost gleefully of having "stumbled upon, as it were, the only family in North West America" who can yield the kind of insider information on Native American life that will make him famous. He makes the acquaintance of "Mr. Johnston" in the Sault and gains "temporary quarters at his house," and meets "several intelligent members of his family." The year was 1822, and Henry uses all his "ardor and assiduity . . . pressing the advantages . . . to interrogate . . . Jane's family [*sic*] who promise to be useful subjects of information during the day, and to test my inquiries in the evening." Robert Parker makes the astute observation that "we can see Henry Schoolcraft's publication of traditional Ojibwe stories as cultural theft. It seems no coincidence that as he revised the stories for publication, Henry also played a leading role in negotiating a series of treaties to steal Indian lands."[52]

Henry became a well-known ethnographer and author of studies of Native Americans.[53] Despite his ostensible interest in the Anishinaabe, he did not engage in friendships with them in the way that John Johnston did. Beyond his marriage to Jane and connection to her family members, Schoolcraft formed no enduring bonds with Native people. Mostly, he viewed them as a means to an end. He collected data about them, not unlike one netting butterflies to impale and study under a microscope, reminiscent of the character Stein in Joseph Conrad's classic novel, *Lord Jim*. Stein believes his objects are beautiful even as he kills them.[54]

It must be said that Jane may have desired marriage to a white man, though possibly not an American, given her father's deep antipathy towards the Yankees. Though John Johnston never became an American citizen, he understood diplomacy and gradually accepted Henry as his future son-in-law. The Indian agent was a charismatic man who no doubt worked doubly hard to ingratiate himself into the good graces of Jane's father and mother. Given the downward drift of Native status in the northern Great Lakes region after the War of 1812, it is possible Jane saw marriage to Henry as an alternative to a way of life she feared was fast disappearing. Also key to the prospective union was a shared passion for books and the ambition for a literary and writing life.

They were married in 1823, at which time Henry held the position of Indian agent for the U.S. government in the Sault Ste. Marie region. After the Schoolcrafts' wedding, Jane's parents built an addition to their cedar log house in the Sault for their beloved daughter and her new husband. In 1827, Jane and Henry built what was considered a fine mansion. They called the place Elmwood, and Jane appears to have been happy there, living near her parents and in the land that she called home. In the first years of marriage, Henry was capable of warmth, and even silliness towards his wife. In 1825, when traveling, he writes: "I had been dreaming of home, and stepped in my canoe, with my mind filled with the Subject. / Oh Jane, Jane, Jane! / When shall I see thee again / To smile or to speak, to rejoice or complain."

Jane, too, writes poems about missing Henry. There is the lovely verse "Neen-awbame," or "Absence." "Say dearest friend, when light your bark, / Glides down the Mississippi dark? / Say, do thy thoughts e'er turn on home? / As mine to thee incessant roam."[55] Schoolcraft can be flirtatious, as in these two lines scribbled in the margins of a letter and signed in one of her pen names: Leelinau. This one was sent to Henry from Mackinac: "My earrings are gone, in the Wars of Fate—/ And a pair of red-drops I would not hate. Leelinau."[56]

Schoolcraft experiments with different poetic forms, including this witty acrostic, again to Henry:

A thing of glitter, gleam, and gold,
Loose thoughts, loose verse, unmeaning old,
Big words that sound a thousand fold;
Unfinished scraps, conceit and cant,
Mad stanzas, and a world of rant.[57]

A romantic gloss on this marriage will not carry it far. Schoolcraft's playful letter about her earrings may have been an attempt to cheer Henry up when his career as Indian agent was on the skids.[58] Another poem written while on Mackinac shows her devotion and despair when he is away: "Welcome, welcome to my arms, / All that constitutes life's charms; / Welcome day of sweet emotion, / To my heart of deep devotion— / Desponding hours of grief away."[59]

Henry's long absences, sometimes months at a time, wear on Jane as the years pass by. Many of her letters beseech him to spend more time at home. This one is dated November 22, 1831:

> The Boat arrived this afternoon & I was made happy by the reception of your letters, but alas! Not as happy as I should have been had you said there was a probability of you returning home.—What necessity is there of your going to Detroit ... ? A man may be seen too often as well as too seldom for his own good. [B]ut pardon me my dear Husband, I know I have *no right* to speak, but out of the fullness of the heart, the mouth finds the utterance—And if ever I required support & encouragement since our marriage *it is now*.[60]

It was a good ploy, appealing to common sense. A man should not overdo his welcome in society or with colleagues (extremely sensible given Henry's loquacious nature), but it was to fall on deaf ears. Further, Jane's words "I know I have *no right* to speak" are a sad reminder of how little women in the past possessed the right to simply speak their minds to men.

Despite marital adjustments and the beginning of Henry's ongoing long absences from Jane, she must have been heartened to live next door to her mother, Susan Johnston/Ozhaguscodaywayquay in her earliest years of marriage. In later years on Mackinac, Anna Jameson comments that Schoolcraft speaks "with fond and even longing affection, as if the very sight of this beloved mother would be sufficient to restore her to health and strength. 'I should be well if I could see my mother'" seems to be the predominant feeling.[61]

That was 1836. The strong bonds between the poet and her mother signify more than a touching relationship. The yearning, nay desperation—as will become clear—to return to the safe arms of her parent reveals the depth of trauma Jane was experiencing by the time she had been living on Mackinac nearly five years. By sheer will, she musters the energy to rise above the "delicacy of her health and the trials to which it is exposed" and return home to the Sault and to Ozhaguscodaywayquay.[62]

Even before moving to Mackinac, Jane's letters evince the challenges she had with Henry as a husband. On one of his long absences from home in 1829, she reminds him that she is about to give birth, and clearly beseeches him to return. He writes back: "It is the order of providence that man should be active, & woman quiescent." We may suppose that Henry is ignorant of the violent action of giving birth and many other activities women engage in. He also makes the unconvincing statement that she is the object of his undivided attention. Jane responds with intelligent subtlety. She speaks of his political appointment, saying that if it pleases him, then it pleases her, and then remarks, "I must learn that great virtue of a woman: quiescence."[63] Do we detect her ironic tone, even as she submits to his pronouncement? Absolutely.

Gender inequality made it difficult for female poets to find a public forum in the early and mid-nineteenth century. Yet women did publish, though mostly in newspapers. One of Henry's friends extolled the power of Schoolcraft's verse (though her authorship appeared only under pseudonyms) in Henry and Jane's one-issue literary magazine. *The Muzzeniegen*, or book—its translation in English from Ojibwe—was passed around to a select number of friends. One friend, Mr. Trowbridge, asked Henry if he might share her work with others. Trowbridge made it clear that he would wait on Henry's and Jane's approval together. Also clear is that Henry alone responded that Jane's poetry was to stay under wraps.[64]

It was a likely shock to Jane to leave her beloved St. Mary's River woodland, much highlighted in her poetry, for the bustle of Mackinac. Henry and Jane moved to the island in 1833, where Henry had the responsibility as agent for a larger region in Michigan than before. Anna Jameson describes where the Schoolcrafts lived:

> On a little platform, not quite half way up the wooded height which overlooks the bay, embowered in foliage, and sheltered from the tyrannous breathing of the north by the precipitous cliff, rising almost perpendicularly behind, stands the house in which I find myself a grateful and contented inmate. There is an avenue of fruit trees, the gate on the end opening on the very edge of the lake.[65]

Schoolcraft's personal geography is important; she struggled to connect to the island, but it was her home for nine years. Her friend, Jameson, would leave us with a line drawing of the fort and the face of the Schoolcrafts' many-chimneyed home. She was an artist capable of lovely and precise line drawings of Mackinac and frontier America, from Niagara to the Great Lakes and parts of Canada. Anna kept her sketchbook at the ready wherever she traveled. Before photography, Jameson captured the view of the Schoolcrafts' home; it is titled *Island of Mackinaw—Indian Village*. This detailed artwork reveals Jameson's fine observation with pencil and conte stick. The sketch also includes the garden, a huddle of trees near the house, and wigwams and figures below on the beach. Brian Dunnigan includes this drawing in his book *A Picturesque*

Situation, and though he does not identify the house as the Schoolcrafts, an obvious matchup can be made when compared with later photographs.[66]

The Schoolcrafts' home, known as "the United States Indian Agency House," would eventually burn down, but it was located east of the old Indian Dormitory, now the Manoogian Art Museum.[67] Jane's home occupied the lot of what is today "the Ann Cottage" in front of the marina.

Jane Schoolcraft and the Complex Racial Ties in the Great Lakes

Schoolcraft's time on Mackinac as seen through the eyes of Jameson is yet another example of sisterhood at work on Mackinac. Her ebullience regarding Schoolcraft is evident: "we shall soon be the best friends in the world!"[68] Beyond Jane and Anna, future generations reap the fruit of this unlikely friendship. From Jameson we get some answers as to who this quiet poet was, this woman who asked questions of her own race and left us a major body of work that has been largely unread. As has been indicated, her years on Mackinac were not easy ones.

She struggled with the conflict of loyalty and her own racial identity. Schoolcraft was by heritage both Irish and Anishinaabe, but she identified more closely with her mother's culture. Though Schoolcraft read the English-language classics bestowed on her by John Johnston, she lived and engaged in her mother's culture on a daily basis. There are no records of Jane's warmth towards her father, while multiple references to Schoolcraft's connection to Ozhaguscodaywayquay exist. Jane's identification as daughter of a full Ojibwe is apparent throughout her life. Equally apparent is the traitorous action Jane's own husband takes repeatedly against the Anishinaabe, causing struggles of loyalty for Jane. At what level did she process his part in the exodus of the American Indians from their land, and how much was she truly able to separate herself from that cultural and physical theft? As the resident Indian agent on Mackinac, Henry oversaw the annuities Indians received, while separately angling for land sales, to their great detriment.

Just as there were Cherokees who found it hard to reconcile the betrayals by the white man during the infamous "Trail of Tears," so Jane must have suffered under the gradual knowledge that Henry was working closely with Governor Lewis Cass in President Jackson's cabinet to oversee the takeover of Indian land in the vast Michigan territory.[69] Henry was instrumental in persuading the Anishinaabe to sign the Treaty of Washington, wherein they gave up over thirteen million acres in Michigan territory to the U.S. government. Henry signed the treaty in 1836. Up the street from where the Schoolcrafts lived, Agatha Biddle and other Odawa met at the Biddle house in a summit, discussing their fears regarding this devastating treaty.

Schoolcraft's written word is a powerful testament of the wrongs being done to her people. Regarding the fog of blandishments doled out by the United States, Schoolcraft is, in many respects, the face of her Native culture in Michigan regarding the broken trust of her white brethren. Living on Mackinac in the 1830s, she relates to Jameson her fears as to what is happening to the Anishinaabe, and she pens such thoughts, yearning for a place where "No crimes, no misery, no tears / No pride of wealth; the heart to fill, / No laws to treat my people ill."[70]

The Australian writer Michael A. McDonnell has examined the Anishinaabe strategy for domination of the Great Lakes region. He notes their competition with encroaching Europeans and the nascent republic of the United States, as well as their longtime rivalry with other Native tribes.[71] He rightly claims that this story has been overlooked by Euro-American historians. However, his study of the Native networks focuses on the prowess and success of the male Indian, and leaves out the hidden and overlooked story of the Anishinaabe women. Historians have written much about the military and the exploits of men in the western Great Lakes, and more recently included the exploits of the male Anishinaabe. Some of these histories have co-opted women's accomplishments as men's own. Here is where the significance of a study of Native women Elizabeth Mitchell, Madeline Laframboise, Agatha Biddle, Elizabeth T. Baird, and Jane Schoolcraft lies.

Further, in terms of culture and sheer population in the Great Lakes region, the Anishinaabe as a whole people, male and female, were greatly harmed. It is well to guard against a cavalier attitude towards the real suffering experienced at the hands of the Euro-Americans. Schoolcraft voices this in her work, and Jameson echoes it in her eyewitness accounts, as do Juliette Kinzie, Margaret Fuller, and Harriet Martineau. In the nineteenth and twentieth centuries, there is quantifiable evidence of the boarding schools alone, which Indian children were forced to attend, and of their punishment if they did not acquiesce to white assimilation. That is the tip of the iceberg of two centuries worth of severe prejudice leveled towards Native Americans.

Writing for the National Park Services from the University of Pennsylvania, Doug Kiel explores the power shift after the War of 1812, the "Indian fighter" Andrew Jackson, and his Indian Removal Act in 1830. The fur trade that had prevailed in the

Michigan territory for hundreds of years was giving way to farming, and concomitant with that, the belief that the life of the Indian who hunted in the forests as a way of life was invalid.[72]

As both Ojibwe and Irishwoman, Schoolcraft's challenges were representative of the complex social, religious, and racial challenges of the Métis in the nineteenth century. It is helpful to examine on a personal level how she struggled with community, and with her white husband. The conflict in her marriage manifested in several ways. She loved Henry but became embittered by his long absences, along with his job that invited the anger and sorrow of Indigenous people. The indignities against them were felt on many levels. Jameson comments on a council meeting on Mackinac she attended with Henry where fifty-four chiefs were present:

> The council was convened to ask them if they would consent to receive goods instead of dollars in payment for the pensions due to them on the sale of their lands. . . . So completely do the white men reckon on having everything their own way with the poor Indians, that a trader had contracted with the government to supply the goods which the Indians had not yet consented to receive, and was actually now on the island, having come with me in the steamer.[73]

That government representative happened to be Henry Schoolcraft. Jameson's concern over religious indoctrination is felt in her observations. This author of *Legends of the Madonna as Represented in the Fine Arts* was objective enough to write that one Métis man at the council "had been carried early to Europe by the Catholic priests, had been educated at the Propaganda College at Rome." That man was the only person other than Henry Schoolcraft to have had a chair to sit in at the council meeting.[74] Jameson cannot help but add that "The mean, petty-trader style in which the American officials make (and *break*) their treaties with the Indians is shameful."[75]

It is not difficult to imagine how torn Jane Schoolcraft was regarding her husband's dealings. As superintendent of Indian Affairs, Henry was determined to remove the Indigenous people of Michigan from their homeland, and wrote: "Like most of our Northern Indians, they require the proper course to be pointed out and can readily be induced to conform to it."[76] Richard Bremer, biographer of Henry Schoolcraft, noted:

> The history of his [Henry Schoolcraft's] efforts to persuade the Michigan Indians of the benefits of leaving their homeland would prove the fatuity of that remark.

The Saginaws, scattered by smallpox and ravaged by hunger, refused to reduce their reservation period. The Chippewas and Odawas of northern Michigan adamantly opposed removal even after a delegation of their chiefs had visited the Southwest. Many of the Maumee Odawas and the Swan Creek and Black River Chippewas found flight to Canada a preferable alternative. What the Indians themselves wanted, however, did not strike the superintendent as a serious consideration, and he wrote Lucius Lyon that their removal could be satisfactorily accomplished as early as the (white) people of Michigan desired it.[77]

Early in her years on Mackinac, there is evidence that Schoolcraft tried to become part of the island community. Church life formed one such attempt on her part. By 1835, there were only irregular services held at the Old Mission Church. The church itself had formally folded but was used on and off for services—and quite wonderfully, for theatrical shows.[78]

As reported by one Dr. Charles Gilman visiting from New York, Henry read lessons and presented a sermon at one of these occasional services at the church. That Sunday worship provides a fine example of the mixed society of Mackinac, including soldiers in uniform, "well dressed gentlemen and ladies; behind them were a few persons in more common dresses, with here and there an Indian, either in blue or white blanket coats."[79] It is remarked that there were a few more Native people standing near the back staring "with utter unconcern at the worship."

It is likely that Jane Schoolcraft was also in the congregation, participating in the service and supporting her husband, who was at the pulpit that day. Some of Jane's poetry professes an earnest belief in Christianity; other poems have a desperate religious feel to them, more strait-laced and pious than genuine. Certainly, no one theme dominates her poetry. Schoolcraft writes most powerfully about personal loss, that of her two children and of her fears at witnessing the plight of her Ojibwe people. Other subjects cover historical ground,[80] and it is noteworthy that she also writes much joyful verse that celebrates nature and invokes us to join her in a reverence for the earth. All of her written stories are based on Native life without specific Protestant or Catholic context.

Separate from her writing, Schoolcraft followed up on her interest in community involvement by joining a band of Native mothers in a Protestant praying circle. In *Historic Mackinac*, editor Edwin O. Wood discusses a religious revival on the island that began in 1824 under Amanda and William Ferry's ministry.[81] He also speaks of how the school had begun to falter and by 1837 had closed down; classroom numbers were shrinking as many of the Native Michigan student families felt forced to leave their state. Their land had been taken.[82] The Presbyterian Ferrys had been proud of the distances some of their students traveled for education at their school on Mackinac.[83] The correlation between the declining number of Indigenous people traveling to Mackinac to attend Amanda and William Ferry's church and school and Henry's actions advancing the removal of the Indians in the Michigan region is clear.

In his study of the Mission Church on Mackinac, Wood relates that there were regular Sunday-school classes, "cottage prayer meetings in the village, work among the soldiers at the garrison (there being at that time no post chaplain), occasional days of fasting and special prayer, [and] a Maternal Association."[84] Of that last maternal group that met, he elaborates:

> This was a praying band of mothers anxious for their children. I find mention of one of their meetings held at the home of Mrs. Henry R. Schoolcraft, a lady of half-Indian blood, educated and refined, and devotedly pious. The meeting was attended by as many as fourteen members, four of whom were Indian mothers loving Christ and the souls of their children—the exercises being interpreted to them [by] Mrs. Schoolcraft.[85]

In discovering this church meeting at her own home, I was heartened to imagine Jane's connection to other women on the island. It must have been meaningful to the Native women present to have Schoolcraft translate the written word for them. But as there is only one mention of her engagement this way, and given the faltering church life of the Protestant ministry at this time and the evidence of Schoolcraft's gradual isolation, it would seem that her attempt at spiritual support with other women was short-lived. More is the pity as Jane had lost two beloved children and no doubt would have benefited from ongoing prayerful empathy from other mothers who had experienced the same kind of loss in that age of high infant mortality.

Given Jane's particular standing in town, it is probable that mingling with her new community would have been strained from the start. In the nineteenth century no woman had it easy asserting an identity that was not subservient to that of her father or husband, and further, Schoolcraft knew she was viewed most singularly as the Ojibwe wife of the Indian agent on Mackinac. There were other married women who were Anishinaabe on Mackinac, including Agatha Biddle, and some years earlier

Madeline Laframboise and Elizabeth Mitchell, but with a crucial difference. While Biddle, Mitchell, and Laframboise had married honorable businessmen in the fur trade, Jane was married to a man whose huge ego and adversarial action towards the Native people could not be missed.

It is little wonder that she felt he had put her in a jeopardized position. In the years living on Mackinac, her fears would be outlined in letters to Henry:

> There is a great deal of talk, I am told, going on in the Indians attempting hostilities this summer after the payments are over, it is said, some have been imprudent enough to say they will set fire to the Agency &c. &c.

In this same letter she later states, "we have turns of *fear* at night," and later, "I am afraid that the *threats* made and making will end in, *no joke*."[86] Here was a woman living alone with her young children much of the time, and as Jameson remarks in her chapter about Mackinac, there was ear-splitting noise many a night during her stay with Jane. The annuities to the Anishinaabe often came in the form of liquor.[87] Outside the general store and near the Agency House (the Schoolcraft's home), the intoxication-fueled disturbance could be extreme. Jameson describes the "yells and whoops," and Schoolcraft expresses her discomfort and revulsion, most of which masks fear.

With possible retaliation against the wife of the Indian agent not far from her mind, it becomes difficult for her to cope. While living on Mackinac, Schoolcraft tries for a distinction between herself and the visitors who received their paltry annuities. This attitude reveals her dual identity and the confusion it caused. She was both Indigenous woman and wife to the white "Indian agent" on Mackinac. In the mid to late 1830s, Jane formed an addiction to laudanum.[88] It is likely that it was first prescribed for Schoolcraft as a way to deal with her conflicted life, made worse by a largely absent husband and very real fears of what could be a perilous situation. Laudanum was a pernicious drug, an opium derivative served up to men and women alike in the nineteenth century. Famous addicts include the English poets Coleridge, Shelley, and Byron. Such writers as Mary Gaskell and George Eliot were also known users of the drug.[89] As is true of narcotics in most cases, the treatment for nerves was far more deleterious than the anticipated cure.

When Anna Jameson first arrived at the Schoolcrafts' home on Mackinac, Henry's comment regarding his wife's unwell state was true. The combined effect of drug use along with the loss of her young son, the theft of her written word, and the ongoing theft of Ojibwe land did her no favors. The singular good news was that in a matter of days, the very presence of Anna Jameson at the Schoolcrafts' home buoyed Jane's spirits, drew her out of her illness and depression. If in the end it was a brief reprieve, her restoration was also remarkable.

The Journey Out: Wilderness, Empowerment, and Legacy

Jameson had expected to go alone with several voyageurs to explore the region north of Mackinac, but at the last minute, Schoolcraft expressed a desire to join her. Once that decision was made, Jane became a whirlwind of organization and action.

The journey itself stands out as a desperate attempt on Jane Schoolcraft's part, a chance to flee the stultifying atmosphere as wife to the Indian agent on Mackinac, and a fleeting few weeks of reconnection to self. This would encompass her return to nature, to heritage (including her mother, sister, and brothers in the Sault), and the invigorating new friendship with Anna Jameson. The timing for the trip to the Sault was largely dependent on an available bateau and voyageurs to assist with rowing. Schoolcraft and Jameson had exactly one hour to prepare for the next several weeks in the Upper Peninsula. Jameson is informed by her friend that they will travel some ninety-four miles by water, twice the distance it would have taken to go by land, but this way they'll avoid the heavily forested terrain that is full of the dual enemies of bear and mosquitoes. Of the five voyageurs who are hired on, four are disinclined to industry. As soon as the sail is hoisted just beyond the harbor of Mackinac, the men get out their cards and the keg, and are falling asleep. Halfway through the journey, the men will again put up their oars and refuse to go forward. Jane takes the initiative to shake them awake and urge the party forward.

A young man of eighteen is put in charge as he is the most responsible of the lot; however it is clear to Anna that the real officer in charge is Jane Schoolcraft. She supervises the travel, with two nights of hardship on mosquito-infested shores. While the poet is a skilled camper, Anna quite charmingly admits she is not. When they land on Goose Island, she writes:

> Mrs. Schoolcraft undertook the general management with all the alertness of
> one accustomed to these impromptu arrangements, and I did my best in my new

vocation—dragged one or two blasted boughs to the fire, the least of them twice as big as myself.[90]

Earlier in the trip, Jameson did not give herself or Jane any credit. She laments that the men, such as they were, had "two helpless women" aboard. Was this uttered ironically or self-reflexively? Most likely the latter, for sadly women were indoctrinated to think themselves "helpless" and told they were limited to menial status, or in contradictory fashion placed in the position of "sitting pretty," frozen, atop a pedestal. It is unsurprising that Jameson retreats briefly to the cliché of "helpless women."[91] Yet, they are anything but, and this adventure, coupled with the progress of the weeks beforehand on Mackinac, refutes the tired trope. Schoolcraft, too, recognizes her strength. She is in a situation where once again she can be action-oriented and useful, as indicated in a letter she sends Henry stating that it is a good thing she is on this trip as Jameson is not the camper she is. Schoolcraft declares, "I feel delighted at my having come with Mrs. Jameson" as she does not "know how to get along" in the wilderness.[92]

The pair makes the choice of where they will stop for the night, and Jane navigates the setup of camp on shore. She builds a large fire to fend off the mosquitoes (Jameson doing her best to follow Schoolcraft's order to gather tinder). The flames keep the bugs at bay for only so long, and some hours later the small band of travelers returns to their boat tied up until morning. Even there, Jane is full of exertion, singing hymns with the designated "captain" in order to keep him awake.[93]

As for Jameson, she falls asleep, yet will wake often with the lovely sense of being taken care of, being safe, although she realizes they are in complete wilderness. That Schoolcraft is in charge and clearly in her element lends a sense of right action to the experience. Jameson seems to recognize that Schoolcraft has been restored. *And she herself*, as well. In shock after migrating to Toronto in an unhappy marriage, she feels a lifting of spirit. The sensibility of independent adventure prevails. On the second night out, she comments on Lake Huron "studded with little islands . . . with the richest, loveliest, most fantastic vegetation, and no doubt swarming with animal life."[94] Using her writing case as a pillow on the boat, she ponders:

> I cannot, I dare not, attempt to describe to you the strange sensation one has,
> thus thrown for a time beyond the bounds of civilized humanity, or indeed any

humanity; nor the wild yet solemn reveries which come over one in the midst of
this wilderness of woods and waters. All was so solitary, so grand in its solitude,
as if nature unviolated sufficed to herself.[95]

It may be noted that this is a white European woman speaking of her reverence of
nature. So, too, is this reverence in full evidence in Jane Schoolcraft. Owing to an
overly sentimentalized view of Indigenous people communing with nature in film
and contemporary story, there is legitimate cause for treading lightly here. Fear of
labels is a valid argument, and yet this connection with the earth, water, plants, and
animals was no label but rather a lived experience for the Anishinaabe, and often,
it may be argued, for Europeans and all sentient beings. Anna records the Ojibwe
belief in the animate spirit of trees and the "spiritualization of the whole universe."[96]
Consider how relevant Jameson's conversation is in the twenty-first century when
the universal web, the very connection between all living matter on earth, is at long
last being acknowledged, at least from an environmental standpoint.

Jameson's image of nature in an unviolated state might well describe Jane
Schoolcraft returned to the comfort and power of those images she puts forth in
her own poetry. We have only to look at her words as a young poet regarding her
beloved Michigan pine: "Ah beauteous tree! ah happy sight! / That greets me on
my Native strand," or in any number of her stories.[97] "The Three Cranberries," for
instance, highlights three women who are in danger. The only one to survive is she
who climbs a "thick spruce" that hides her from the enemy. In essence, the protagonist
turns to nature for survival.[98]

Schoolcraft's heritage and ties to nature strengthened her in that crucial trip
north, one of her last attempts to become the inventive woman she had once been.
Jameson completes the image of Schoolcraft and herself, the restored writers and
adventurers, with these words:

> Two days and nights the solitude was unbroken; not a trace of social life, not a human
> being, not a canoe, not even a deserted wigwam, met our view. Our little boat held
> on its ways over the placid lake and among green islands; and we its inmates, two
> women, differing in clime, nation, [and] complexion.[99]

What the reader of this passage takes away is that despite their differences, these
are women who are supporting one another in good faith. Jameson ends on

the intriguing note of them traveling "in a new-born world."[100] Insofar as being women in charge of an utterly challenging and potentially dangerous situation, they certainly were inhabiting a place that their sex might well feel was liberating, a world "new-born."

Discussions of setting up camp in the two nights on the lake—fires to be built and lighted, supper cooked for the two children and six adults, camp broken, and the iffy question of which way the wind is blowing—if at all, ensue. On the second night, they travel through the dark hours. "Thus we floated on beneath that divine canopy. . . . it was a most lovely and blessed night, bright and calm and warm, and we made some little way, for both wind and current were in our favour."[101]

After the party reaches the Sault, Jane Schoolcraft and children go to stay with her mother, Ozhaguscodaywayquay, on one side of the St. Mary's River, and Anna is invited to stay on the opposite side with Charlotte and her husband, the Reverend MacMurray. Yet merely an hour or two later we find Jameson and company paddling across the river to dine with Jane and Mrs. Johnston. Jane/Bamewawagezhikaquay is vibrant in every way and serves as "interpreter" for her mother, who speaks no English. After dinner, the group heads out to visit the wigwam belonging to her uncle Wayishky, who is considered "a great man." They walk a short distance to his home, which is in "Chippewa form, like an egg cut in half lengthways" and with "wattles and boards; the whole covered with mats, birch-bark, and skins; a large blanket formed the door or curtain, which was not ungracefully looped aside."[102]

Here is a team, Schoolcraft and Jameson, bringing to light the frontier and Native life of the 1830s. Once again, Jameson's written account includes her artwork. In a deft graphite drawing she reveals the lodge belonging to Jane's brother. Throughout this visit and ones to come, the history of the Native people is conveyed to Jameson in translations by Schoolcraft, confidences that "Mrs. Schoolcraft [Jane] whispered me."[103]

Jane's zestful demeanor fairly leaps off the page. We cannot help but compare this with Anna's first knock on Henry Schoolcraft's door when he informs her that his wife is ill and has not left her room for some days.[104] What Anna witnessed in her time on Mackinac was anything but a drug-addled woman incapable of fending for herself. Anna identified with Jane's renewal, though in her own particular way. After all, the English author had left her home in Toronto to take on a large and uncertain adventure. In short, she, like Schoolcraft, was striving to move on to new purpose in life. In their time together, each woman felt she was helping the other. Anna remarks on being there to assist her "sister-woman" in time of need. At the same time, there was Schoolcraft assisting Jane throughout the journey, from camping in the wilderness to translating the Ojibwe language in the Sault. There is something profound and altogether human in one person lending a hand to the other.

Apart from the devastation of her home in the fire when she was young, Jane Schoolcraft's most challenging period came after the early years of her marriage. She had grown up with mother, kin, and neighbors who were Ojibwe and was uncomfortable in the white culture her husband immersed her in on the island. Henry writes condescendingly to her about her own culture; he changes the profound and direct language in poetry she writes and even disparages her "Indian" and "uneducated" ways to her own daughter, *after* Jane's death. His letters make clear that he is trotting her out as an "exotic," a "Northern Pocahontas."[105] He believed it was a feather in his cap to show off his wife as an Indian; it bolstered his career as an "Indian expert."

Schoolcraft sometimes traveled with her husband, and Detroit was one of their destinations. John Ball met the Schoolcrafts in 1837 at a boarding house in Detroit. He had this to say:

> Mr. Schoolcraft, whose wife was a half-breed of the Johnson family. She did not often appear at the table, though well educated in England and a real lady, in her manners. When she found herself cut by some of the white ladies when in Washington, she could never get over it, but rather retired from company.[106]

Throughout her adult life, Jane experienced overt racism directed towards her by men and women. We can appreciate her wariness of most Euro-American women and that she was uncomfortable in their orbit. Anna Jameson was the exception.

A Revealing View of Society: The Language and the Lives

When on Mackinac, Jameson roamed the island. The Schoolcrafts owned a private carriage, and Anna outlines her time with them, including "delicious drives. . . . no more than three miles in length. . . . a perpetual succession of low, rich groves."[107]

During her walks she observes the thousands of Anishinaabe arriving on the shores of Mackinac for their annual annuities, including an elderly gentleman whose meditative state she watches with awe.

> The most striking personage in this group was a very old man, seated on a log of wood close upon the edge of the water; ... [his head] decorated with a single feather—I think an eagle's feather, his blanket of scarlet cloth was so arranged as to fall around his limbs in graceful folds, leaving his chest and shoulders exposed; he held a green umbrella over his head (a gift or purchase from some white trader) and in the other hand, a long pipe—and he smoked away, never stirring, or taking the slightest interest in anything that was going on.[108]

She examines the birchbark canoes that are flat-bottomed and elegant in shape and manages to get herself invited into wigwams. People were attracted to her extroverted personality and keen interest in cultures other than her own. Jameson uses sign language to communicate in the wigwams and to note the range of goods "in tidy order" from bags of woven grass to a large coffee pot of "queen's metal."

She is both frank and coy about the honor of "being permitted to be present, or, as the French say, to *assist*" at the council meetings she attends with Henry. At one of the meetings an Ojibwe beseeches the Indian agent to hear him out about land payments the U.S. government owes his tribe. However, Henry shushes him up and tells him not to speak further "on that subject."[109] The Anishinaabe are frank as well in their reaction to the meetings: "The Indians themselves make witty jests on the bad faith of the Big Knives."

Jameson's intelligent footnotes, alluded to earlier, are one of the joys of her work, whether shedding a light on the small steamboats on the Great Lakes, which make "horrible and perpetual snorting like the engine on a railroad," or her agreement with Washington Irving's view of the voyageurs with "the steersman [who] often sings an old French song with some regular burthen in which they all join, keeping time with their oars. When spirits flag or relax in exertion, it is but necessary to strike up a song of this kind to put them all in fresh spirits and activity."[110] In case we are not familiar with the term "long knives," there is her footnote explaining its etymology, referring us to the year 1794 when the Indians near the Miami River suffered badly "from the sabers of cavalry."[111]

Just as visitors to Mackinac in the twenty-first century might note several types of sailboats in the marina one morning, and then delight in a completely different batch a week later, so Jameson draws us into the ever-changing scene on Mackinac in the 1800s. After commenting on the Indian lodges and canoes one day, she cannot resist letting us know that "I forgot to tell you that yesterday afternoon there came in a numerous fleet of canoes, thirty or forty at least; and the wind blowing fresh from the west, each with its square blanket sail came scudding over the waters with amazing velocity; it was a beautiful sight."[112]

This was a rare period in Great Lakes history. Never again would people witness dexterously manned canoes in such numbers by Indigenous clans in the Mackinac harbor. With warmth and vivid details, Jameson conveys a continuum of life that is forever preserved. We learn about the distinction of tribes who come to Mackinac, and where they are from. From the west come the Winnebagos and the Pottowattomies, and from the east of Lake Michigan in Arbre Croche are the Odawas. The latter, she tells us, are more agricultural than the other "Lake Indians."[113]

As ever, the weather presents drama on Mackinac. She describes what she calls a hurricane when sitting one day with her "Irish friend" at the "mission-house. . . . The billows came rolling with might, flinging themselves in wrath and fury" and "the expanse of the main lake was like the ocean lashed to fury."[114]

Jameson personalizes her journey in distinctive ways. Her book is not just social history but a revelation of how a woman of the early nineteenth century used her extended trip to Mackinac, the Sault, and the entire upper Great Lakes region to map out how she was going to live a future rewarding and contented life. Her friendship with Jane Schoolcraft lent her courage and knowledge. If Anna was searching for role models of women who managed on their own (as she would be doing in the near future) then Jane's lessons on the autonomy of particular Indigenous women found a ready ear.

From reading about America before her move to North America, Jameson had assumed that the Indian woman was no better off than the most menial of servants, a virtual slave to her husband. In a conversation on the subject, Jane begs to differ, and says there are some examples of parity in Native marriages. Moreover, not every woman is forced to marry. Schoolcraft shares a story of one who chooses the sun as her Manito and is in effect "married to the luminary" and provides for herself, building her own wigwam and hunting and gathering for herself.[115] Jameson learns that "Heroic women are not rare among the Indian," and though she does note that many of the women she sees on Mackinac give a submissive impression, Schoolcraft lets her know that "female chiefs, however, are not unknown in Indian history."[116] Jameson is thrilled "with her [Jane's] new ideas," and will continue her search for selfhood through communion with Jane and her Native family.[117]

Their conversation together often settles on a form of social history of the Native people on Mackinac. This leads to a discussion between Jameson and the Schoolcrafts of the tragedy of firewater given to the Anishinaabe. When there is drunkenness among them, Jane relates that the Indian women "have taken away their husbands' knives and tomahawks, and hidden them—wisely enough."[118]

While we may draw conclusions about women of all stripes as passive peacemakers, this view is tempered by the activist voice and action of other minorities Jameson meets on the journey that shapes her history. During her visit to Niagara, she is struck by the power and passionate stand that a group of African American women take when violence erupts after a runaway slave is caught. The women throw themselves into the fray "fearlessly between the Black men and the whites. . . . One woman had seized the sheriff, and held him pinioned in her arms." When one man threatens to shoot her, she "gave him only one glance of unutterable contempt" and collared him in such a way "as to prevent his firing." Jameson speaks with a Black woman who states that while she believed there would be freedom in the North, she now fears it is not so, but that she will "find some country where they cannot reach us! I'll go to the end of the world, I will!"[119]

It is an unforgettable voice, part of an anthem to the republic that she should change her course, abolish slavery once and for all. It would be another twenty-six years before the Civil War. These African and Native American lives recorded by Jameson are crucial documents.

Anna's surprise at how intelligent and literary Schoolcraft is discloses her own background biases. Jameson, as a middle-class woman from the Continent in the 1800s, had her own preconceived notions about the "red man," as she sometimes refers to Native Americans. While she lapses into a romanticized view of the Anishinaabe, revealed particularly in descriptions of his "wild dancing," among other features she describes, her analytic brain more often rises above this. She recognizes that most people have cultural prejudices, and that there are moments when she is no different. Jameson trains her eye on an expansive worldview, and she makes clear that her mind was broadened by Jane Schoolcraft.

Following the connection between Jameson and Schoolcraft leads to the understanding that there are many ways to describe what constitutes history itself, multiple definitions available to us when shaping and restoring what happened in the past. One example of a new paradigm that came to my attention was Jameson's interest in the childcare views and practices of the Native people who traveled to Mackinac. It may be agreed that how parents raise children in a community matters; the approach and input directly affects the next generation of citizens and leaders in any given area. Hence, childcare is a significant perspective to include in a history of Mackinac or any setting in the young United States of the 1800s.

Jameson addresses this with due seriousness, and she witnesses Schoolcraft as an outstanding parent. Anna writes of how on Mackinac "the general reverence and respect of [Native] children for parents is delightful; where no obedience is exacted, there can be no rebellion; they dream not of either, and all live in peace in the same lodge." That last bit on the total lack of rebellion between child and parent and utter peace at home is certainly a rosy view, whether a description of an Anglo family or the Anishinaabe in a wigwam on the beach. Yet her overall observations are worthy ones. She notes that the Native people who come with family members while delivering pelts and meeting with the Indian agent foster independence in their children. "They say that before a child has any understanding" of incorrect behavior, "there is no use in correcting it, and when old enough to understand, no one has a right to correct it. . . . The will of an Indian child is not forced. . . . I hear no scolding, no tones of command or reproof."[120]

Schoolcraft makes clear to Jameson, by example, that there are no ill effects from this "mild system," and indeed the latter marvels at how "the inherent sentiment of personal independence grows up with the Indian from earliest infancy." Her view of parenting that forms the character of the young would have been corroborated by living for a time with the Schoolcrafts. She refers to Jane's "two sweet children, about eight or nine years old." Further evidence of loving parenting occurs when Schoolcraft travels by bateau to Sault Ste. Marie, after Jameson's stay on Mackinac. Stopping for the night at the entrance of St. Mary's River somewhere between Neebish Island and the mainland, the party is beset by mosquitoes, as indicated earlier. Anna is struck and deeply touched by Jane's solicitous attention to her children:

> But whenever I woke from uneasy, restless slumbers, there was Mrs. Schoolcraft, bending over her sleeping children, and waving off the mosquitoes, singing all the time a low, melancholy Indian song.[121]

All this, Jameson further informs us, "while the northern lights were streaming and dancing in the sky, and the fitful moaning of the wind, the gathering clouds, and chilly atmosphere foretold of a change in weather."[122]

While still on Mackinac, Jameson observes that Jane always speaks to her children and to her "Indian Domestics" in the "Chippewa tongue." Building on this, Anna discusses the Ojibwe language and grammar. She remarks on the sound of Schoolcraft's voice, "sweet and musical to the ear, with its soft inflections and lengthened vowels, but very complex. . . . subject to strict grammatical rules." Earlier in her visit to the island she writes of the "plaintive modulations reminding me of recitative," and of the softening of the aspirates. Instead of a firm vowel, for instance, in saying Manito, the proper pronunciation elongates and softens the vowel to become "mo-nee-do."[123] Here is a true wordsmith paying attention to the diversity of language.

Jameson remarks that much of what she hears from Native people is an unwritten language, a truism of many tribes in the United States, even today. Therefore, it is remarkable and valuable to history that Jane Schoolcraft wrote down many versions of her poetry in the Ojibwe language, perhaps a form that she created. One such version is preserved in her poem "To the Pine Tree." The differences in cultural perspective between the Euro-American and Native worlds are related in subject matter and even in word choice. When Jameson describes the beauty of Mackinac, she goes right to her Irish childhood, and the low, rich groves of the island have "alleys green, dingles, and bosky dells."[124] As a young teenager, Schoolcraft was taken by her Irish father to London and to Dublin. When abroad, she was terribly homesick. Looking back to that time, she writes of approaching her native Northwoods land after being away:

To the Pine Tree
The pine! the pine! I eager cried,
The pine, my father! see it stand,

As first that cherished tree I spied,
Returning to my Native land.
The pine! the pine! oh lovely scene!
The pine that is forever green.

Ah beauteous tree! ah happy sight!
That greets me on my Native strand
And hails me, with a friend's delight,
To my own dear bright *mother land*

Oh 'tis to me a heart-sweet scene,
The pine—the pine! that's ever green.

Not all the trees of England bright,
Not Erin's lawns of green and light
Are half so sweet to memory's eye,
As this dear type of northern sky
Oh 'tis to me a heart-sweet scene,
The pine—the pine! that ever green.

The italics of "mother land" in the poem are my own. It is worth mentioning that while historically a male usually prefers referring to his country as the fatherland, a female perspective often takes her own sex as the guidepost in her perspective. Further, we may take into consideration the Anishinaabe's reverence of the earth, often thought of as "mother earth."

Here is "To the Pine Tree" once again as Schoolcraft wrote it down in three stanzas in her Ojibwe translation:

Shing wauk! Shing wauk! Nin ge ik id,
Waish kee wau bum ug, sjhing wauk
Tuh quish in aun nau aub, ain dak nuk I yaun.
Shing wauk, shing wauk No sa
Shi e qwuh ke do dis au naun
Kau gega way zhau wus co zid.

Mes ah nah, shi egwuh tah gwish en aung
Sin da mik kea um baun
Ka gait suh, ne meen wain dum
Me nah wau, wau bun dah maun
Gi yut wiau, wau bun dah maun een
Shing wauk, shing wauk osa
Shi e qwuh ke do dis aun naun.

Ka ween ga go, kau wau bun duh e yun
Tib isht co, izz henau gooz ze no an

Shing wauk wah zhau wush co zid
Ween Ait ah kwanaudj e we we
Kau ge gay wa zhau soush ko zid.[125]

A Woman in a Thousand

In her social history of Mackinac and the Great Lakes region, Anna Jameson pays attention to the Indigenous men as well as the women.[126] While on the island, she comments on the sheer loveliness of the young men she sees or meets. Her attention indicates an artist's close attention to and interest in the human form. She feels she cannot move her pencil fast enough in her sketches. The net result is a superb record that is the sum of the polymath Jameson: social historian, visual artist, art critic, and engaging travel writer.

> I should not forget to mention that the figures of most of the men were superb; more agile and elegant, however than muscular—more fitted for the chase than for labour, with small and well-formed hands and feet. . . . [A young warrior's] spear lay across his knees, and he reposed, his head upon his hand. He was not painted, except with a little vermilion on his chest—and on his head he wore only the wing of the osprey: he sat there—a model for a sculptor.[127]

Jameson makes her artistic intentions clear: "There was not a figure among them that was not a study for a painter; and how I wished that my hand had been readier with the pencil to snatch some of those picturesque heads and attitudes."[128] Whether it is a Jameson or a Catlin, the artist's image is often all we have of a visual scene before the advent of photography. In Jameson's case, in which history is recorded in word and image, the reward is twofold.

Jameson's friendship with George Johnston, Jane's brother, is noteworthy. They formed an easy camaraderie and shared a mutual admiration of one another. Raised in the same house with Jane and their mother, Ozhaguscodaywayquay, he stayed closely connected to his Ojibwe roots. Jameson first met George on Mackinac when he was serving as the interpreter for Henry at Native council meetings she attended. At that time, Jane's brother let her know that his brethren on the island enjoyed Anna's warmth and interest in them. She passed on George's report: "The Indians like me, and are gratified by my presence."[129] Poking fun at her limited language skills, she writes, "we hold most eloquent conversations." She mentions a range of subjects to which she nods, smiles, frowns, and gestures. Still, she uses the Native words she has learned, and like most people, the Ojibwe of Mackinac appreciate how she took the time to try to learn their language. Whether speaking of their children or frowning when asked for "English milk, (rum or whiskey)," she is fully engaged and rewarded with the first of two Indian names bestowed upon her. On Mackinac, she is given the name Ogimaquay (English Chieftainess).

When spending several weeks in the Sault, Anna is delighted that George shows her the beauty of St. Mary's River. While leaning on his arm, she watches the small canoes "popping like corks" over the cataracts. Afterwards, she takes him up on his dare that she shoot the rapids, and describes her ride with a Native canoeist. His "astonishing dexterity [keeps] the head of the canoe to the breakers" and guides them between small passages of rock as they descend the falls. Her adventurous spirit is in full evidence, and Jameson is given a second Ojibwe name: Odawyaungee, or "the woman of the bright foam." After this honor, Anna declares: "I am Chippewa born."[130]

Jameson is fully at home with Jane Schoolcraft's family: "A cousin of mine (I now have a large Chippewa cousinship)," she states drolly, and with evident pride.[131] Realizing how many days have slipped away while visiting at the house of Jane and her mother, she comments, "I have been too long on the other side of the river; I must return to our Canadian shore, where indeed I now reside under the hospitable roof of our missionary." That residence belonged to Jane's brother-in-law, Pastor MacMurray, and Charlotte, who, as stated earlier, was Jane's sister.[132]

Throughout her weeks with Schoolcraft and her family, Schoolcraft shares a number of stories and songs with the English author, one of which is titled "Ojibwe Quaince." Anna marks down the score, and the words are as follows: *Aun dush wwn do we nain, Git-chee mo / ko-maum since Kah zah wah da mood we ya / ya hah ha we ya hah ha.* She includes Jane's Ojibwe and a rough English paraphrasing. It is intriguing that this song gives a frank if cynical turn to the courtship between a "Longknife" (white man) and a woman, perhaps echoing some of Schoolcraft's own felt experience when Henry disappears for months at a time on his various Indian agent business trips. Jameson records Schoolcraft's translation of the song:

Hah! What is the matter with the young Long-knife? He crosses the river with tears in his eyes. He sees the young Chippewa girl preparing to leave the place; he sobs for his sweetheart because she is going away, but he will not sigh for her long; as soon as she is out of sight he will forget her![133]

As for other men with whom Jameson engages on this journey, Henry Schoolcraft himself figures largely. Jameson is anything but blind to his charisma and his influence on Mackinac. If she has suspicions regarding his poor treatment of Jane, she is careful to tread lightly. As a woman in a man's world, she is keenly aware of his powerful position. There is evident effort on her part to stay on his good side so that she may have news of Jane. It is only in her book, published after she travels back to London—at a safe remove, one might surmise—that she is free to discuss his wrong dealings with the Anishinaabe. This she witnessed in the Ojibwe council meetings she attended and in general communication with Jane and Henry. Jameson may not have been aware that Henry had also formed a pattern of vindictiveness towards others, often those caught in the crosshairs of one of his adversarial battles.[134]

The cultural association of women on Mackinac in the first half of the nineteenth century is made vivid in remarks by Anna Jameson and Elizabeth T. Baird. Jameson offers a cultural reading of what she has witnessed on Mackinac in language that is inviting. Of the bark cradle, or *tikinagan*, that she sees in one Native lodge, she states: "and as for the gay cradle of the baby, I quite covet it—it is so gorgeously elegant."[135] We have only to turn to the description of another Anishinaabe cradle, as observed fifteen years earlier by author Elizabeth T. Baird, to see the continuum: A child carried in a *tikinagan*, as it is attached to a board worn on a mother's back, contains "a bed of a mixture composed of fine dry moss, old cedar wood and a species of reed, commonly called cat tail."[136] Baird, a Métis who lived on Mackinac for twelve years, gives far greater detail than Jameson. Regarding shared crafts of the Anishinaabe women, it was a given that Schoolcraft was skilled with a needle, as evidenced in sewing shirts for the soldiers when she visited the island as a teen. It is likely that she, like Madeline Laframboise, Therese Schindler, and Agatha Biddle, were each taught as young girls to be handy in bead and quillwork. Beyond a continuity of skilled craftwork among these three Native women, there were differences, none perhaps more obvious than Schoolcraft's writing skills and literary talent. Of the six remarkable Anishinaabe Mackinac women in the nineteenth century—Mitchell, Laframboise, Schindler, Biddle, Schoolcraft and

Baird—just two were literate: Baird and Schoolcraft. Unfortunately for Jane, the chance of meeting sister Métis writer E. T. Baird would not come to pass, as she left the island nearly a decade before the poet's arrival. One can imagine how pleasantly surprised Schoolcraft was when at last a writer whom she could connect with came to stay at her house on Mackinac.

The eventual visit with Jane's mother and sister was a happy one for all parties, but months later Jameson would write movingly of the highwater mark of that journey: the two nights and three days when she, Jane, two children, and several voyageurs paddled through the wilderness of the old Northwest. That adventure might well represent the wilderness journey of two women and their attempt to stake out a firm identity in a world that would have none of it.

Picking up on the thread of Jameson moving on to a life of relative freedom and continuing artistic expression, the English author who had enlisted all of her "womanly sympathies" towards the plight of Schoolcraft may well have worried at a later date that she had failed in helping the poet set a new course in life. In years to come it would not have been lost on Jameson that while she had arrived at a peaceful place in life, her brilliant songwriter, poet, and tale-spinner friend had neither the same literary successes nor a peaceful life. Jameson, remarking on the last time she saw Schoolcraft:

> Handling her paddle with singular grace and dexterity, [she] shot over the blue water, without venturing once to look back.

As it happened, Schoolcraft wept along with Jameson when it came time for the friends to part. When Jameson writes of leaving Mackinac, "O—at Mackinaw! That fairy island, which I shall never see again," she is nonetheless still with Jane Schoolcraft as they make their way north to Jane's family in the Sault.[137] Some weeks later (Jameson does not give precise dates), she gives a stirring description of her last sight of Schoolcraft, one that strengthens our sense of Jane's emotional warmth, courage, and physical dexterity. Jameson records that there were

> more last affectionate words from Mrs. Schoolcraft. We then exchanged a long farewell embrace, and she turned away with tears, got into her little canoe, which could scarcely contain two persons, and handling her paddle with singular grace and dexterity, shot over the blue water, without venturing once to look back![138]

Jameson watches Jane's "little canoe skimming over the expanse between [the white spray of the rapids]; and this was the last I saw of my dear good Chippewa mamma!"[139] Until this passage towards the end of *Winter Studies*, it would be easy to assume that it is Jameson who took up the maternal stance in this culturally significant friendship. We have been made aware of Jane's difficulties, and so it is with a jolt that it becomes clear that Jameson, too, found support, even maternal strength in Schoolcraft herself. The mutuality of such a friendship between women of different races in this era hits home. As does the empowerment of one by the other.

Jane Schoolcraft returned to Mackinac after that interlude with her mother, sister, brother, and newfound friend, Anna Jameson. In the next five years, her last on earth, the poet would experience a number of life changes.

When first married to Henry, it is unlikely she imagined ever leaving her homeland in Michigan and being made to live in New York in an empty house. She described it as such because neither her children nor her husband (Henry gone for the most part) were there with her. They moved away from Mackinac because Henry had been ordered to leave his post as Indian agent. Charges of corruption had been leveled by Mackinac resident Michael Dousman, trader Robert Stuart, and Edward Biddle, who was husband to Anishinaabe resident Agatha. To make matters more complicated, charges against Henry by Jane's brother William were leveled as well.[140] He was Jane's youngest brother and he lived in close proximity to the Schoolcrafts when they were first married in Sault Ste. Marie. One of the stories Jane passed on to Anna Jameson, titled "The Forsaken Brother," prophesies her sadness over the falling out between her husband and her brother William. His name in Ojibwe, Miengun, has the English translation "Wolf." It is possible that the rift in 1838 came about, in part, as a result of William's understanding of Henry's overall dishonesty. The poignant story by Schoolcraft looks at a fictional youngest brother in a family—much like William, eleven years younger than Jane. This youngest brother is abandoned by his older siblings and taken in by a family of wolves. The young man, already turned into a half-wolf, appeals to his older sister for help. She becomes involved with a man whom she marries and soon forgets to help her younger brother, who then turns into a full wolf and disappears forever into the forest.

This story is one of three by Schoolcraft that Jameson included in *Winter Studies*. Each is a strong and affecting narrative, but of the group presented, "The Forsaken Brother" is most fully realized as an emotionally resonant narrative. Schoolcraft ends on a note of mourning. The older sister weeps for her lost brother the rest of her days. Jameson comments on the simplicity and power of Schoolcraft's work.[141]

While most of Schoolcraft's poetry was written before Jameson's visit, her Ojibwe tales appear to be an ongoing part of her writing life. Some of her stories appeared in Henry's papers and edited versions of his wife's work. The telling feature is that Schoolcraft also gave Jameson her stories, some of which do not reflect the editing changes that husband Henry made. This makes Jameson's record of Schoolcraft's work all the more valuable.

While it was known that Henry exhibited sly tactics with many of the Anishinaabe, few realized the extent to which his own wife was subjected to his venality. The Indian agent was capable of belittling her talents and telling her that he and others found her wanting. He does not honor the singular education she received in a multicultural home, and in 1830 has this to say to her in a letter:

> Brought up in a remote place, without any thing which deserves to have the name of a regular education, without the salutary influence of society to form your mind, without a mother, in many things, to direct, and [a father who] made even your sisters & brothers and all about you bow to you as their superior in every mental & and wor[l]dly thing."[142]

It is mean-spirited of Henry to suggest that her own mother was of no import in Jane's upbringing. The very reverse of this statement is true, given Henry's adulation of Ozhaguscodaywayquay in his own memoirs, and in Jameson's many references to Schoolcraft speaking admiringly of all her that her mother represents. If anything, Jane's assertive side was not unlike her mother's, whose extensive (and highly successful) maple sugar business, along with full-time nurturing of her children gave her daughter much to emulate and admire.

In the article "Bicultural before There Was a Word for It," Margaret Noori comments on the sadness Jane felt when Henry insisted her young children be sent to boarding school. As Noori points out, the abuse of Indian children in these establishments was widespread, including rape and physical torment.[143] As late as the early 1980s, Holy Childhood School in Harbor Springs, Michigan, forced cultural assimilation and beat children who were caught speaking their Native tongues.[144] Noori assumes Schoolcraft's son and daughter were shipped off to an "Indian" institution. However, Janey and John attended elite East Coast prep schools, which did not level the physical abuse known in the government schools for Native people.[145] Still, the so-called civilized East Coast boarding schools were hardly free of racial prejudice, and there, too, existed possible violence towards Indigenous children.

It was after Janey and John, Schoolcraft's two remaining children, had been placed in boarding school that Henry was fired from his position as Indian agent on Mackinac. The corruption charges involved a federal investigation, some of it implying that he had been "cooking the books," keeping annuities for himself, monies meant for the Ojibwe or for the U.S. government.[146]

Without a job in 1841, Henry took to the road, trying for the public lecture circuit, in which he would lecture on "Indian culture." The Schoolcrafts left Michigan and moved to a house on Nineteenth Street in New York City. He left Jane alone in a setting where she felt no connection to her surroundings. The absence of the natural world she loved in Michigan, a universe of nature that she had written about often, affected her deeply. Her husband had spent a large part of their marriage traveling in pursuit of career advancement, but in this instance, it was seemingly to run from his own possible state of humiliation. Yet he recovered faster than Jane, who also felt Henry's shame acutely. More significantly, the removal of her children and her own permanent removal from the land she loved cut her to the quick.[147]

Once the Schoolcrafts moved permanently to New York, Jane's health began to worsen. Nonetheless, Henry was determined to go to London. She languished in her new home, and at last, in 1842, made a journey to visit her sister Charlotte in Dundass, Ontario.[148]

Back in a woodland setting with her sister, Schoolcraft must have found succor, but it was too little, too late. She may have been overwhelmed, felt undone when considering that she would have to return to a new abode in the east, and again without her children. Jane was found dead, sitting up in a chair one morning in her sister's home. When Henry learned of her death, he briefly considered sailing home for her funeral and for the sake of his children. He changed his mind, however, and toured Paris, Brussels, and Frankfurt, and after this returned to England for another six weeks. He had decided to look for a publisher abroad as well, hoping for a book on his "Indian Tales," the ones that Jane had written and translated for him.[149] When the book was published, she was unattributed.

There is no record of the physical cause of Jane's death, but one cannot help but think that heartbreak contributed to her departure from this world. The imagistic poem she wrote in both Ojibwe and English a year before her death regarding the absence of her children is a heartrending foretelling:

Nidaanisen e / My little daughter
Nigwizisens e / My little son
Ishe naganagwaa / I leave them far behind
Waasawekamig / A faraway place
Endanakiiyaan / My homeland
Zhigwa gosha win / Now
Beshowead e we / It is near
Ninzhifke we ya / I am alone
Ishe izhayaan / As I go
Endanakiiyaan / My homeland

Several forms of this poem may be found in the Schoolcraft papers in the Library of Congress. Henry gives a version that is much padded compared to the powerful and bare-bones translation that most closely aligns with Jane's Ojibwe words. Additionally, Margaret Noori remarks that the "pattern of repetition" in Schoolcraft's translations "echoes hand-drum songs still heard today."[150]

Though possibly small consolation for Schoolcraft at the end of her life, she spent her last days with sister Charlotte in Ontario. The poet had remained close with her siblings throughout her life. Her three sisters in particular would have appreciated Schoolcraft's poem that was paean both to the sister-women of the world, and to the regenerative power of nature that her Ojibwe heritage taught her. The verse starts this way:

By an Ojibwe *Female* Pen
Invitation to sisters to a walk in the Garden, after a shower

Come, sisters come! The shower's past,
The garden walks are drying fast,
The Sun's bright beams are seen again,
And nought within, can now detain.[151]

The last stanza invokes the sisters to look at "the breeze of hope," and allow "life's mix'd scene itself, but cease, / To show us realms of light and peace."[152] There are many such strong and stirring poems in her canon. Another one that stands out is also set in northern Michigan and contains these lines:

> Lone island of the saltless sea!
> How wide, how sweet, how fresh and free
> How all transporting—is the view
> Of rocks and skies and waters blue
> Uniting, as a song's sweet strains
> To tell, here nature only reign.
> Ah nature! Here forever sway
> Far from the haunts of men away
> For here, there are no sordid fears,
> No crimes, no misery, no tears
> No pride of wealth; the heart to fill,
> No laws to treat my people ill.[153]

The poem speaks powerfully to the laws that have done damage to her Native people. To those who know the islands of the Great Lakes, these lines also summon their eternal beauty. The imagined island in question sets up twin symbols that Schoolcraft wants us to take to heart. This place where "here nature only reign" followed by "Ah nature! Here forever sway / Far from the haunts of men away" calls to mind her experience and belief in nature as a haven far from the machinations and politics that have wreaked havoc in her beloved Michigan. The "crimes" and "laws" that "treat my people ill" could no longer be whitewashed.

Jane Schoolcraft's time on Mackinac did not end well, yet she had formed a strong association with island life, as evidenced by her association with Anna Jameson. After the many weeks she spent on-island and in the Sault, the English author wrote Schoolcraft a letter sent by care of Henry. Compulsive saver that he was, he kept that letter to Jane, which reads: "As long as I live, the impression of your kindness, and of your character altogether remains with me; your image will often come back to me, and I dare to hope you will not forget me *quite*."[154]

Anna had sensed that she might not hear back from her friend. We know Schoolcraft did write letters to select people, her sister Charlotte and Henry included. Given her friendship with Anna, it is likely she would have written back, yet Jameson received no letter. It is possible that Schoolcraft's controlling husband—who had a habit of taking what had been written to and by Jane and filing such papers away as his own—did not show her Jameson's heartfelt missive. Whether or not Schoolcraft saw Anna Jameson's letter is unknown, but in Henry's papers there is a letter from Jane that reveals how much Jameson's presence meant to her: "Poor Mrs. Jameson cried heartily when she parted with me and my children; she is indeed a woman in a thousand."[155] It is high praise for anyone, and it may be too much to hope that Henry shared his wife's sentiment with Jameson.[156]

On Mackinac, Schoolcraft may not have spent time with fur traders Laframboise and Schindler, or humanitarian Agatha Biddle, but surely the four women knew each other. In and of itself, this knowledge created agency and authenticity for this trio of Native women. Laframboise, Biddle, and Schindler were leaders in business and humanitarian outreach in their communities, while Schoolcraft led with literature, her valuable gift of Native stories, poems, and song that preserved the Anishinaabe heritage. This gift was first shared among a large number of readers by Anna Jameson, who wrote extensively about Schoolcraft and her work.

Bamewawagezhikaquay, Schoolcraft's Ojibwe name, translates as *The Sound the Stars Make Rushing through the Sky*. One does not associate sound with a falling star, and yet we have no difficulty sensing the power and beauty of such stars "through the sky." So it is with Bamewawagezhikaquay, whose name and work suggest that which has been largely hidden from view. Yet once known, such a star is unforgettable.

1. A leader in the Mackinac community, Elizabeth Mitchell was a farmer, a fur trader, and a woman torn between loyalties. Her friends also noted that she was never seen without her tall beaver hat with a single feather.

ELIZABETH MITCHELL, OIL PORTRAIT BY MELISSA CROGHAN, 2019.

2. The home of Elizabeth and David Mitchell was the largest residence on Mackinac in the early to mid-1800s. Elizabeth hosted the wedding ceremony of Josette Laframboise and Captain Benjamin Pierce, the daughter and son-in-law of Madeline Laframboise. Today Cindy's Riding Stable on Market Street sits on the former grounds of the Mitchell house.
COURTESY OF MACKINAC STATE HISTORIC PARKS COLLECTION.

3. Therese Marcot Schindler, sister to Madeline Marcot Laframboise, was an entrepreneur who expanded her fur-trading business as a widow and owned a maple sugar business on Bois Blanc Island. Her businesses gave jobs to islanders on Mackinac. Therese and Madeline, who were Anishinaabe, lived next door to one another on the island until Madeline built her own grand home near the marina.
COURTESY OF WISCONSIN HISTORICAL SOCIETY.

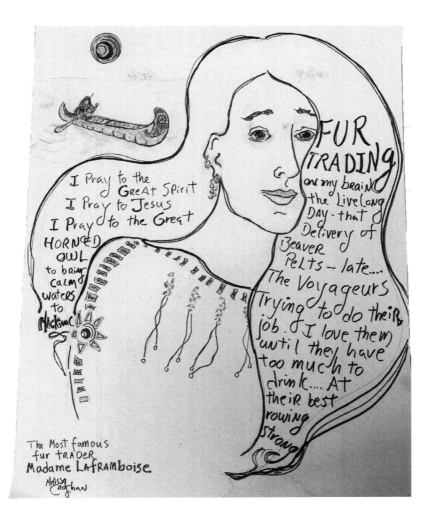

I Pray to the Great Spirit
I Pray to Jesus
I Pray to the Great HORNED OWL to bring calm waters to Mackinac

FUR TRADING on my brain the Live Long Day - that Delivery of Beaver Pelts - late.... The Voyageurs Trying to do their job. I love them until they have too much to drink.... At their best rowing strong

The Most famous fur tRADeR Madame LaFRAMboise

Melissa Croghan

4. Madeline Marcot Laframboise, the Odawa fur trader, was highly respected by such thinkers as Alexis de Tocqueville and Margaret Fuller. No woman before or after approached her visionary reach in the fur-trading world. This influential trader was also a philanthropist who started a school for Anishinaabe girls on Mackinac. She experienced great tragedy in life: the murder of her husband, and in 1821, the death of her daughter Josette in childbirth. After losing Josette, she lived year-round on the island. Descriptions of Madeline by other women of Mackinac testify to her brilliance, dependability, and wit.

MADELINE LAFRAMBOISE, PORTRAIT IN PEN AND INK BY MELISSA CROGHAN, 2014.

5. *Wigwams on the Beach* would have been a familiar view to islanders in the 1830s. In 1836, Anna Jameson parked herself with sketchbook in hand on the Mackinac waterfront and created this drawing. The gregarious nature of the author of *Winter Studies and Summer Rambles* occasionally got her invited into the tipis. While on Mackinac, she lived first with the Schoolcrafts, and then for a month with Jane Schoolcraft's Ojibwe family in the Upper Peninsula of Michigan.
COURTESY OF TORONTO PUBLIC LIBRARY.

6. This photograph was taken in Elizabeth Therese Baird's early middle age, most likely in Green Bay, Wisconsin, when she and husband Henry had achieved a measure of prosperity. The Anishinaabe woman gained attention with her memoir that takes a close look at Mackinac culture and life, including unforgettable studies of her grandmother, Therese Schindler, and her great-aunt Madeline Laframboise. E. T. Baird grew up on Mackinac and did not shy away from writing about the colorful Elizabeth Mitchell, or emotional travail in the households of Agatha Biddle and Therese Schindler.
PHOTOGRAPH CIRCA 1850–1860. COURTESY OF WISCONSIN HISTORICAL SOCIETY.

7. Ste. Anne's Church was the brainchild of Madeline Laframboise, who donated property at the east end of town for the erection of this historic Mackinac building.

AFTER THE RAIN, OIL PAINTING, MELISSA CROGHAN, 2013. AUTHOR'S COLLECTION.

8. Agatha Biddle was an Anishinaabe woman who grew up on Mackinac. Her mother, Marie Le Fevre, was a well-known storyteller, and her stepfather was a man whose booming voice could be heard all over town. Perhaps as a result, Agatha was composed and quiet. She worked tirelessly for the rights of her Native kin and those in need. She was present at the Treaty of Detroit in 1855, which encouraged fishing and hunting rights for the Anishinaabe.

PHOTOGRAPH, CIRCA 1850. COURTESY OF MACKINAC STATE HISTORIC PARKS COLLECTION.

9. Captain Benjamin Pierce married Josette Laframboise in a ceremony held on Market Street at the home of Elizabeth Mitchell, who mentored the bride's mother, Madeline. Captain Pierce, who was the brother of President Franklin Pierce, assisted Madame Laframboise in building her Mackinac home. That house has been preserved and today is the Harbor View Inn.

PORTRAIT OF CAPTAIN PIERCE, CIRCA 1825. COURTESY OF MACKINAC STATE HISTORIC PARKS COLLECTION.

10. Biddle House. Agatha's home on Market Street was often full to bursting with guests. Public notary Samuel Abbott wrote about how the house was "crowded with Indians, receiving shelter and food." She and Edward Biddle built the house in 1822, and though much of the original structure burnt down in 1910, it has been restored and today houses the Native American Museum. Notably, the Biddle House was a stone's throw from Elizabeth Mitchell's home, underscoring the close community of Anishinaabe on Mackinac.

11. Juliette Kinzie was "one of the best known writers associated with early Mackinac," according to historian Edwin O. Wood. Her social history, *Wau-Bun*, meaning "the dawn" in Ojibwe, gives an honest look at the Great Lakes region in 1830, including Kinzie's meeting with Madeline Laframboise. The author, a Connecticut woman, had married a former Indian agent. After moving to the wilds of the old Northwest, she would sleep with two pistols under her pillow at night.

OIL PAINTING OF KINZIE, 1856; ARTIST GEORGE HEALY. COURTESY OF THE JOE BYRD COLLECTION, JULIETTE GORDON LOW MUSEUM, GIRL SCOUTS OF THE USA.

12. Jane Johnston Schoolcraft was an Anishinaabe poet whose short, creative life included stories, songs, translations, and the original "Hiawatha." She had a rough time coping with racism during her obligatory travels with husband Henry, whether to Detroit, Washington, or New York, and was happiest in her homeland of northern Michigan.

THIS PORTRAIT IS THOUGHT TO BE A PHOTO OF AN ORIGINAL WATERCOLOR PAINTED WHEN SHE VISITED NEW YORK WITH HENRY IN 1825. COURTESY OF THE BENTLEY HISTORICAL LIBRARY, UNIVERSITY OF MICHIGAN.

13. Ozhaguscodaywayquay, also known as Susan Johnston after her marriage to poet Jane Schoolcraft's father, owned a profitable maple syrup business in northern Michigan. She and Jane were a mother-daughter team who preserved Anishinaabe stories. Anna Jameson, who was close to Schoolcraft, wrote that the poet felt that she "should be well," her health restored, if only "[I] could see my mother." Painting, 1827, from *Sketches of a Tour to the Lakes*, by T. L. McKenney.

COURTESY OF THE CHIPPEWA COUNTY HISTORICAL SOCIETY, SAULT STE. MARIE, MICHIGAN.

14. This oil portrait reveals the cheerful mien of John Johnston, father of poet Jane Johnston Schoolcraft. This ambitious Irishman saw that marrying into an influential Ojibwe family in Sault Ste. Marie would further his career as a fur trader. A deal was struck with Chief Waubojeeg, though his daughter, Ozhaguscodaywayquay, was initially stricken by the arrangement and ran away from Johnston soon after marriage. Her father threatened to cut off her ears if she did not return to Johnston.

PORTRAIT IN BELFAST BY JOSEPH WILSON, 1789. RESTORED IN 2006 BY THE DETROIT INSTITUTE OF ARTS, THE PAINTING HAS BECOME PART OF THE COLLECTION OF THE CHIPPEWA COUNTY HISTORICAL SOCIETY IN SAULT STE. MARIE.

15. The United States Indian Agency House, Jane Schoolcraft's home on Mackinac, was lovingly rendered by her friend Anna Jameson in a conte stick sketch. The picture was drawn when the polymath Jameson, who was art critic, social historian, visual artist, and travel writer, stayed with Jane and Henry Schoolcraft in 1836. The Englishwoman and the Ojibwe poet became fast friends, one of the only close friends Schoolcraft would have in her lifetime.

16. This portrait of Anna Jameson, a colored etching by an unknown artist, is thought to have been created approximately six years before she met Jane and spent time on Mackinac and in Sault Ste. Marie. It captures the confidence and intelligence of the author-artist, who would befriend Schoolcraft. Each would offer the other valuable support during a tough period in their lives.

CIRCA 1830, ETCHING, UNKNOWN ARTIST. COURTESY OF THE TORONTO PUBLIC LIBRARY.

17. During Jameson's travels in Michigan's Upper Peninsula with Jane Schoolcraft and her family, she wrote and sketched steadily, preserving a record of the way of life in the 1830s. Jameson's drawing *Ojibwe Women Constructing Birchbark Canoes* reveals the way Anishinaabe women were active engineers. They not only built canoes, but lodges as well. The chiaroscuro in this artwork gives it power.

CIRCA 1836. COURTESY OF THE TORONTO PUBLIC LIBRARY.

18. The "radiant genius & fiery heart" of Margaret Fuller, as described by her confidant Ralph Waldo Emerson, was surely on display when Fuller trekked to Mackinac. She was besotted with the island and its people and would write at length about its culture and the manner of east meeting west in her book *Summer on the Lakes*, published in 1844. While on Mackinac, Fuller stayed at Madeline Laframboise's house and wrote about the famous fur trader. She would also summon the "poesy" of Jane Schoolcraft, the two writers having more in common than might at first be gathered.

19. This profile view of Constance Fenimore Woolson, taken when she was fifty-four, is one of the few photos she liked of herself. She spent three summers on Mackinac as a teen, and Fenimore—as Henry James fondly called her—would write about the island for years afterward. Her articles and the novel *Anne* explored the beauty and complicated society of Mackinac. Her work garnered positive attention from critics and attracted a new wave of visitors to the island.

DEPARTMENT OF COLLEGE ARCHIVES AND SPECIAL COLLECTIONS, OLIN LIBRARY, ROLLINS COLLEGE, WINTER PARK, FLORIDA. COURTESY OF SPECIAL COLLECTIONS, ROLLINS COLLEGE.

20. The stone monument Anne's Tablet on Mackinac is not just a tribute to Constance Fenimore Woolson, it is also a testament to the power of story. The carving honors Anne, the titular character in Woolson's bestselling novel set on Mackinac. This monument is framed by an opening in a wooded area that looks down over the harbor.

PHOTOGRAPH BY MELISSA CROGHAN, 2016. AUTHOR'S COLLECTION.

21. Rosa Truscott Webb's devotion to Mackinac was
eventually recognized by its residents. She found
inventive ways to keep the core community alive as it
transitioned from a fishing industry to a tourist trade.
This founder of the Mackinac Island Public Library also
recognized that the schoolchildren and their families
needed a community center. The Great Depression did
not make things easier when she went to work raising
funds for the "Community House" in the former
headquarters of John Jacob Astor's American Fur
Company. Not only did she persevere with the support
of many island women, but she brought Girl Scouts of
America to Michigan.

PHOTOGRAPH OF WEBB BY MELISSA CROGHAN, 2020.
COURTESY OF MACKINAC PUBLIC LIBRARY.

HONOR LIBRARY FOUNDER—This bronze tablet at the
old Astor House, Mackinac Island, honors Mrs. Rosa S.
Webb, lower left, founder of the D. A. R. Library there.
Above: Mrs. O. W. Laidlaw, Tecumseh; Mrs. G. D. Schermerhorn, Reading. Below: Mrs. Webb and Mrs. D. A. Blodgett, Washington, D. C.

22. In 1936, the *Detroit
News* wrote an article about
Rosa Truscott Webb and
her establishment of the
Mackinac D.A.R. Library. The
Daughters of the American
Revolution helped to fund
the project. The ceremony
honoring Webb announced the
opening of the D.A.R. Library
on Market Street. A bronze
tablet was presented to Webb by
Daisy Blodgett, underscoring
the supportive community of
women.

PHOTOGRAPH 1936, COURTESY OF *THE DETROIT NEWS*.

23. Daisy Peck Blodgett is pictured here in top hat and equestrian attire in front of her longtime Mackinac home that brought her unexpected happiness. Though her husband, Delos, was forty years older than she, they had three children together, built their summer cottage, Casa Verano, and were active philanthropists in Grand Rapids. Daisy carried forward that activism on Mackinac in many charitable causes. Her daughter, Helen Erwin, and grandchildren, Hope Goodwin, Hal Erwin, and Eileen Croghan, would live in the West Bluff neighborhood as well.
PHOTOGRAPH, 1895. COURTESY OF MACKINAC STATE HISTORIC PARKS COLLECTION.

24. After Stella King graduated from nursing school in Chicago, she returned home to Mackinac and in the following decade was often the only healthcare professional on hand. Other than the two-year period when she worked for Daisy Blodgett in Washington, DC, Nurse King lived and worked on the island until her death. From handling a surprise bear in her path when traveling by carriage to the Blodgett cottage to her years as a midwife delivering countless babies on island, she was one who could handle every kind of emergency.
PHOTOGRAPH, 1925. COURTESY OF DWIGHT LAPINE.

25. Daisy Blodgett was adventurous in multiple ways. Beyond her philanthropic contributions, she was an athletic woman, an outstanding equestrian who fostered the horse culture on Mackinac. When the sport of bicycling became a national craze towards the end of the nineteenth century, she became a full-fledged enthusiast. As Daisy undoubtedly deduced, the sport gave women new independence in fashion and movement. And never more so than on Mackinac Island, where the ban of cars even today promotes biking as a chief mode of transportation.

STUDIO PORTRAIT ON MACKINAC, CIRCA 1898.
COURTESY MACKINAC STATE HISTORIC PARKS
COLLECTION.

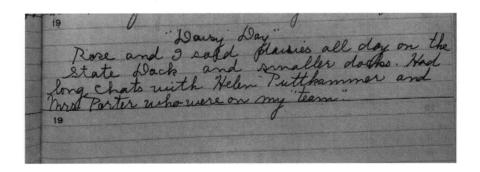

26. Participation in the early, annual Daisy Day charity on Mackinac, raising funds for the island Medical Center. Helen Blodgett Erwin Papers, with diary entry by Helen in her daykeeper, August 21, 1936.

COURTESY OF MELISSA CROGHAN.

27. This watercolor of Stella King reminds viewers of the Medical Center that was at long last built on Mackinac, and of Nurse King's tireless work on behalf of island patients in need of care. King assisted Blodgett in the Daisy Day charity that resulted in the healthcare center, and further, she was instrumental in establishing the annual Lilac Day parade. The nurse lived most of her life right in town on the corner of Market Street and French Lane. If those who knew her remember a stern, sometimes dour woman, they are also eternally grateful for her service. She and many other Mackinac women carried forward work that has ties to the Indigenous humanitarians nearly a century earlier. Stella King herself was Anishinaabe, a fact she was not comfortable sharing, owing to the racism of her age.

PHOTOGRAPH OF THIS PORTRAIT BY MELISSA CROGHAN. COURTESY OF THE MACKINAC ISLAND MEDICAL CENTER.

28. Lumber baron Delos Blodgett was married to Daisy Peck Blodgett. He was an abolitionist, a supporter of women's rights, and founder of several Michigan towns. He supported Daisy in all her charitable causes. The couple built the cottage pictured here, Casa Verano, in 1893. She would outlive him by thirty-seven years.

PHOTOGRAPH, CIRCA 1900. COURTESY OF BRUCE GOODWIN.

29. Helen Blodgett Erwin, age twelve, on her horse riding with dogs along the shore road near Arch Rock, Mackinac, 1907. Helen, the oldest daughter of Daisy Blodgett, was a memoirist and poet who lived next door to her mother in Cragmere, a cottage along Pontiac Trail on the West Bluff. Her daykeeper and other journals are a valuable record of life in Washington, DC, and on Mackinac Island, 1900–1950. Of particular interest are her documents on Daisy Blodgett.

COURTESY OF MACKINAC STATE HISTORIC PARKS COLLECTION.

30. Emma Ford and her husband, Joseph, were instrumental in initiating the hospitality business on Mackinac. In the 1890s, she ran a restaurant on Main Street, where the present day Chippewa Hotel stands. Ford was an entrepreneur and a Black civil rights leader who fought against Jim Crow laws and the discrimination of women throughout the state of Michigan.

CHAPTER SIX

Margaret Fuller (1810–1850)

R alph Waldo Emerson declared that his confidante and colleague Margaret Fuller possessed "a radiant genius & fiery heart," and this was what attracted so many people to her.[1] There is hardly a better description of the visionary social reformer, translator, early feminist, and author. Despite her connection to Emerson and her work as editor of the Transcendentalist magazine, *The Dial*, Fuller was only too ready to take leave of New England when the opportunity arose in 1843. She jumped at the chance to explore the Great Lakes when she was invited to accompany her friends James and Sarah Clarke. For several years, she had in mind the studies of Mackinac published in books by both Harriet Martineau and Anna Jameson.[2] Fuller was intrigued by the big Lake country and a young America's dramatic movement west. Her own book, *Summer on the Lakes*, published in 1844, was the result of her four-month journey from Niagara to Lakes Erie, Michigan, and Huron.[3] She devoted the last large section of this work to Mackinac.[4] During her time in the Midwest, Fuller gives a view of the island and the Great Lakes as a microcosm of a fast-changing nation. She sets out to understand the part women play in "the newest new world" of the old Northwest, and the status of the Indigenous population of the region.[5]

Fuller's narrative is both entertaining travelogue and analysis of the state of freedom for women and Native Americans. Her vignettes introduced a new approach to travel writing, one that interspersed narrative description with poetry, literary allusions, and dialogue of fictional characters who illustrated her journey. There are high-minded sections followed by down-to-earth observations of key historic figures such as the fur trader Madeline Laframboise, with whom Fuller stayed on Mackinac.

This East Coast author got an education the second she landed at Laframboise's house. She lets us know that the society there is entirely new to her, and that some of the other boarders who hailed from La Pointe and Arbre Croche, Michigan, were traders, "men who had become half wild and wholly rude, by living in the wild." Yet she learns that they had "a store of knowledge to impart" with their "good-humored observing."[6] Her experience in the Northwest opened her eyes, and we are the recipients of her expansive perspectives. *Summer on the Lakes* is a passionate hybrid work that contributes to the social history of America in the mid-nineteenth century.

Margaret was born Sarah Margaret Fuller, May 23, 1810. Her insistence at age nine that she would answer only to "Margaret" was a sign of her strong-minded personality. Yet here as in so many instances in her life, she offered her opinions in a lively, winning manner. In the case of her preferred name, she emphasized her wish a year later in a letter to her father, Timothy Fuller: "PS I do not like Sarah, call me Margaret alone, pray do!"[7]

Timothy believed it was his duty to educate his oldest daughter in ways that were generally denied to a girl in 1820. Nonetheless, he was often stern with her and quick to judge her actions. An outspoken lawyer and congressman who spent half the year in Washington, he sent letters of instruction home and kept his oldest daughter at her desk working hard. In that same year, young Margaret would translate Oliver Goldsmith's *The Deserted Village* into Latin and fully comprehend *The Aeneid*. As a prodigy with vision and ambition, she soared in her studies of foreign languages, history, and literature. Self-educated in many areas, she schooled herself in the classics, translating Virgil from Latin. She would later become a recognized expert in Goethe and German romanticism.

In years to come, Emerson would replace Timothy as an often-censorious father figure to Fuller. Long after his death, she would write that her father "was a tyrant in his own home."[8] By comparison, Emerson, though belittling women as he sometimes did, was not a tyrant and offered her an uncommon friendship. He was immediately impressed with Fuller when in 1839 he attended one of her "Conversation" soirees in the Boston area. Excluded from universities and all male intellectual clubs, she had started her own club, which was open to all and described as a "Ministry of Talking." She began conducting her popular "Conversation" classes among the erudite Boston women, with men joining later. Among the subjects she taught were Greek mythology, education, and history of art. She led discussions on ethics, religious creeds, and "the ideal." Her conversations on the relations between men and women led to a fifty-page essay with a focus on the state of marriage and the status of women in society. This was published in *The Dial*, the fabled Transcendentalist journal begun by Emerson. Among Fuller's many followers were artist Sarah Freeman Clarke, who later traveled to the Midwest with her; Bronson Alcott, the father of Louisa May Alcott and founder of a utopian commune; and the Peabody sisters, who encouraged mid-nineteenth-century educational reform.[9] Fuller charged $10 a ticket for her soirees. Right at the get-go she had twenty-five takers. She was declared a "born leader," and James Freeman Clarke would write, "How she did glorify life to all!"[10] He also declared that when speaking, her words were quite as "finished and true" as a written sentence and yet she conveyed a perfect "air of spontaneity."[11]

Fuller is remembered for a number of "firsts." In 1845, she published her landmark book about women's rights in America, *Woman in the Nineteenth Century*.[12] In it, she writes about how women in the mid-nineteenth century were essentially owned by their husbands: "There exists in the minds of men a tone of feeling toward women as toward slaves."[13] This view was qualified in a number of ways in her book, including: "As the friend of the negro assumes that one man cannot by right hold another in bondage, so should the friend of Woman assume that Man cannot by right lay even well-meant restrictions on Woman."[14] *Nineteenth Century* was not without critics who faulted Fuller for a lack of feminine modesty, but there were many who gave it high praise, including Henry David Thoreau and Edgar Allan Poe, a well-respected, and often tough, critic.[15]

Fuller was the first woman foreign correspondent at Horace Greeley's *New York Tribune* and the first female book reviewer at a number of national magazines. Her work as editor of *The Dial*, chronicled American thought and brought it to a new plane. Fuller would eventually diverge from her confidant Emerson in the philosophy of that movement.[16] While Emerson often focused on introspective exploration of self, Fuller, after her trip out west to Michigan, began to believe that this view of self must be tempered by wide social reform.

In Margaret's journey to the Midwest, she would spend nine days alone on Mackinac. She then charged off on a trip by bateau to the Upper Peninsula of Michigan, and returned to the island several days later after a tour of Sault Ste. Marie. Her time on Mackinac offers valuable insights. In *Summer*, she pondered the illustrated records of the Anishinaabe: "At present the only lively impress of their [Native American] passage through the world is to be found in such books as Catlin's and some stories told by the old travelers, of which I purpose a brief account."[17] Fuller was likely unaware of scattered sketches and paintings of the Anishinaabe in the region at the time.[18] One book with illustrations she had read was *Winter Studies and Summer Rambles* by Anna Jameson. *Winter Studies* possessed dynamic pen-and-ink drawings of Mackinac and Sault Ste. Marie. As for Fuller's book, it had its own fine illustrations created by Sarah Clarke.

While several strong biographies of Fuller have been written, the focus on her productive years has centered mostly on her life in New England and in Europe. Little has been said about her connection to Mackinac, where she met the remarkable humanitarian and fur trader Madeline Laframboise. Fuller would stay with this "widow of a French trader" in her own home, where she sometimes took in boarders and had started a school for Native girls.[19] She is "a great character," Fuller wrote, and "Indian by birth and wearing the dress of her country."[20] Laframboise and her sister, Therese Schindler, were the only individuals to prevail as independent fur traders once John Jacob Astor and his American Fur Company set up camp on Mackinac in 1815. Adding to the trader's achievements, she eventually managed to work with the Fur Trade Company while holding fast to her own highly successful business.

Besides her brilliance in the fur trade, Fuller notes that Laframboise "spoke French fluently, and was very ladylike in her manners." She spoke numerous Native languages, and while she undoubtedly had excellent manners, she also exhibited a lively curiosity about life. Fuller records how in one instance, Laframboise demanded to see Sarah Clarke's pencil drawings and then asked if she could "borrow the sketches of the beach" to show the Native people who were living in wigwams on the shore.[21]

Of the Indigenous people Fuller met, Madeline Laframboise made a large impression on her. Margaret, who was driven to a high bar of success herself, was duly impressed by the obvious ambitions of this "shrewd woman of business." Others were dazzled as well, and not just by Laframboise's business prowess, but as someone Great Lakes residents approached "to get her aid and advice." Here was a woman to whom visitors to the island "were all the time coming to pay her homage."[22] Those people ranged from French writer Alexis de Tocqueville to the Indian agent Henry Schoolcraft and Chicago businessman Gurdon Hubbard, along with countless women whose names have not been recorded. Three writers, Elizabeth Therese Baird,[23] Juliette Kinzie, and Margaret Fuller, have done more than any other of this era to preserve and advance the figure of Laframboise in the annals of Great Lakes history.

While Margaret was honored to have made the acquaintance of Laframboise, she lamented that she would never be able to meet another Native resident, Jane Schoolcraft, who had died the year before Fuller arrived. Yet the poet's presence is felt in Margaret's several references to her in *Summer*.[24] She comments on Anna Jameson's extensive discussion of Schoolcraft in *Winter Studies and Summer Rambles*. Fuller is less clear about the other members in Schoolcraft's Odawa family, and her confusion leads her to assert that the poet's brother George Johnston was "almost the only white man who knew how to regard with due intelligence and nobleness, his connexion with the race."[25] Nonetheless, Fuller has eagerly read Jameson's account and wishes for even more "history of this ancient people." She is intrigued by the knowledge Schoolcraft has shared with Jameson, such as the way a sister Odawa became a "chieftainess in her own right." Taking a realistic perspective, Fuller notes that more common than the chieftainess are the many Indigenous women she witnesses on Mackinac whose "forms [were] bent by burthens."[26] It is worth noting the connection between Jameson and Fuller even though they never met one another. Here are two writers with one (Fuller) building on the earlier work of the other. Together, their work resulted in key records of nineteenth-century Mackinac.

In Massachusetts, Fuller was the only woman to be editor of *The Dial*. Invited to be part of Emerson's male-bastion club of Transcendentalism, she was so "honored" because he considered a discourse with Margaret "the most entertaining conversation in America."[27] As their friendship grew, she became familiar with his Transcendentalist thought, the philosophy that espoused belief in a personal God and in the divine nature of humanity in men and women. She and Emerson were fast friends, writing hundreds of letters to one another and going on walks at Walden Pond. Another fan of hers was Nathaniel Hawthorne, and she visited him often in Concord. Henry David Thoreau, too, was part of the Transcendentalist group. When he was still a young man, Fuller, as editor of *The Dial*, rejected an essay he submitted. Yet she encouraged him to revise and generously published one of his early poems. Years later he, like Fuller, would visit Mackinac.

If Thoreau's trip to the Great Lakes in 1861 was precipitated by the hope of healing his tuberculosis, Fuller's journey nineteen years earlier was inspired by a need to see beyond her privileged world in New England. While her friends, the Clarkes, met for a family reunion in Chicago, she traveled on her own to Mackinac. After her week-plus stay as an unchaperoned upper-middle-class woman on Mackinac—still considered unusual in Fuller's time—she made an even more daring move. Buoyed by reading of the long trip Anna Jameson made with Jane Schoolcraft to the Upper Peninsula of Michigan, and by Harriet Martineau's trip to Mackinac, Fuller went on an independent expedition in the Great Lakes. At first leery of the voyageurs who would chauffeur her by canoe to north country, she grew to admire their wit and their endurance. She chronicled their hard lives, along with the Anishinaabe she met.

When Fuller arrived back on Mackinac, she was happily surprised to see Sarah Clarke there to greet her. *Summer on the Lakes* brings to life the explorations on Mackinac by these two women, Margaret with pen and paper always in hand, and Sarah with her sketchbook. The second edition of Fuller's book would include seven of Clarke's drawings. Fuller was close to the Clarke family, including James, a theologian and writer who published Margaret's first literary review in the magazine he edited, the *Western Messenger.* Fuller also met and traveled with James and Sarah's brother, William, whom she formed a romantic interest in when he performed the duty of guide in their journey to Chicago. For the most part, Margaret and Sarah roamed Mackinac together, one day arranging for "a canoe excursion" in the lake with Native guides. One of the guides was "the chief's son, a fine looking youth of about sixteen, richly dressed in blue broadcloth, scarlet sash and leggings, with a scarf of brighter red than the rest, tied around his head, its ends falling gracefully to one shoulder." According to Fuller, once out on the lake, the guides rowed "us into the path of the steamboat." However, the entire party, Fuller along with Clarke, were in high spirits and managed to laugh at the near collision. Of her companion Sarah, she writes that she is "one who sees all, prizes all, enjoys much, interrupts never."[28] One cannot help but smile at that last observation, for Margaret, with her strong personality and conversational bent, would have appreciated few interruptions.

Summer on the Lakes received high praise from famous publisher and editor Horace Greeley. The editor stated that the travel book was evidence of Fuller as "one of the most original as well as intellectual of American women." Like Martineau and Jameson, who traveled to Mackinac before her, Fuller had garnered a reputation as a distinguished thinker before she journeyed to the Great Lakes. Unlike the British writers, she did not have a bestselling book at the time of her trip. Fuller explores social reform in *Summer on the Lakes* and makes a plea for change, especially where treatment and understanding of Native Americans are concerned. She observes how their "condition" in life has been harmed by the white man. Her colleague Emerson had written a letter in 1838 to President Van Buren regarding the "sham treaty" that resulted in the removal of the Cherokees from their native land in Georgia. While he advocated educating the Indian "in the arts and customs of the Caucasian race,"

Margaret, who met and spoke personally to many Native people in her journey to Mackinac, had a different viewpoint. In *Summer on the Lakes*, we see her belief that the Indigenous people had their own culture with an intrinsic "worth and civility."[29] On Mackinac, she enumerates the ways the Anishinaabe represent the very "greatness" of "this American continent."[30]

Regarding Fuller's prestigious position at Greeley's newspaper, it is well to remember how she helped a number of men to get published there, including James Nathan and Ellery Channing. She had become a famous writer and had clout. Several years after her time on Mackinac, Fuller was sent by the *New York Tribune* to cover the revolution in Italy. Sailing to Europe in 1846, she met with luminaries such as Harriet Martineau and Thomas Carlyle in Britain, and in Paris, "Madame Sand" (George Sand) and her lover, the composer Frédéric Chopin, before she pressed on to Italy.[31] There she would meet and find happiness with Giovanni Angelo Ossoli, an Italian marquis who was eleven years younger than she.[32] Fuller wrote pamphlets and leaflets about the upcoming revolution and sent dispatches home to Greeley's *Tribune.* She became immersed in the politics of the country, its anti-papist and anti-Austrian movements. After marrying Ossoli, with whom she had a child, she wrote her mother that he was "a man wholly without vanity," adding that "In him . . . I have found a home." This was quite an admission for the thirty-nine-year-old intellect who had formerly despaired of ever finding a marriage to one of like mind and heart. She also wrote at this time: "I am no longer young, yet still so often new and surprising to myself."[33]

Tragedy struck after her time in Italy. In 1850, she set off by ship to return to America. A storm rose at sea when Fuller was close to home, and she, Giovanni, and their infant son died. The shipwreck occurred off Fire Island, New York. Thoreau was so stricken that he searched for her body, but only her trunk, which contained some papers—minus the history of the Roman republic she had penned—was washed ashore.[34]

Her friends and colleagues Emerson, Clarke, and William Henry Channing published two volumes, *Memoirs of Margaret Fuller Ossoli*, that emphasized her personal life, and in a manner of speaking, Fuller's contemporary Julia Ward Howe did the same. Howe, the author of "The Battle Hymn of the Republic," may not have done Margaret any favors as that memoir published a number of the writer's somewhat desperate letters to an unrequited love.[35] By the early part of the twentieth century, Fuller's contributions to society both as a critic and social historian had gone into decline.[36] Megan Marshall's superb biography of the writer has restored her to a place of deserving recognition, particularly her life's work on the East Coast and in Italy.

In her journey to the old Northwest, Fuller had sensed that she arrived almost too late to rescue some of its knowledge, in particular the literature of the Anishinaabe. She mourned:

> Yet, ere they depart, I wish there might be some masterly attempt to reproduce, in art or literature, what is proper to them, a kind of beauty and grandeur, which few of the every-day crowd have hearts to feel, yet which ought to leave in the world its monuments, to inspire the thought of genius through all ages.[37]

Thankfully, there was Jane Schoolcraft, who preserved the literature of her people, and there was Anna Jameson, who preserved the words of Schoolcraft. Fuller appreciated the history that she witnessed, and related her wonder at the sight of so many wigwams on the beach of Mackinac and the canoes of the Anishinaabe approaching daily for their annuities. She understood the consequences of an unequal society and gives an "expression of the sorrows of unequal relations."[38]

Her book *Summer on the Lakes* represents a literature of witness, testimony to the lives of those who had few rights in the eyes of the U.S. government. Margaret Fuller takes a look backward and forward at the same time. She scoops up the champion women of Mackinac and the writers who documented them, in particular Jameson and Schoolcraft. She makes their contributions felt in America's "life-blood [that] rushes from east to west and back again from west to east."[39] Together these nineteenth-century writers cohere in a sensibility that illuminates the untold story of women on Mackinac and in the Northwest territory.

Informed and energized by her island sojourn, Fuller had returned to the Northeast with a new perspective. She deserves recognition for capturing a record of a nearly lost literature and history. In *Summer on the Lakes*, she conveyed her observations to the community of letters and ideas that were shaping America. In many ways, Fuller's life was as brief and brilliant as that of Native writer Jane Schoolcraft, who died at age forty-two. Of the Mackinac poet, Fuller had written: "By the premature death of Mrs. Schoolcraft is lost a mine of poesy."[40] Margaret could not have guessed that her own sudden departure from life would occur when she was but forty years old.

PART III

The Continuum

Into the Twentieth Century

CHAPTER SEVEN

Constance Fenimore Woolson
(1840–1894)

I n 1840, a few years before the deaths of Mackinac authors Jane Schoolcraft and Margaret Fuller, Constance Fenimore Woolson was born. In the nineteenth century, Woolson's contribution to American letters was widely recognized. Today she is once again gaining attention for her work. What has not been addressed before is her exploration of a racially mixed family on Mackinac Island in the novel *Anne*. Readers in the Midwest, Britain, and New England were introduced to the complex life of Anne Douglas and her Native stepmother and half siblings. The publication of that novel would inspire future stories of Anishinaabe in the Great Lakes. This study of Woolson also reveals how *Anne* and other publications by Woolson gave birth to the promise of Mackinac and the Great Lakes as a desirable travel destination for the rapidly urbanizing Midwest.

A memorial to the author stands at Woolson Rampart in Sinclair Grove on the East Bluff of Mackinac. It was erected by her nephew and niece, Samuel and Katherine Mather, in 1916.[1] Katherine and Woolson were frequent travel companions, and Sam and his beloved aunt wrote to each other frequently. A successful industrialist from Cleveland, his communications with her reveal telling events in her life up to the time she died.

To date, "Anne's Tablet" is the only monument that honors a woman in history on Mackinac.[2] That the stone tablet is of a fictional character is testament to the power of story, and in particular, Woolson's novel, *Anne*.[3] The popular novel had a long serial run in *Harper's Magazine*, published both in England and America before presented in book form.[4] The monument on the island is a meditative spot cloaked in foliage on three sides. A carved relief of Anne is framed by the opening in this wooded area that looks down over the harbor. This figure reaches up to touch the bough of a spruce tree that forms a border to the words etched in stone. In chapter five of *Anne*, Woolson wrote:

> She loved the island
> and the island trees
> she loved the wild larches
> the tall spires of the
> Spruces bossed with lighter green.
> Hear the rustling
> And the laughing of the forest
> And the wash of the water
> On the pebbly beach.[5]

The engraved words at "Anne's Tablet" conjure another Mackinac poet who wrote about trees: Schoolcraft and her poem about the pine trees of Michigan. Mackinac author Margaret Fuller, with her Transcendentalist background, would also have appreciated this memorial paying homage to the natural world. Certainly, Fenimore Woolson carries forward a theme of honoring nature that is intrinsic to Mackinac. In turn, her attention to the forests and glorious vistas of the lake would add to the promotion of the island.

Fenimore, as she often liked to be called, was born in Claremont, New Hampshire, to Hannah and Jarvis Woolson. Scarcely was she ushered into the world when three of her older sisters died of scarlet fever. Though her life was spared, Constance Fenimore felt the grief of her family at a young age. It is little wonder that her mother was broken for many years and that the family often prefaced remarks with "If I live."[6] Her father had a literary bent and was considered "something of a wag"; however, he followed in his own father's footsteps and went into the family business of stove manufacturing. He was never happy peddling the "Woolson Stoves" but was able to make a tolerable living for his family. Devastated by the death of the young children, the Woolsons left Claremont, stopping first in Cooperstown, New York, where Hannah's grandfather had been a strong-minded judge. The judge was father to Constance's famous namesake, James Fenimore Cooper.[7] Her good friend Henry

James would always call her Fenimore, an act that strengthened her connection to the historic author, Cooper, yet asserted her own authority as a writer.

Woolson would have read the stories of Cooper's protagonist, Hawkeye, who figures in five of his novels. Like Hawkeye, her heroines are most contented in the wilderness. For Fenimore, Mackinac Island represented a literal and metaphoric wilderness that she longed for. It is no surprise that Anne, the titular character of her hugely popular book, finds that no matter how far she travels, she is most at home on the island where she grew up.

Woolson's childhood years on the island provided her with valuable inspiration for her work. She did not live year-round on Mackinac as did her main character, Anne, but she spent three summers there, beginning at the impressionable age of fifteen. Despite biographical references to a family home on the island ("they had a cottage") there is no evidence that the Woolsons owned a cottage on Mackinac.[8] The confusion may have arisen because there is a cottage, Crow's Nest, that was owned by a distant relative of Woolson.[9] The myth could easily have been fostered by the doubly confusing fact that Crow's Nest is on the East Bluff, directly across the road from Anne's Tablet. It would seem logical that this was the home of Constance and her family but for the fact it was built in 1900, six years after her death.

Though the Woolsons did not own a cottage, they found lodgings in town for several summers. She and her parents and siblings boarded with another family who had rented the United States Indian Agency House.[10] During the economic panic of 1857 and the depression preceding the Civil War, the Woolsons' family stove business suffered, and they could no longer afford to spend the season on Mackinac.[11] Woolson never forgot the delights of the large and historic Agency House, and it assumes grand proportions in her future published work. The novel *Anne* is a key document of the post-fur-trade era on Mackinac for multiple reasons, not the least being its setting of the historic Agency House and the American Fur trading buildings on Market Street. Woolson connects the fur-trading frontier to the succeeding fishing industry, and peoples the novel with merchants, many of whom were the descendants of fur traders. In chapter 2, she gives us a lively dance held in the large hall of the former trade warehouse where the "Chippewa," the fishing superintendent, and the military on Mackinac congregate with others. This study of *Anne* takes up Woolson's revelations of the multiple racial and class levels of society.

It was during her three girlhood summers on Mackinac that the future author had a view of community life that would reappear in fictional dress in *Anne*. It was in those summers, too, that she had an initial vision of being in print. She and a close friend, Zephaniah Spalding, worked together editing a "manuscript newspaper." At this time, Fenimore also penned a poem she acknowledged was inspired by "Hiawatha." Little did Woolson know that the authorial source behind this fabled poem was none other than the poet Jane Schoolcraft, who had been a Mackinac resident for nearly a decade. In yet another remarkable connection, these two writers had both found a muse in the same setting. Both lived in the United States Agency House, though Woolson would come to know its charms thirteen years after Schoolcraft was there.

Several literary icons owe Woolson a debt, including Edith Wharton and Willa Cather. Fenimore Woolson is credited as the first American woman to craft fiction applying the technique of empathetic realism, a form of narrative that George Eliot, William Dean Howells, and Charles Dudley Warner were making popular.[12] The writer developed realistic characters in her stories, figures who also possessed empathetic features that appealed to the reader. Sentimentalism was to be avoided. Successful women writers of literary realism in nineteenth-century America include Sarah Orne Jewett and Rebecca Harding Davis, the latter with her acclaimed *Life in the Iron Mills*. Born nine years after Woolson, Jewett was also a frequent traveler in Europe, and was most likely acquainted with the older woman's work. Jewett's often anthologized masterpiece "The White Heron," set in Maine, was first published in 1886, years after Woolson's short stories "St. Clair Flats," and "The Old Agency," along with the novel *Anne*, all three of which are set in the Great Lakes.

There were numerous male literary critics who tried to make the case that women had not the intellect to pursue serious fiction writing. Hardly true, as would be proven in the upcoming years. When books by women outsold the men's in Woolson's era, male authors such as Nathaniel Hawthorne wrote jealously of "those damn women scribblers." Even Henry James, who was a close friend of Woolson, could not bear it when her novel *Anne* outsold his *Portrait of a Lady*. In order to remain his friend, she had to downplay her own talents and success.[13] As a whole, most men bridled at the intelligence of a female colleague. Insecurities and the male ego may have played a part there, but it would be unfair to cast full blame their way. Most white males had been raised for generations to believe it was their right to own all the power behind the governing laws and societal behavior. It took a strong and secure man to admit to equality between the races and the sexes. There were such men, of course, but they were not the majority.

Aside from becoming a seamstress, domestic worker, teacher, or governess, the only path open in Fenimore's era was marriage. The road to becoming a writer if you were female was rocky indeed and ruled by the male literati. While Henry James belonged to an exclusively male literary club and his stories were immediately published by *Harper's* and *The Atlantic*, Woolson's languished for several years before being considered seriously for publication. It was the death of her father, Jarvis, that promoted her all-or-nothing attempt to market her work. She adored him and would always remember fondly his charming if impractical approach to life. Rather than take the train on trips with his daughter from their home in Ohio to Mackinac and other beauty spots, he insisted on traveling by carriage, because this afforded him close details of bird, tree, and landform. After the family stopped spending all summer on Mackinac, Fenimore made a point of returning when she could.[14]

Jarvis died unexpectedly in 1869 while Fenimore was on Mackinac. Though he was unwell at the time, he had insisted she go to the "Great Turtle," perhaps vicariously wishing to be there with her. He left the Woolsons no money after his death, and it became Fenimore's job to provide for her sister, younger brother, and their mother. She became a writer who supported herself entirely by her pen. Woolson had always admired another writer who did the same: Mary Ann Evans, better known by her pseudonym, George Eliot, author of the critically acclaimed and popular novels *Adam Bede* (1859), *Mill on the Floss* (1860), and *Middlemarch* (1871–1872).

Woolson's first book was the winner in a children's literature contest with a cash prize of $500. Published in 1873, it was titled *The Old Stone House*. The children's book featured a heroine, Anne March, whose last name was a tribute to Jo March, the strong protagonist in Louisa May Alcott's *Little Women*. Fenimore was not pleased with her prose in *The Old Stone House* and would never admit to authorship in future years.[15] This attitude suggests a writer who held herself to high standards, even regarding her fledgling work.

Three years earlier she had published short pieces for the first time, and under her own name, an accomplishment in a century when such well-known writers as George Sand (Aurore Dupin) and George Eliot had to hide their authorship under male pseudonyms. These two pieces by Woolson were printed by *Harper's*. One was set in the Utopian community of Zoar, Ohio, a place she had visited with her father, and the other, "Fairy Island," was set on Mackinac.[16] Those who come to Woolson's work and wish to read about a place where lovers "find each beyond the boundaries of an oppressive social world" would do well to look at "Fairy Island."[17] Throughout her career, Fenimore's Mackinac stories and nonfiction pieces imparted the sensibility of a natural and spiritual existence outside a prohibitive society.

She had met her friend Zeph Spalding on the "Fairy Island" when she was a teen. Two years older than she, he also summered on Mackinac. His father, Judge Spalding, was an abolitionist who made speeches in Cleveland about fighting for the Union at the start of the Civil War, and it is likely that the belief in equality and human welfare in Zeph's family appealed to Woolson.[18] By the time of the war, the friendship between Zeph and Constance had blossomed into romance. She was smitten with the young man and would later model characters after him in *Anne*, *The Stone House*, and other stories she wrote. Just as Zeph was a handsome blond boy, so Erastus in *Anne* has "bright blue eyes, golden hair, a fine spirited outline." Anne's best friend, Erastus, or Rast as he is called, is further described as an "Apollo Belvedere" by the Lieutenant's wife at a dance held in the old American Fur trade warehouses on Market Street.[19] Fenimore and Zeph became engaged with the understanding that once the war was over, they could marry. This engagement is only hinted at by Woolson. Uncertainty reigned in the nation, and perhaps the pair thought discretion was the best course to pursue.[20] Following their time together on Mackinac, Zeph joined the Seventh Regiment and went off to fight in the Civil War.

The war made its way into her oeuvre and left its mark on Woolson as a young woman. Characters in *Anne*, and short pieces such as "Rodman the Keeper" and "The Old Agency" feature war veterans or those killed in battle. She was twenty-one when the Confederacy attacked Fort Sumter, and soon enough she and the entire nation were reeling. Her belief in the fight against slavery was apparent in her activity over the following four years. Fenimore would write "[The] war was the heart and spirit of my life," and she volunteered at the Soldier's Aid Society of northern Ohio, sang at fundraising concerts for the Union Army, and became for a time a postmistress.

Following the success of "Fairy Island," Fenimore moved to New York and lived with her brother. It would not do to stay in the city unchaperoned. Once there, she used her connection to her great uncle, James Fenimore Cooper, to appeal to magazines for freelance work. She was soon commissioned to write six pieces about the city for the *Daily Cleveland Herald*. She found herself writing about the upper crust. Her good friend Flora Payne and her husband were on their way "into Mrs. Astor's Four Hundred" and no doubt supplied Fenimore with grist for her writing.[21] The boarding house where Woolson stayed was not far from the mansions of John

Jacob Astor and Robert Stuart, Astor's right-hand man in the fur-trade empire business on Mackinac.

Woolson milked this New York milieu for all it was worth. She dispatched smart send-ups of New York gentlemen: "the Manhattan uniform—incomplete without a variously shaded brown appendage curving over the upper lip and ferociously waxed at the end." And another lively example:

> "Rip Van Dam!" Did anyone ever hear of a more astonishing title? It was of no use to tell that he was a staid dignified burgher of pious and portly presence. His name is against it, and we will not believe it.[22]

It is not clear from Woolson's letters exactly how or why her engagement to Zeph fell apart, only that it did so. It is apparent that after the war he was in search of new horizons. He found them in Hawaii and was posted there as the U.S. consul in 1869. Several years later he became a partner in the West Maui Sugar Association. In 1871, Zeph married a sugar heiress, a younger woman by the name of Wilhelmina. Woolson was truly shocked by the marriage of her old sweetheart.

She would vent her distress by writing about Wilhelmina in her own fiction, notably in a story titled "Wilhelmina." The young protagonist waits out the Civil War for her sweetheart.[23] Eventually this character releases him from the engagement, having discovered he has fallen in love with a dimpled, sixteen-year-old girl. It is safe to say that romantic relationships in Woolson's fiction are largely unhappy affairs.[24] Yet a short time before she died, Woolson would write Sam Mather from Italy about her Mackinac pal and first love: "I should like to see [Zeph] again. If I could get him *alone*, I daresay we should have a very funny and friendly talk. But, meanwhile, we should both be inwardly thinking, 'Great heavens—what an escape I had!' It was only the glamor of the war that brought us together."[25]

After losing Zeph, Fenimore shied away from marriage. Beyond her obvious heartache, other factors affected her disinclination to marry. For the rest of her life, she feared that family history made her prone to serious illness. She would write her relatives, including her devoted nephew, Sam Mather, that theirs was a family who must take more care than others against illnesses such as tuberculosis.[26] To her mind, marriage seemed to add to the risk exponentially.

In her own parents, she had witnessed how the death of children affected families. In addition to her three sisters who died as infants and toddlers, she had two more adult sisters who died shortly after they got married. Georgiana's death came after giving birth, and another sister, Emma, nursed her consumption-ridden husband only to contract the same disease and perish soon after he did. Fictional characters who sacrificed for love show up in Woolson's work. In her novel *Anne*, the mother of the protagonist dies young after having sacrificed her health for the sake of her husband.

Separate from health concerns, Woolson wondered at the mental confinement women endured after marriage. She would witness three dear female friends, one of whom she encouraged to marry, who changed drastically after becoming the property of their husbands. Flora Payne, who married the future secretary of the navy, William C. Whitney, had been someone Woolson and her friends pictured as a future musician and scientist.[27] Woolson watched in horror as her friend, once vivacious and intellectual, was expected only to showcase her husband, and year after year became a more diminished being.

Add to this Constance's introverted personality along with her incipient deafness, and we begin to understand how she remained single in an age when such a thing was unacceptable. As the years passed, she subsumed male-female relationships into her fiction writing, where they found a dramatic life. Nonetheless, she would always feel that perhaps she had missed out on love and adventure of the kind that her peers had discovered. When Woolson learned that the writer she most admired, George Eliot, was living in happy cohabitation with G. W. Lewes, she felt positively churlish. She wrote resentfully of the devotion Eliot was to find with her true love, a man she would live with for the rest of her life.[28]

Woolson's religion also provided her with a degree of guidance in her life as a single person. Her experience as a youth at Grace Episcopal in Cleveland would sustain her. She was active there in outreach during the Civil War, and her romantic side enjoyed the ceremony of her church, its stained-glass windows, vestments worn by the priest, stirring rituals, and the so-called "smells and bells" deployed in Catholicism and high church Anglicanism. Equally, she took to heart her religion's belief in a God who saw no difference in rich or poor, color or creed.

In keeping with her belief system, Fenimore demonstrated an empathy extending to all humankind. The characters in her work were likely to be of modest means, and she was known as one who would stop on the street to help strangers in need. Woolson's fiction includes a number of narrators with great compassion for others. Her narrator Martha, in "Ancient City," pays attention to freed slaves and a character who cross-dresses. That story was published in 1874 when Woolson was still a relatively young writer. Her marginalized characters range from "Old Fog," accused of murder in "Peter the Parson," to "Miss Grief," whose title character is deemed eccentric, in part, because she is a brilliant writer.[29] Though Woolson's early writing bears the mark of "religious fiction," she soon made a career decision to stick to the school of naturalism. Adhering to some of those tenets, she often avoided an omniscient narrator. Woolson preferred to let readers arrive at their own conclusions regarding protagonist action.

Woolson was introduced to Henry James when both were visiting London. Already he had forsaken America as the place he called home, and over time, she would become an expat too. She was in her late thirties when they met. In him she found an intellectual equal, and the two formed a close and companionable relationship. Over the fourteen-year span of their friendship, they frequently chose to stay in the same place abroad, whether it was London, Venice, Florence, or the Riviera. Fenimore was easily his closest female friend. Understanding the mores of the time, she and James were discrete about spending time together publicly. Her reputation would have been ruined had the wagging tongues of nineteenth-century society assumed a love affair between the two.

While James lived off his inherited wealth, Fenimore supported herself entirely by her writing, an anomaly for women of this time. Scholars today believe James was sexually attracted to men, but wherever the pair landed they made sure they were lodged near each other. Sometimes they had separate hotels, or if at the same one, Henry James had a suite downstairs to Constance's upstairs rooms. Florence was a favorite setting for the two authors to do their serious writing and to enjoy life. In 1887, James "took pleasure in the daily commerce with Fenimore Woolson." By this time, she was struggling with deafness, and it is possible she appreciated the clarity and resonance of his voice. A year later, James published an essay titled "The Art of Fiction." To her delight, Fenimore Woolson was one of the three authors he highlighted.[30] When James and Woolson were living in Geneva near one another, his sister, Alice James, wrote that she was certain her brother was flirting with Woolson. In the meantime, Henry was busy writing that he was deeply engaged with a fencing master: "lessons twice a week, in the art of thrust and parry." Though she misperceived her brother's attentions to Woolson, Alice was devoted to Fenimore's writing. In addition to reading everything she could from George Eliot, Dickens, Flaubert, George Sand, and Tolstoy, she listed "Miss Woolson" among her favorite authors.[31]

Chief among the ingredients of the friendship between Fenimore and Henry James was their shared worldview on several levels. They appreciated the ways in which travel could enlarge one's perspective of the world, and they acknowledged a mutual respect for one another's daily writing schedule. It appears that in the early years of their connection, Woolson hoped for marriage. Fenimore's letters do not reveal that she was aware of his sexual orientation, but as time passed it was clear to both that marriage was not in the cards for them. As an unmarried state was hardly the norm at this time, they commiserated in their mutual spinsterhood, as it were. James even describes Woolson as such. She was his "distinguished friend [and] a *meticuleuse*" or old maid.[32] Other references by him were less kind. There was then, and is now, no such derogatory term for unmarried men, who were often cavalierly referred to as "a confirmed bachelor." Like Hawthorne, James was most often uncharitable in his remarks and attitude regarding the successful woman writer.[33] When in a burst of enthusiasm Woolson shared a particularly enthusiastic fan letter regarding her novel *Anne*, James responded by immediately putting her in her place as a mere female author. Never mind that while the reviews of the day praised James for his refined style, they lamented that his characters showed little action and lacked heartfelt emotion. In contrast, Fenimore's *Lake Country Sketches* were described by reviewers as having "a strength such as has not informed any women's writing, that we remember in some years of American magazine literature; and a force and freshness that has belonged to few men in that time."[34]

Her novel *Anne*, a resounding success, was serialized for eighteen months at *Harper's Magazine*, and Woolson's reading public grew with each installment. Fan letters and excellent critical reviews followed her wherever she traveled. While in Sorrento, Italy, she received a letter and contract that writers in that age could only fantasize about. Not only was there a check of $1,000 from *Harper's* for a book publication—twice what she'd been paid for the serialized format—but also a bid to retain her as their writer, asking for first refusal for all her future books. After James wrote a stinging response to her ebullient news, she reacted in a pleading, submissive tone: "My work is coarse besides yours. Of entirely another grade. . . . & any little thing I may say about my own [writing] comes from entirely another stratum, and is said because I live so alone, as regards to my writing, that sometimes when writing to you, or speaking to you—out it comes, before I know it."[35]

Perhaps the groveling tone was the price Woolson believed she had to pay in order to be accepted by those who made the rules for literary and social acceptance, James being one. Author Anne Rioux remarks that Fenimore's reaction was no doubt an expression of fear; she could not risk losing his friendship, on both a personal and professional level.[36] Though Henry James did praise her writing when she was alive, he did not promote Fenimore's legacy after her death. Theirs was a complicated relationship.

As a perceptive writer and traveler, Woolson was aware of the ways Americans or Europeans had a tendency to think themselves a cut above other cultures in the world. One of Woolson's many journeys to distant lands brings this home and demonstrates the author's responsible understanding of such biases. Sam Mather, her nephew who appreciated Woolson's deep connection to Mackinac and the Great Lakes—and who supported his aunt in a number of ways—had offered to pay for the trip she longed to take to Jerusalem, followed by a trip to Egypt and Jordan. Her letters from that journey affirm what her readers benefited from in her capacious worldview. In 1890, she wrote to friend and editor Henry Alden of the "intelligence and dignity" of the people of the Middle East: "I can't look down upon them as I used to,—from a superior Anglo-Saxon standpoint.... in traveling widely over the world, and living for years in foreign countries; one inevitably loses one's old standards, and comfortable fixed prejudices and opinions."[37]

Interestingly, she also points out that she was inspired to go on this trip after reading about the explorer Lady Hester Stanhope. After being on horseback for three days and visiting the Holy Land and Jordan, she wrote in 1889 to Sam Mather: "Don't ask me how I arrived. . . . but think of Lady Hester Stanhope." In the nineteenth century, few female role models were known or made public, and just as Woolson took courage from Stanhope, so the author of *Anne* would become a role model to many who saw such territory as the Great Lakes and Mackinac as a distant and unknown vista. Even for those who lived closer to the island, Woolson established a model of diversity in her fictional characters that reflected the complex mixed races and culture of Mackinac and its surrounding communities.

Woolson's paean to Mackinac, "The Fairy Island," was wildly popular with readers. It fairly explodes with reverence for Mackinac, including attention paid to the Indigenous people who were its first residents. Here is Woolson describing how the Anishinaabe named the island. She reiterates her mantra about the sense of freedom one experiences on the island:

They gave to the beautiful island the name of Michilimackinac, or the 'Home of the Giant Fairies.' Life is long on Fairy Island, and life is free and careless.[38]

After the story was published in 1870 by *Putnam's Magazine*, she received many letters in response to her description of Mackinac's natural wonders, health virtues, and destination for romance. The narrative piece advanced the public relations of Mackinac, and after its publication intrepid travelers made their way for the first time to her beloved island. The momentum would only build with yet another piece in *Putnam's* on the mysterious beauty of the island's "Wishing Springs," published in 1872.[39] Three years later more tales of Mackinac emerged in her book *Castle Nowhere: Lake Country Sketches*.[40] The wide availability of her Mackinac-focused work coincided with the expansion of steamship lines and the railroads. It is no coincidence that as word got out about the invigorating air and beauty of the island, well-off families began to investigate and see to the construction of cottages overlooking the lake on the East and West Bluffs.

It was after "Fairy Island" was issued, and following *Lake Country Sketches'* publication in 1875 that more than thirty cottages were built on the two island bluffs.[41] Cottagers, overnight visitors, and new residents to the village would discover the island in the early twentieth century. It was less the trickle effect than a steady uptick in summer population and overall popularity of the place. Woolson's bestselling articles and books had secured her a place in the New York literati and spread the word of the wonders of the Great Lakes.

To a large degree, the kind of lively, careless life in "Fairy Island" referenced the voyageurs whose time had come and gone by 1865, when Woolson summered on Mackinac. Certainly the author romanticizes those figures, yet she does such a good job of it that her narrative is a stirring one. The narrator presents herself as a visitor to the island who encounters several ancient *grandperes* who recount the "old times" on Mackinac. They "told us merry tales of the fur-traders, their wild adventures of the far west, and their gay meetings at Mackinac twice a year." The reader is then treated to a wizened voyageur's "piping voice" singing an old boating song:

> Row, row, brothers, row
> Down to the west;
> On, on, we go,
> Pause not for rest.

Mackinac assumes the persona of a sweetheart:

> Soon the night
> Will veil from sight

The distant heights of Mackinac
Farewell, farewell.
Ma belle, ma belle.

The ancient voyageur makes clear that the "[fur-]loaded bateaux" return twice a year:

Afar we go,
Towards ice and snow,
With wolf and bison must we war,
But smiling Spring
Again will bring
The distant heights of Mackinac.[42]

Woolson captures more lost pieces of history in her recollection of "the little chapel attached to the Fort, where for more than twenty years the Reverend John O'Brian, a clergyman of the Episcopal Church, officiated. On Sunday morning the bugle call, echoing from the height, called the villagers. . . . [who] were seen ascending the steep, graveled pathway to the garrison. . . . the commandant in full uniform, and the services began with full responses, both musical and spoken, from hundreds of deep bass voices."[43]

It was during a visit back to Mackinac at age thirty that Woolson wrote "Fairy Island." By the time she was there researching her piece for *Putnam's*, the military chapel had been turned into a "drill room." As Woolson records change on Mackinac, her love of the island is unwavering. She invests this narrative with passion, illustrating her own religious faith and open-mindedness. At times, the two converge.

Like Anna Jameson, who also wrote about "the famous Indian spiritualist, Chusco," Woolson shares with her readers stories of his lodge on Round Island, "where strange lights appeared, and where the whistling wind swept over the circle of silent Indians, sitting with bowed heads to receive the manifestations of the spirit."[44]

Writing forty-four years earlier, Anna Jameson gave a more expansive account, one that tells of Chusco's conversion to Catholicism and his decision to give up alcohol. Fenimore may have been overly romantic when describing Chusco, but she had no trouble noting that at the fort, "those old-fashioned officers, you know, were much addicted to the bottle."[45]

The persona in "Fairy Island" is a conflation of the author and an imagined narrator. One can quibble over the exaggerated content of the piece, yet what penetrates is a voice of felt emotion. In this essay by Woolson, the brain and heart are knit together as never before in her work. It anticipates both *Lake Country Sketches* and her novel *Anne*. In each there is a heroine who inhabits Mackinac. Her writing is full of drama and naturalistic detail, and Woolson pulls off the hat trick of imparting a mist-colored view of the past, a nostalgia that attracts tourists of her day and future citizens to the island.

Her Mackinac stories such as "Fairy Island" announce that the past matters—the daily life of long-ago women residents, fur traders, or soldiers. After this story and others by Woolson were published, transportation there improved. As her popular works were circulated, train travel became more popular, along with charter steam-boats to Mackinac. Senator Ferry, son of the island's leading Protestant missionaries, Amanda and Reverend William Ferry, proposed a bill to set aside 1,000 acres of federal land to be preserved as a public park.[46] Five years after Woolson's popular "Fairy Island," President Ulysses S. Grant would sign a bill in 1875 that established Mackinac as the nation's second national park.

In "Fairy Island," the narrator walks us past "houses on the beach . . . venerable and moss-grown, while behind them stand the deserted warehouses of the fur-trad-ers, once so filled with life and activity." Woolson follows the thread of change on Mackinac. She focuses more than once on the old Indian Agency, a place that had once known abundant activity in the days of Schoolcraft, Laframboise, and Biddle.[47] Her later anthology, *Lake Country Sketches*, features the remarkable story "The Old Agency" with ties to the heroics of the Napoleonic era.[48] Its emotionally resonant setting may be attributed to Woolson's own history of having lived in this very house for a number of summers in her youth. The place burned down in 1872, and today the imposing "Anne's Cottage" is in the same lot as the former home of Woolson.[49]

The three principal characters in her story "The Old Agency" include Jacques, Father Piret, and the narrator of the story, who tells us: "After some years of wandering in foreign lands, I returned to my own country. . . . The summer was over, but there came to me a great wish to see Mackinac once more; to look upon the little white Fort where had lived my soldier nephew, killed at Shiloh."[50] We do not learn that the narrator is a woman until nine pages into her story, but once known, the persona bears a strong resemblance to Woolson herself.

Two wars are invoked in this moving fancy at the Old Agency House: the nephew who died in the Civil War, and the mysterious Jacques, a grenadier under Napoleon. The former merely sets the stage for the story of the latter, who takes up residence in the deserted Agency House. The last Indian agent had departed some years earlier, and the squatting Jacques is deemed harmless even by the fort commandant, who investigates and decides that the old grenadier is "a quiet, inoffensive old man." The major permits him to live gratis in the former Indian agent's home. By looking the other way in this instance, the fort commandant demonstrated an example of kindness and a helping hand to the underserved of the Mackinac community.

The strength of "The Old Agency" rests in the pathos of the soldier, Jacques. A man with virtually no material goods to his name, this former soldier finds solace in telling his story to a sympathetic ear, one Father Piret. Father Piret, in turn, will reveal Jacques's past to a sympathetic woman who wonders—as does the reader—at the mysterious circumstances in which the soldier lives at the old Agency House. Once the challenging plot is sorted out, strong character studies emerge. Character and setting give the narrative its power. Jacques has been holing up in the Agency House for some years, and while he is a known eccentric, the islanders accept him. The story unfolds—as told to the narrator by the equally eccentric Father Piret, who is dressed as "a Roman Catholic priest, albeit slightly tinged with frontier innovations." He sometimes dons "a cloth cap embroidered with Indian bead-work" and wraps himself "in a large capote made of skins with the fur inward." This priest holds both female narrator and reader as a captive audience in this clever embedded story within a story. Very gradually Jacques's secret past is revealed.

The story leads off with a factual epigraph stating that the buildings of "The United States Indian Agency on the Island of Mackinac were destroyed by fire, December 31, at midnight." Following this information, the narrator makes a bold lament: "The old house is gone then!" Obviously distressed, this narrator draws the reader in with a vow that the Agency House "shall not depart into oblivion unchronicled." The Agency House was a boarding house in the 1860s and until the fire that destroyed it twelve years later. It had given Woolson a place to stay many years beyond her teen summers on the island. The author's own connection to the place is visceral, and indeed the house becomes a character in its own right.

Woolson does not mention poet Jane Schoolcraft, and it appears she was not aware of the poet's residence at the Agency House. Yet our knowledge of the Schoolcrafts' life in the historic home forms a powerful subtext to "The Old Agency."

The house connects the two writers, and Woolson lovingly describes the flower beds created with "infinite pains" by the early agents, with the "prim arbors" and "cherry-tree avenue" that led to a home that she recalls having warm carpets and candelabra on its high mantel.

She also corroborates some of Jane's fears when her husband, Henry Schoolcraft, alienated Native people coming for their annual annuity payments. These annuities were given in return for the vast lands ceded in the Treaty of 1836 and in other treaties. Woolson describes a time when there was a tall stockade surrounding the place, and how unhappy the Anishinaabe were with the "government pittance." She writes of the "loaded muskets" trained on the Native people as they came to receive their payments. There is more than a little truth to her understanding that "The officers of the little Fort on the height, the chief factors of the fur company, and the United States Indian agent, formed the feudal aristocracy of the island."[51] While there were complex layers of race and culture, the top tier was undisputed, as Ojibwe Mackinac trader Madame (Madeline) Laframboise and others over the course of the century knew well.[52] In the novel *Anne,* Woolson also takes up her study of society in a discussion of Fort Mackinac, which was "the castle of the town, and its commandant by courtesy the leader of society."[53]

The narrator in "The Old Agency" meets Father Piret on a steamer that is traveling across Lake Erie and up the "brimming Detroit River, through the St. Clair Flats, and out into broad Lake Huron." Woolson ramps up the drama: "a gale met us and for hours we swayed between life and death." Given the authenticated shipwrecks in the Great Lakes recorded over time, the fictional drama hits home. Adding to the connection between Father Piret and the narrator is the truism "In times of danger, formality drops from us."[54]

Together these two will sit and talk outside on the piazza of the Agency House, noting the masthead star of a far-off schooner, and behind them the lighted windows of the fort. The "white chimneys of the Agency loomed like ghosts," while the "evening sky retained that clear hue that seems so much like daylight when one looks aloft."[55] The ambience provides a dramatic backdrop for Piret to speak of island history—for instance, "the battle which took place on Dousman's farm, not far from the British Landing." He, in turn, listened when Jacques revealed that he had been in battle with the Emperor Napoleon and was a French grenadier, replete with saber, horse, and total devotion to the famous man. After Waterloo and then St. Helena, Jacques was a broken man and left the Continent for a new life in America, "wandering as far as Mackinac in his blind pilgrimage." He spends his days at the Agency House reliving the glory days with Napoleon. Woolson gives us an island setting that lends itself to stories of strife and valor. Most intriguing is the voice of the unnamed narrator, whose mysterious backstory is never shared. On the one hand, her voice is silenced by that of the priest and soldier, and on the other, hers is the voice that we remember. Her words guide the story.

By story's end, the impression left upon the reader is of an island redolent with people like Father Peret, Jacques the grenadier, and our strong female narrator. Their similarities stem from having lived fully and loving Mackinac Island. "The Old Agency" begins as a lament for the past, but closes with a sense of beauty and wholeness.

Following the success of "Fairy Island" and *Lake Country Sketches*, Woolson published *Anne*, a sprawling Victorian novel. Fenimore's heroine, Anne Douglas, is not one to sit by the hearth darning socks. Born on Mackinac, she is a young woman who lives for roaming the island forests. We see her sledding down Fort Hill Road at breakneck speed with her childhood friend Rast, or racing with her younger siblings for the sheer pleasure of feeling her limbs fly. She is a true innocent, an island girl who has a challenging time once she leaves Mackinac for the wide world beyond. Her rich aunt insists that she attend a French finishing school in New York, where she is misunderstood by snooty classmates. Anne perseveres and becomes a teacher in Cleveland, after which the novel shifts dramatically, and not entirely successfully, into a detective mystery with an unclear narrative direction. There is a grand love story, and Anne's true love, Heathcote—in name, reminiscent of Heathcliff in *Wuthering Heights*—is accused of murder. Anne manages to find the killer and restore her lover's good name. Loose threads are hastily tied together, and the end of the novel finds Anne and Heathcote returned to Mackinac, where they are all set to live happily ever after.

If today's reader finds the middle sections of the book a challenge, most readers and critics in the Victorian age relished it. In 1889, the *Hartford Courant* commented on Woolson's "three years in writing *Anne*, which story has all the evidences of care and thought in its construction." The article for the "Bookbuyer" section of the paper also wants us to know that "the author's early years were spent in Cleveland, Ohio, and on the island of Mackinac, in the connecting lakes Huron and Michigan."

Anne was Woolson's first serious novel and her most autobiographical one.[56] She mined her girlhood summers on Mackinac, her close relationship with her father, and unhappy experience at a girl's finishing school in New York. Anne chafes at being closed out of a real university where men were privileged to attend, but finally is restored at the end of the novel by her deep ties to the island. Woolson herself felt rejuvenated when traveling back to Mackinac after her experiences in New York. Never again would she write about nature in the rapturous tones witnessed in her protagonist, Anne. With "the wild forest her background, the open air and blue straits her scenery," the heroine recites from Shakespeare and feels at once energized and at peace "among the cedars." A reading audience found Anne's interpretations of "Juliet, Ophelia, Rosalind, and Cleopatra" enticing, as did her childhood friend in the novel, who wishes to be "as handsome as the trees" so that he may join her.[57] Here is yet another publication by Woolson that teases out the natural beauty of Mackinac, inviting all who visit her literature to visit the island in person.

The first ten chapters of the book set on Mackinac are by far the strongest, and bear two noteworthy features. As in "The Old Agency," Woolson places her characters in the once historic house on Mackinac. Detailed descriptions of the United States Agency House ring with verisimilitude. Anne is also part of a biracial family. While she is white and happens to be the oldest child in her family, her father has remarried, with five offspring in all. Anne's biological mother and her father's second wife are dead. Anne's stepmother, Angelique Lafontaine, was Métis, and Anne adores and cares for her four younger Native half-siblings who are the offspring of the second wife. The action of these children is rendered with full attention to character. Anne, at age seventeen, is the caretaker of three young boys and thirteen-year-old Tita, with long black braids, who always wears her comfortable moccasins and is sometimes attired in clothing with beadwork. Writing with realism about family dynamics, Woolson shows Tita competing with Anne for her father's attention. Mr. William Douglas is a former U.S. Army surgeon, a New Englander, who spends most of his time birding and examining the flora "across the island," not unlike Woolson's own father, Jarvis, who preferred being in nature to running the family stove business.

Tita is a vivacious girl who teases her young brothers by pretending to be a ghost when she is not curled up with books in her corner of the house "lined and carpeted by furs" near the fireplace and an old secretary. She speaks her mind and sometimes swears, causing her father to approach Anne about disciplining her younger sister. When he says that the thirteen-year-old Tita will soon be a woman, Anne counters: "Oh no, father, she is but a child," bringing to mind the difference between a young woman's perspective and a male one. Even in the mid-nineteenth century, young Native women were married off at ages thirteen and fourteen. Mr. Douglas thinks about having married Tita's mother when she was hardly older than the girl is now, while Anne defends the girl's right to youthful behavior. Woolson's delivery of social history in novelistic form brings to mind the power of American literature when employed responsibly.

The villagers of Mackinac figure significantly in the story, including shopkeepers; Dr. Gaston, the Protestant minister who is Anne's teacher; and the compassionate Lois Hinsdale. Hinsdale, the superintendent of nursing on the island, becomes jealous of Angelique, Douglas's second wife to be. The small island society recognizes that Lois hopes in vain for the hand of Mr. Douglas. The villagers claim she might as well have "been hunting loon with a hand-net." Woolson drolly adds that though Lois is seven years older than the man she loves, "women of forty-one can answer whether that makes any difference." Age forty was considered to be teetering on old age in 1850, the approximate year when the novel is set.

The setting of the novel draws the reader in, opening with an evening winter scene of the parade ground of Fort Mackinac covered in snow, and the distant lamp in the darkness of the mostly shuttered shops in the village. It is Christmas Eve, and after an organ practice in the small fort chapel, Anne and her father walk down the steep steps wearing their fur-lined overshoes, making their way into the large hall at the old Agency House. Inside is the "great fire of logs," with nearby "rattling dormer windows," and the "crowded, and comfortable" study that Anne and her father inhabit with "dried plants, wampum, nets, bits of rock, half-finished drawings, maps, books and papers that were scattered about or suspended from the wall."[58] This is a home filled with character, and Anne's sense of loss registers keenly when she must leave family and island behind to attend school in the east.

Anne is a convincing study of a separate and sometimes blended East Coast and Great Lakes ethos. Over time, Anne's father, a crusty New England dreamer, has become deeply attached to Mackinac. Mr. Douglas appreciates its fauna and flora, and in his career as island surgeon and then, briefly, as postmaster, he participates fully in the island community. No novel set on Mackinac before *Anne* had taken an honest look at the layered culture and mixed races of the region, including perspectives from the East and the Midwest.

When the novel moves into a scene where the fur-trade warehouse on Market Street has been turned into a lively dance hall, the reader is treated to the different classes of society and racial diversity: "the military element presided like a court circled," with these characters described as "first families." Nearby, giving life to the dance, are the Métis—"French girls," as Woolson refers to them—who dance with "sparkling black eyes." Though the "Indians" are first described as standing at the sidelines, the calm dignity of the Native "old grandams" is contrasted with the more restless East Coast women. The grandams sit on a long bench along the walls.[59] *Anne* does not shirk from controversial subjects. There are testy exchanges among the islanders regarding their aspirations as to what sort of marriages their children should enter into. They reject the "transient soldiers" at the fort in favor of "the most desirable suitors for their daughters," who are the young men of Scottish descent who are fish merchants. Woolson tracks the change in island livelihoods, from a frontier of fur trade to the prevalence of a fishing industry.[60]

By the middle section of the novel, Anne has left Mackinac, and Woolson experiments in writing about an urban setting and suspenseful action. At 540 pages, *Anne* may be a long narrative, but it follows the travails of a heroine who remains vibrant throughout. Nineteenth-century readers embraced this coming-of-age story with a protagonist who was a thinking woman, both action-oriented and compassionate. By the time she wrote *Anne*, Woolson could well afford to write a book that experimented with a picaresque form coupled with realism and even a detective story. By achieving publications in *Putnam's*, the *Atlantic Monthly*, and *Harper's*, she was viewed as a respected writer. This serious recognition encouraged the populace to take her at her word and long to visit the Great Lakes. Her novel accomplished a dual goal: Woolson promoted the beauty and charm of Mackinac, and she made sure her readers were educated in the cultural diversity of the region. This she explored in her focus on the Douglas family and their connection to island industry and community.

Prone to the kind of depression that afflicted her father and would result in suicide for her brother, Woolson had an extended period of serious melancholy when her mother died.[61] She felt the loss keenly, having assumed the role of primary caregiver of her mother since Jarvis's death ten years earlier. Clara, her one sister still alive, stepped up to the duty of caring for the depressed Constance. Clara insisted that they take an extended journey to Europe, and gradually the new surroundings vanquished the gloom into which Fenimore had sunk. Though self-supporting for some years, she accepted her nephew Sam Mather's generous donation to his two aunts for a trip abroad in 1879. This was her first trip to the Continent, and it did not take long before she began to fall in love with the "Old World" settings.[62] In her later life, Woolson sought warm places to live: the Riviera, and various settings in Italy. She spent years in these places. Yet Britain, too, beckoned—though no doubt more for its culture than lovely weather. Early in her friendship with Henry James, she spent one happy winter and spring in Salisbury, England. She felt at home in the cathedral town and was able to write all day and spend evenings with James.[63]

Beginning at age forty, Woolson lived peripatetically in England, France, and Italy. The losses she had faced in her homeland contributed to a desire to escape to Europe. In addition to the death of her parents, five Woolson siblings had died of scarlet fever and tuberculosis, then known as "consumption." The counsel for avoiding tuberculosis, which Woolson thought her family prone to, was healthful air and warm climes. Terrified of the same fate (her letters to her nephew Sam testify to this), she followed the medical advice of the day.[64] In her early middle age, Fenimore traveled to the Great Lakes and Mackinac, believing it to be the tonic she had known in her youth. Long after she stopped visiting the island, its physical and spiritual benefits show up in her fiction.

She never forgot Mackinac, and one letter to Lieutenant D. H. Kelton, written nearly two decades after her family stopped summering on the island, reveals the way she followed its news and publications. From Florence, she wrote: "I have recently had far away here in Italy a most pleasant hour of recollections and old associations, revived by your 'Annals of Fort Mackinac'—for which please accept my best thanks." She asks him to remember her to any of her old acquaintances, if they are still there. She writes that the best compliment she could give Capri is that its sunsets remind her of those on Mackinac. She closes the letter with a hopeful assurance to her friends there: "tell them that I shall certainly come back some day."[65]

Perhaps she was thinking of Mackinac both at sunset and at nighttime. In an article in *Harper's* about the island, she describes approaching by boat: "It rose before us in the moonlight, its high cliffs and bold dark outlines looking far more romantic and wild than anything we had seen on the freshwater seas. The little Fort on the height and the little village seemed fast asleep."[66] When Woolson's fictional boat, the *Columbia*, blows its whistle, a crowd appears on the dock, and "the sensible, middle-aged woman" who had not planned on going ashore claims that "something in the moonlight bewitched me." Later, on the west shore of the island, she joins her young niece and one Major Archer in making "an offering to the fairy, and drink[ing] three times from the fountain." The party throws in bluebells and a knot of ribbon, and someone pins a ten-cent scrip to an overhanging branch. They make their wishes, and according to general wisdom not everyone reveals what they asked for.[67]

The short story "Miss Grief" is one of Woolson's best pieces.[68] Compelling and witty, it is set in a vague part of Italy, and highlights a writer seeking validation of her work from a vain, successful male author with inherited wealth. "Miss Grief" is the male narrator's name for her, though her real name is Montcrief. She is an older woman in her forties, the narrator tells us, and the young, successful author, bearing huge similarities to Henry James, is struck by the originality and force of Miss Grief's stories. He agrees to help her publish them on the condition that she revise the work, modifying the strong voice and making it fit the prescribed meek women's stories that are being published at the time. She refuses to compromise her work in this way and does not get published. During their numerous meetings, Miss Grief also counsels him about his writing, and he is aware that she is the only person in his life so perceptive about his books. She dies soon after he tells her to drastically change her work. The narrator keeps the stories she has given him, still not publishing them, but pulling out her manuscripts to read many times over the course of his life.

Six years after Woolson's death, James would publish his much anthologized "Beast in the Jungle." As in a number of his other short stories, the principal female character is partly modeled on his close confidante, Constance Fenimore Woolson, and meant to reveal her as a lovelorn old maid, "who wasted away for want of James' affections." The reviewer Amy Gentry of the *Chicago Tribune* further comments that the short fiction reveals James's "own anxiety" on a number of levels. Though it is certainly a masterpiece, she comments that "'Beast in the Jungle' is also monumentally solipsistic." Gentry hits home with her observation regarding Woolson and James: "Yet intellectually, the two were equals, such that James had to make it a condition of their friendship early on that, professionally speaking, he was Woolson's mentor, never her peer—or, God forbid, rival."[69] It is not easy to give him a pass on his misogynistic acts.

Woolson did not suffer the same publishing fate as Miss Grief in her famous short story, for she was well published when she met Henry James. Yet as a female writer, she encountered condescension and bias throughout her career. In her later work she seems to have partly internalized the mythos of timid prose by women. Additionally, when one examines some of Fenimore Woolson's stilted language in the last two thirds of *Anne*, the books by her famous namesake, James Fenimore Cooper, come to mind. In reading *Last of the Mohicans*, the freshmen and sophomores in my class at the University of Pennsylvania got a quick lesson on the turgid prose in many parts of Cooper's novel. Their reaction was loud and clear. Not one to give up easily on Fenimore Cooper, who contributed to the canon of American literature in multiple ways, this struggling instructor then taught his last work, *The Pioneers*. That novel delivered a far more palatable Deerslayer (his multiple names include Hawkeye and Natty Bumppo). This is not to say that Fenimore Woolson inherited some of her great-uncle's prose style, but that perhaps she was influenced by it.

Most of Woolson's short stories reveal sharply drawn characters. Their economical style stands in contrast to the prose in the middle and late sections of her novel *Anne*. In their regional breadth, they surpass other stories of the period, and the best of them rival Sarah Orne Jewett and her collection *Country of the Pointed Firs*. Woolson's *Lake Country Sketches* are memorable, especially "Jeanette," the central character in a story set on Mackinac; "Solomon"; and "St. Clair Flats," set on the lake of the title. Many of the characters speak with refreshing honesty about their lives. She takes on serious social commentary and domestic abuse in her novel *Jupiter Lights*, and racism in her story "Rodman the Keeper," where a cemetery caretaker and former Union soldier reveal the extent to which inhabitants from the North could be as alarmingly bigoted as those in the South.

In her forties, Woolson became increasingly deaf, just as her father had been. By her early fifties, the deafness contributed to her isolation and loneliness. She could no longer indulge her love of singing or attend the opera. In 1894, she either fell or leapt to her death from the balcony in her bedroom apartment in Venice. She had influenza at the time, was depressed and struggling with financial woes. Worse, she was befuddled by laudanum, used by men and women alike to calm nerves or to hope for sleep. The pernicious drug, a mix of opium and alcohol also thought to have contributed to Schoolcraft's late-life malaise, certainly did not help Woolson's state of mind. At her death, her family was devastated, and Henry James as well. He traveled at once to Venice, where he gathered up her black silk gowns and carried them to the nearby canal. Several stories attest to him rowing out in a gondola and tossing the dresses overboard. Apparently, they rose to the surface repeatedly, no matter how strenuously James tried to poke them down.[70] Woolson's reputation and strength as a writer defies drowning; there is much that needs to surface and be said about her standing in American letters.

The tributes to Woolson after her death were many. Abroad, the *Glasgow Herald* wrote: "Miss Woolson's death is a distinct loss to American Literature," and closer to home, author Charles Dudley Warner, who had admitted to borrowing some of her ideas early in his career, would write movingly of how "She was a sympathetic [and] refined observer, entering sufficiently into the analytic mode of the time, but she had the courage to deal with the passions, and life as it is."[71] Current readers, writers, and critics have begun to notice Woolson's value as an author of her time and ours. Of *Castle Nowhere: Lake Country Sketches*, the writer Margot Livesey comments that Woolson never lost sight of the loveliness of life even as she was "always remaining keenly aware that beauty in no way mitigates hardship."[72]

The women of the Great Lakes who people this study sometimes traveled far from home, but most returned to their land of origin, even if by pen alone. By the time Woolson was in her forties and fifties, she no longer traveled to Mackinac, but as so many of her stories, letters, and the novel *Anne* attest, she was there in mind and spirit. The letters to her nephew Sam speak of her personal attachment to "The Great Turtle," and her work, from "The Old Agency" to "Fairy Island" and *Anne*, advanced the understanding of mixed-race families on Mackinac.

Brother and sister Sam and Kate Mather, who were both close to their aunt until her death, wrote expansive instructions for the creation of "Anne's Tablet" to be undertaken. They created a fund to be directed to the Mackinac Island State Park Commission for care and upkeep of the "Constance Fenimore Woolson Memorial." This directive included words that uphold the values of Woolson herself. The area at Anne's Tablet was to have "wild and informal trails rather than symmetrical and park-like [with] rigidly trimmed edges" and plants "represented by moss, pink, phlox subulate, the Indian tobacco," along with an arborvitae planted and maintained at the bluff's edge.[73]

Each year this place of honor, Anne's Tablet on Mackinac, attracts thousands of visitors, many stumbling upon the statue of her heroine unaware of Woolson as an American writer. Once a summer, a ragtag group of poets and poetry lovers gathers at Anne's Tablet and recites poetry. Outwardly modest, this event bridges the past with the present. The abiding spirit of the author prevails. The participants and visitors sit on the bank at the cliff edge or on the low semicircle bench. Food and drink are in good supply, and better yet, the passion of the spoken word. Fenimore Woolson would approve.

CHAPTER EIGHT

Rosa Truscott Webb
(1853–1942)

osa Truscott Webb stands out as one who preserved the social fabric of
community on Mackinac as it evolved from fishing industry to holiday
destination. When tourism became Mackinac's chief industry in the
early twentieth century, the fundamental core of school, library, and
community activities could easily have been lost. Webb was the founder of the island
library, and she led the movement for the first official community center. Recognizing
that the island youth needed a common space for after-school activities and sports, she
became their advocate, speaking up tirelessly on their behalf. Her civic reach extended
beyond Mackinac, and she was responsible for initiating Girl Scouts of America in
Michigan. Her leadership improved the opportunities for girls in Michigan and
greatly changed the cultural landscape of Mackinac.

In 1866, the same year Rosa Truscott's family moved permanently to Mackinac,
Elizabeth Cady Stanton and Susan B. Anthony initiated the American Rights
Association, which promoted the goal of suffrage for all humankind, regardless of
gender or race. As a young teen, Rosa may not have been aware of that organization, or
of the previous attempts to gain equal rights for women and African Americans that
had begun with the nation's independence from Britain. Black men would receive the
vote in 1870, but women, black or white, would have to wait nearly fifty years before
handed that privilege. In 1872, Susan B. Anthony cast a vote for Ulysses S. Grant for
president; she was arrested and brought to trial for her action. Rosa Webb underwent
a very different life-altering change. The death of her husband in 1882 forced her to
reevaluate women's rights, and the obvious connection to how she would make a
living. By 1887, women's suffrage was taken seriously by many, though the vote put

through to the U.S. Senate at that time failed. Still, the succeeding years saw women begin to enter public life, and the widowed Rosa (age twenty-nine) decided she could move forward to better her community.

If the first and second wave of early Mackinac women ranged from traders and scribes to farmers and social historians, it became the mission of the third group of Mackinac citizens, most of whom watched women fight for equality, to forge a society in the fields of healthcare, education, business, and horse culture. Three of the major leaders in these areas were Rosa Truscott Webb, Daisy Peck Blodgett, and Stella King. These women knew each other well, and despite their different backgrounds, they worked together on behalf of Mackinac. It was not only Webb's seniority that led the group, but her vision and self-driven action. This overlooked history begins with Webb's unquiet voice.

In many instances, she singlehandedly championed improvements to civil society on Mackinac. That unquiet voice was variously firm—all business—or suddenly homey, and even pleading. She could be genuinely downcast or sound exceedingly grateful and jolly. Her actions are documented in letters and in the local island paper, as well as the Lansing, Flint, and Detroit newspapers. Whether stopping in at the bank or the fledgling "Community House" at the John Jacob Astor House, as the former base of the American Fur Company was known, she would take any opportunity to speak up on behalf of her projects.[1] She wrote dozens of letters to influential people on Mackinac and was an activist in the cause of educational development. Regarding the well-being of the young people, she wrote to Wilfred Puttkammer, director of the fund for the historic Beaumont Memorial in 1931, prefacing her bid for support with an indication of his standing in the community and following this up with an earnest plea: "The youth have nowhere to go." They are "roaming the streets."[2] That letter along with others was part of her push to turn the unused fur-trade buildings into the island's first community center. This was an unusual idea at that time, and but one example of her indefatigable efforts to effect positive civic change.

At first glance, Webb appears to have led a somewhat peripatetic life. Marriage and tragedy sent her off-island to make a home in places as various as Texas and Iowa. Yet a close look reveals that she lived away from Mackinac only six of the approximately seventy-five years she spent there. The Great Turtle had exerted its pull and lured her home after each monumental change or loss that she experienced. Webb was born in Port Hope, Ontario, in 1853.[3] Her mother, Sophia Bates, was a native of that region, and her father was born in Plymouth, England. Sophia and George Truscott moved to Chicago when the four Truscott children were young. George and his brother-in-law, John Bates, had started up a wholesale fishing enterprise together, with John operating from Mackinac and George at the family-owned business in the city.[4] As wholesalers, Bates purchased the fish from myriad fishermen in the Great Lakes region surrounding Mackinac. Meanwhile, George oversaw the delivery in Chicago of fish on ice or salt, to sell in the city at wholesale prices. At age thirteen, Rosa and her family moved to Mackinac when it appears that George and his brother-in-law had switched places in the business. At this time, 1866, there was also a family-owned store on the island. Most likely, Rosa would have been put to work in the store, perhaps in retail and inventory. This prepared her for the savvy understanding of numbers she demonstrated when later at work buying the Astor House and trading warehouses from the state so that the island could have a library and community center.

Rosa Webb came to Mackinac in a time of bustling enterprise. The fur-trade business had closed its doors by 1840, but its vestiges and the historic warehouses on Market Street left their mark on the girl. As a child, she would have seen scattered wigwams along the shoreline, and she may well have met Native American Agatha Biddle, a person of great repute on Mackinac. Biddle lived on Market Street, and the Truscott family house was at the end of town on the east side. It was a Victorian with bric-a-brac design work between the pillars and a picket fence bordering the yard. Just as it is today, Mackinac is a small town, and most were aware of, or friends with, one another. The Truscott home was near Mission Hill, or as it came to be called, Truscott Street, named after Rosa's family. Rosa spent most of her life in that spacious cottage with a wraparound front porch. There on Truscott Street, her parents had made a home, along with her sister and brother, and eventually Rosa's children and grandson. It was the perfect setting, far enough out of town that Rosa could find respite as she planned the next move in her island projects, and close enough that she could walk ten minutes westward and be in the thick of action, downtown.

Growing up with a family store on the island, Rosa had plenty of opportunity to observe islanders who needed to figure out ways to create a well-rounded, self-sufficient community. Trade alone, as in her parents' fishing business and other enterprises, did not offer islanders a life of music, books, dancing, and other forms of culture. Schooling took place in the old Indian Dormitory, but there was no access to community space for youth activities on the island.[5]

At age nineteen, Rosa met and married the builder William Disbrow. It was 1872, and the couple moved to Munising, Michigan. Despite the beauty of the north country, its falls and pictured rocks, Webb's life there was marred by hardship and loss. Her son, Edwin, was born in 1873 and a year later her husband died, his stated death given as an accident, perhaps one at an industrial site.[6] Her return to Mackinac soon afterwards marked the first of her migrations home after tragedy.

She had been resettled at the family residence on Truscott Street with her young son for about four years when she met Charles Webb, an officer at Fort Mackinac. She and Captain Webb married in 1878, and Rosa moved to Fort Mackinac to live with her new husband. There the couple met and socialized with the Websters. John Webster was an active military man and his wife, Rose, a hotelier. She and Rosa Webb became lifelong friends.[7] The pair may have smiled at their similar names after marriage, but there was considerably more that the two shared. It took daring on each woman's part to marry a soldier. Author Constance Fenimore Woolson comments on the status of Mackinac soldiers in her books, and of the way parents on the island encouraged their daughters to marry fishing company clerks as opposed to the "transient" soldiers at the fort. Certainly the rank of officer conferred a degree of respectability; however Webb's new husband had been "convicted of neglect of duty" by a general court-martial and arrived at Fort Mackinac in November 1877 under arrest and "confined to the limits of the post."[8] We wonder what Rosa Webb thought of her new husband's "negligence," yet his return to active duty after three months' confinement at the fort must have convinced her of his worth. Further, she was willing to give him a chance to redeem himself.

There is another key in the friendship between the Island House owner and the activist. Rose Webster and Rosa Webb recognized in one another the belief in working hard to achieve worthwhile goals. Both were ambitious people, fair dealers, and women with vision. Webster's support of Webb played no small part in the library founder's courage to pursue civic causes. It is a truism that we need role models, like-minded folk to spur us forward; the tough-minded Webster would have offered that strength to Rosa Webb.

Captain Van Allen, a Great Lakes skipper, bought the Island House Hotel in 1865. It is very possible that his daughter Rose helped him to operate the place, for he left the hotel to her in his will.[9] It is telling that Mr. Van Allen chose to bequeath such a major commercial investment to his daughter. He might well have left it to Rose and her husband together, or even simply put it in his son-in-law's name. That he made such a choice reveals a forward-thinking belief in the equality of the sexes, along with trust in his daughter's executive abilities.

After her father's death in 1892, she owned and operated the Island House, making it a gracious architectural wonder and a popular lodging that garnered the label in one newspaper "the best Family hotel" on Mackinac.[10] Under Rose Webster's watch, there was a full orchestra and ballroom dancing, high tea, and two new wings added, the east and west, which give the hotel its distinctive look today. She owned the establishment for an impressive forty-six years, and during that same span, her friend Rosa Webb was working full-time in multiple arenas on behalf of Mackinac. It is often one's younger days that cement a friendship, and clearly this was so for Webb and Webster. Rosa recalls in her journal how she and Rose lived at Fort Mackinac for a year or two. The pair spoke of how they might have to leave the island if their officer husbands were transferred. They joked about how it would be tough if they were transferred down south as they were not used to the idea of wearing light clothing in the winter.[11] Though Rose most likely traveled with her husband to his next post, in the years to come she would manage the hotel while Captain Webster was busy with his military career. She was the sole proprietor until her death in 1938. The story of Rose Webster and Rosa Webb indicates the way Mackinac women such as the hotelier and activist encouraged one another, resulting in the civic growth of Mackinac.

Webb's second husband, Charles, received orders to leave Fort Mackinac in 1880, and after two years of marriage, the couple lived first at Fort Leavenworth and then Fort Riley, both outposts in Kansas. In fast succession, they were transferred to Fort McKavett, Texas, where their daughter, Marcia, was born. In 1882, while stationed in Texas, Captain Webb died from tuberculosis, "lung congestion." With another severe loss to bear, and the second marriage lasting but a few short years, Rosa Webb returned to Mackinac with two children in tow. To support her family, she became a voice and piano teacher at Trinity Episcopal Church.[12] Her engagement with children in extracurricular music lessons revealed to her the need for students to have activities beyond school hours. Yet it took some years of courage for Webb to put her ideas for the betterment of Mackinac into motion. Living in an era where women were expected to keep their heads down, were told it was a man's place to give speeches and make changes, it makes sense that the development of Webb's unquiet voice did not happen overnight.

Her son, Edwin, who attended military academy and served in the Spanish-American War, contracted tuberculosis during his service. After the war, he came home and died on Mackinac, probably in the family home on Truscott Street. With this loss weighing on her heavily, Webb left Mackinac once again. For the next three years she lived in Iowa, where young Marcia attended school and Webb studied music. By 1899, she was back home, again giving singing and piano lessons at Trinity Church. Interestingly, it was not until she was much older that there is evidence of her major efforts to secure a library and community center for islanders. The ratification of the Nineteenth Amendment would have encouraged her sense of women's voice in the public forum and her ability to carry out civic action. She was sixty-six years old when that right to vote was finally granted.

After women got the vote, the activist began to reach out to many islanders, and she wrote numerous letters advocating civic improvements for Mackinac. Significantly, Webb worked side by side with summer residents who lived on the upscale East and West Bluffs, and alongside year-round residents in the village, or town residents such as nurse Stella King. Letters from men and women who supported Rosa, including Wilfred Puttkammer and Daisy Blodgett, attest to the way those who loved Mackinac bridged social classes to work together. The women of Mackinac had long been leaders in education, and certainly Webb's dedication to the cultural education of islanders may be compared with the educational action of Amanda and William Ferry, along with Madeline Laframboise and Marianne Fisher a century earlier. Amanda and William Ferry operated the Mission Church and school, Fisher was also an island teacher, and Madeline Laframboise oversaw lessons in her own home.

In her letters to Wilfred Puttkammer, Webb explained that the town needed a permanent place for the youth to go for such activities as basketball. She also understood how helpful it was for students to have a place to be if family life was tough. She floated the idea of the Astor House to him, promoting it as the "Community House." Her social conscience could be seen in a number of areas. In February 1931, Webb worried about people feeling isolated on the island: "I am afraid we are going to have an open winter here. Ice is not making very well. They are cutting ice, but have been a little unfortunate about ice floating away during the night."[13] Families could not rely on traveling to the mainland, and community connections were more important than ever.

If temperatures were higher than usual that winter, so was Webb's preoccupation with how the island would be able to obtain the Astor House and implement the many repairs it needed. She appealed to Wilfred to write a letter to the island newspaper stating how crucial the Community House would be for the island welfare: "I do not suppose you will want to publish a report in the Island paper, but I feel the people who live on the island do not know how much it costs to maintain it."[14]

Though Katherine Doyle, a summer resident and wife of a Michigan state senator, gives her some hope that Lansing will consider giving aid, Rosa worries that if the state of Michigan takes over the "Community House," many activities will not be permitted there. Webb decides that she is going to have to speak up more boldly than before. She begins making her case known, and on August 3, 1930, the *Detroit Free Press* picks up her story. The paper describes Mackinac resident Rosa Webb, who, "through entertainments of various kinds and subscriptions from residents and summer visitors, $5000 was raised" to deed the John Jacob Astor House over to the Community Association.

Despite that accomplishment, she realizes that she may lose this vital community center after all. Webb communicates with Puttkammer, asking whether he thinks the town will get back the money she has already invested, especially if the state takes over the project. She assures him that the mortgage taken out for $8,000 is down to $3,000 and she has kept up every payment. In the multiple letters she writes Wilfred from 1931 to 1936, she often repeats that she is "sorry to bother you, for I know you are very busy." Never mind that Webb is every bit as busy; she adopts a tone taken by many women of this era who are trying to be heard by those in charge. She prevails upon him, believing he will have a certain amount of pull, simply being a man, and helpfully one engaged in the Island welfare. Her down-to-earth appeal coupled with sharp analysis of finances is a compelling combination.

In a letter to him dated February 14, Rosa presumes he knows that "our island Bank is in the hands of a Receiver." That is to say, the bank is insolvent, and in a government-managed bankruptcy. She discovered this news when going into the bank to check on "our mortgage for the Astor House" (and the site of both the future Community House and the island library). She knows that Puttkammer sits on the board of the historic "Beaumont Hospital" house and hopes that organization may be in a position to assume the mortgage—rather than the failing island bank. She writes:

> This idea occurred to me when I looked over my books and saw what we had received for two years, from the Rummage sales and should this good work continue our share would almost be the amount of the interest we pay at 6%—the mortgage now is $2,332.29 so our interest will be a little less since we have had the house [the "Community House" community center], we have paid our interest to date $796/00. I sincerely wish the little Hospital had had this amount instead of the bank.... There have been repairs on the house—posts under the house, the main part and office were decayed, so that is put in order.[15]

Of her commitment to restoring the community center, the *Lansing State Journal* wrote: "Rosa Webb, a venerable lady" whose "personal interest has resulted in the reconstruction of The Astor House on Mackinac Island, and who was responsible for the organization which has made it a community center. . . . the perpetration of its picturesque history, has, I believe, become a sort of religion with Mrs. Webb, and I am indebted to her [for the history of the place] which otherwise I could not have secured."[16]

There are a number of letters to Wilfred Puttkammer regarding this fervent hope that the hospital board will take over the mortgage. Writing that she "does not know what is in store for the Astor House," Webb tries reverse psychology: "I would never want to do or say anything to ask you to risk any of the money" earned for the little Beaumont Hospital. She adds the ploy, "Put me entirely out of the question."

As it turned out, the Beaumont Memorial was not able to assume the mortgage for the future Community House and the first library. Yet under Webb's direction "the people this winter are doing what they can to earn money, [including] card parties and cribbage (of the latter, a great many men prefer this to bridge)." Eventually Webb and her sister islanders raised enough cash to save the Astor House.

With the support of other women on the island, Webb spearheaded fundraisers to create that first sanctuary of books on Market Street in the old Astor House. Fourteen years after the D.A.R. Mackinac Library opened its doors, the editor and publisher of the island newspaper, Ruth Camp, wrote an article titled "Mackinac's Shoestring Library Helps Itself."[17] That headline aptly describes the activist Rosa Truscott Webb herself. She did not wait on ceremony to see her goals through. Gradually, Rosa learned that others (whether the bank in St. Ignace or downstate government) would not step in to save the day. Regarding the library, she and her island friends were committed to doing the footwork themselves. As to the access to books and reading, no project was more dear to the island women than their determination to create the first library. Rosa Webb was at the helm every step of the way.

In her communications to Wilfred Puttkammer and others—his wife, Helen, and Daisy Blodgett—all of whom were active agents on many civic fronts, Rosa often implies that she may be making a nuisance of herself by writing so many letters regarding the island medical care, education, preservation of the trails, and protection of the youth. Nonetheless, what emerges most clearly is that if she is making a pest of herself, then so be it. Rosa Webb got the job done.

Whether an environmental disturbance or a civic concern, no matter was too insignificant for Webb to tackle. The measure of a woman may often be seen in her daily work; several examples of Webb will suffice. In the same year that the island library opened its doors, the activist speaks of the new park superintendent. He is due to arrive on Mackinac on March 4, 1935, and Rosa is cautiously hopeful as to "whether he will be interested enough to preserve the island trees [that] are left."[18] She has heard from islanders that the entire interior of the island resembles abandoned farmland. Webb admits to a degree of hearsay, wishing she could get into the woods to see for herself. By this time, she was no longer as nimble as in earlier life. At age 82, hiking up the bluff to the middle of the island would have been a treat, and a challenge.

She has been given to understand that "people have been into the woods unseen." She pictures "the blow of the ax" and has several more reports of the wood-cutting in the forests of Mackinac.[19] It was not an unlikely picture in the days of the Great Depression. At this time, Webb writes about the jobs the Works Project Administration has made available for some on the island. The invaluable program known as the WPA was started that year by President Franklin Delano Roosevelt. Webb complains, however, that the WPA is more active in St. Ignace than on Mackinac.

The healthcare of those without status on the island was important to her as well. This often ended up involving the Mackinac women. There is a skirmish regarding the needs of Mrs. Hoban, a longtime islander. When one Mr. Andrews, who sits on the Beaumont Hospital Board and possesses a key to the place, falls ill, he is easily able to obtain a bed and chair from the Beaumont storage. After he got well, these items were not returned. Webb describes Mr. Andrews as a man of "privilege," a man "with a secretary," while Mrs. Hoban has none of these things. When she falls ill, Rosa Webb has trouble securing those same healthcare items and complains that surely Mrs. Hoban is deserving. In her camp, she has a Mrs. O'Brien at the fort who "does a great deal of practical nursing and she felt Mrs. Hoban could be made more comfortable."[20] Wisely, Rosa determines that a better system needs to be devised for distribution of said key to the hospital.

With nothing more in her pocket than the wages from teaching voice lessons and piano, Webb would find a way to send her son to military school and her daughter to Vassar. She persuaded Marcia to transfer from the University of Michigan to attend the latter college, one of the highly esteemed "Seven Sisters."[21] It is not known why she pushed for the transfer from one excellent university to the other. What stands out is that it is likely she sought scholarships for each of her children, and their outstanding education points to Rosa's "can do" attitude in every walk of life.

Another first for Rosa Webb was her launch of the Girl Scouts of America in Michigan. In 1922, Webb entered the first scout troop in the state. Troop No. 1 was begun on Mackinac.[22] Of this achievement, a headline in the *Flint Journal* read, "Girl Scouts Honor First Michigan Leader." The photo caption identifies her as "Mrs.

Charles A. Webb." As it turns out, there were multiple ways in which Rosa Truscott Webb proved herself a leader. In future years, Webb's troop on Mackinac would be instrumental in raising funds for the library. In one instance, a scout creatively dressed up as an infant in a cradle. The girl in her daffy costume was presented at a party with a raffle going towards the goal of starting an island library. Also contributing key funds towards this goal was Daisy Peck Blodgett, a former national secretary for the DAR of Washington, DC. She would give a speech at the official opening of the library. Mrs. George Schermerhorn, the state regent of the Michigan DAR, also gave a greeting at the festive and serious dedication, August 22, 1936. As reported in the *Detroit News*, a bugle call initiated the proceedings, followed by an invocation by Reverend Joseph Ling. The unveiling of the plaque revealed a dedication to the founder of the D.A.R. Library, Rosa Truscott Webb.[23]

For the better part of seventy-five years, Rosa lived a full life on Mackinac. This active woman occasionally ventured off-island, as well. Even in old age, and never mind how freezing the temperature, she gamely made the journey by horse and sled across Lake Huron from Mackinac to the mainland at Mackinaw City. Several journeys to visit her daughter, Marcia, who lived in Flint, are documented in photos of Rosa out on the ice at Christmas: "en route to Flint from Mackinac Island," the pictures read.[24] Although loath to leave her home for any length of time, she was persuaded towards the end of her life to live with Marcia in Flint.

Writing in her journal about Mackinac until shortly before her death, she muses that her dear friends on the island would hardly recognize her now. Though she is living in Flint those last years, it is evident that her love of the island and its residents is enduring. She keeps up with Mackinac news: "I read, and write to fill my time, from what I see in the Mackinac Island pages I read the column over and over. Then I think of the long ago when Rose Webster and I were at the Fort on the island."[25] She muses over her old friendship with the hotelier and comments that Rose and "Lieutenant? Webster have both passed away to go to a better world [where there are] ones who will be waiting for them." She ponders which of her Mackinac friends "will be next to go to the. . . . beyond?" She writes about the Mackinac horses—an occasion when one is in irons and she worries about the situation—and she includes a few words about the time the whole regiment at the fort was ordered off the island in a train of coaches and cars. Above all, she speaks of her old island friends and the kindness they have shown her. She states that she always made a point to greet each person she knew on the street. During her last winter, she and her daughter discuss the Mackinac strawberries (not Webb's favorite fruit it seems) and she eats canned Hubbard squash from the annex area of the island that a friend has gotten to her.[26]

In October 1942, Webb passed away. At her funeral, the American flag was flown at half-mast all over the island. Walter P. Hill, the owner of Bennett Hall and Cottages on Mackinac, testifies to the mourning that took place. In a letter to the activist's sister, he writes:

Dear Miss Truscott,

It was a most wonderful home-coming for Mrs. Webb, and all Mackinac Island paid tribute to her loved memory. The American Flag, Symbol of our Strength, Freedom and Integrity, floated at half-mast from the Fort, the Schools, Business houses, and private homes. As the little Steamer bearing the remains, closed in the boat landing, the little children from the Schoolhouse, formed in lines about the landing space, making a very lovely sight.[27]

Mr. Hill speaks of Mrs. Welcher and Miss Betty Flannigan, who have organized the children to honor Rosa Webb, and of "the beautiful service in the Church [Trinity Episcopal], with wonderful setting, nestling on the side of the hill under the protection of old Fort Mackinac."[28]

Whether inventing games to keep the young people of the island engaged in singing and piano lessons, or fostering an island library and Community House, Rosa was an extraordinary island presence.[29] She and compatriots Daisy Blodgett, Ling Horn, and Stella King carried forward work that has its ties to the Indigenous humanitarians nearly a century earlier.

Today the library has become a true center for study, with lectures, exhibits, and interlibrary loan of books. It sponsors programs on environmentalism and attracts world-class authors to come read, all the while retaining its top priority as a center for the schoolchildren of the island. No longer in small digs at the Astor House on Market Street, the D.A.R. Library found an updated name and a new home at Biddle Point near the boardwalk. Designed by architect Richard Bos, it holds the distinction of being the only known library where it is not uncommon for readers to glance up from their books and see magnificent ore boats passing through the channel. Could Rosa Truscott set eyes on this facility, she would surely clap her hands in delight.

Her life represented an island community's adjustments over the course of evolving industries, the Great Depression, and the Women's Movement. Together, these changes affected the position of women in the nation, and in particular on Mackinac. Webb's actions along with other women became the catalyst for community action that has shaped the island today.

CHAPTER NINE

Daisy Peck Blodgett (1863–1947) and Stella King (1905–1984)

I n the years that Mackinac Island evolved from fishing industry to tourist mecca, Daisy Peck Blodgett and Stella King worked together to bring civic change to the island and to safeguard the heart of the community. Their contributions point to a key definition of leadership ascribed to women: their strength in relationships, and their perspicacity in developing community organizations. One fed the other, and these features powered this pair's success as champions of healthcare. These leaders in community development were from different strata of society, and from outside appearance, unlikely friends.

While King was a single woman who worked year-round on the island as a nurse, Blodgett, married to a lumber baron, was a summer resident and philanthropist. They began working together in earnest during the Great Depression and the economic reality of both mattered greatly during those years. Mackinac depended on the economy created by summer residents such as Blodgett, and an inside look at her life and King's enlarges our understanding of how the island was able to survive. What started as an escape from scandal in Grand Rapids for Blodgett became something altogether different: the island's welfare became her passion. Blodgett would spend fifty-six summer seasons on Mackinac. Stella King came to the island at age fifteen with her family.[1] It was 1920, and her father was attempting to carve out a career as a commercial fisherman in the waning days of that industry.[2] Often the only healthcare provider on Mackinac, she made the island her home for sixty-two years.[3] Stella and Daisy's connection helped them overcome every obstacle as they played large roles in the establishment of a first library, community center, and crucial medical care the residents needed. Daisy also contributed to a lasting horse culture, and Stella, the annual Lilac Festival.

Together, this pair gave their all to Mackinac in the years between World War I and II. When the Great Depression struck, few visitors or residents had money to spend, and downtown shops on Mackinac struggled to survive. More worrisome was the dearth of medical care on the island, which was, at times, dire. Blodgett would bring her experience in starting up two major healthcare facilities in downstate Michigan, and Stella, her years of experience as the island nurse. King was wholly dedicated to Mackinac her entire adult life. As for Blodgett, her lifetime spanned three wars, and she brought a unique national identity to Mackinac. Born into a slave-owning Southern family, she would marry a Northerner, Delos Blodgett. Her husband was an active abolitionist who built a church for the black residents in Grand Rapids, among other acts on behalf of African Americans.[4] Over the next fourteen years together, Daisy came to share her husband's vision of a nation that gave more than lip service to the freedom of African Americans. Delos was also a strong supporter of the Suffragist movement and was good friends with Elizabeth Cady Stanton and Susan B. Anthony. Daisy experienced a great change in perspective regarding the culture she had known as a child, learning from her experiences and becoming a resilient force in any community she lived in.

Blodgett arrived in Mackinac long after its millennia as home to Native people, its history as the chief fur-trading center of the old Northwest, followed by a strong fishing industry. It was in the uptick of visitors in the Victorian and Edwardian eras that she was introduced to the island. Healthy competition between luxury liners and railroad travel became a reality by 1895, making the island suddenly more accessible than before.[5] Through the fin de siècle and early twentieth century America maintained a fairly rigid class structure, yet no matter what class, the vote women gained in 1920 gave them hope for greater parity than before. Beyond rights to protect their own children and improved property laws, they also saw fewer restrictions in clothing and in business opportunities. For the women of Mackinac this meant the chance to participate in community action in ways unavailable to them in the nineteenth century.

In the decades before World War I, Mackinac was influenced by the Gilded Age, a term first used in the 1920s, and derived from the novel of the same name by Mark Twain and Charles Dudley Warner.[6] Published in 1873, it rightly satirized a degree of corruption and political greed of the era to come. The "Gilded Age" referred to "gilding the lily," or attempting improvement on what is intrinsically beautiful. As for the very rich in America, the tendency to spend outlandishly became widespread. Yet it is well to recall that this age, dating from the 1870s roughly to 1900, also fostered steps forward in the nation, both in manufacturing and in philanthropy. There were those like Daisy Peck Blodgett who chose to use their personal wealth to advance social reform. She would contribute breakthroughs in areas of childcare for orphans. After marriage to Delos Blodgett, she also supported the movement for women to have the vote, and together with Stella King, she made great strides on Mackinac in education and healthcare.

The sudden wealth in the Gilded Age saw entrepreneurial Americans spending their money on second and even third homes. The Blodgetts, who settled on Mackinac as summer residents in the mid to late 1880s—with Daisy arriving in 1893—were no different in this respect.[7] The couple had homes in Grand Rapids, in Florida, and for some years, two cottages on Mackinac. They were but one example of the influx of cottagers who built magnificent Victorian houses on the East and West Bluffs. Referred to as cottages, many had five to nine bedrooms, servants' quarters, buttresses, towers, and large wraparound porches with views of the Straits of Mackinac. These Gilded Age families contributed to the economy of Mackinac in multiple ways, ranging from their regular employment of carpenters, painters, plumbers, builders, dray deliverymen, and other services. The Blodgetts and other early cottager families needed groceries and horse care, and many, like Daisy's daughter, Helen Blodgett, were regulars at the early talkies downtown, and engaged in luxury shopping on Main Street and dancing at the Grand Hotel.[8] That hotel, built in 1887, along with the Island House and Hotel Iroquois catered to the upper class and to the many tourists beginning to visit the island.

The people of Mackinac in the 1890s and early twentieth century worked hard to promote the fledgling tourist trade and to maintain the island's core year-round community. It was a precarious balance, and the infrastructure of school and community could have vanished if not for women like Stella King, Daisy Blodgett, Rosa Webb, Helen Erwin, Helen Puttkammer, Ruth Camp, Ling Horn, and many others who were determined that the island not become a mere tourist attraction. As represented by Blodgett and King, that dedication started in the 1890s, in the nexus of the Gilded Age and early twentieth century.

Stella King

She is remembered for her unstinting sacrifice as a nurse on Mackinac. Stella King was the only medical professional on the island for many years. King treated patients for every kind of malady and was the island's chief midwife. Islander Dwight Lapine affectionately remembers: "I am one of Stella's brats. And that's what she jokingly called those of us she delivered into the world." Dwight was one of hundreds of infants on Mackinac whose mothers enlisted King's help during pregnancy and for medical assistance in a number of ways.[9] Trish Martin, proprietor of the Bogan Lane Inn and a columnist for the *Mackinac Town Crier*, recalls that when she was growing up, the kids at school were intimidated by Stella's glowering presence. "She came into the island school and gave the students their immunization shots. Like it or not," Martin admits, "it was a good thing Stella King was there for us."[10]

King did not know Daisy Blodgett when she first came to Mackinac in 1920. It would be a few years before the fifteen-year-old became acquainted with Rosa Webb or the Puttkammers, newspaper editor Ruth Camp, Helen Erwin, and more of the movers and shakers on the island. By 1920, Daisy, at age fifty-seven, and Rosa, sixty-seven, had made major inroads in the areas of education and music, the island horse culture, and community space for the young people. Soon enough, Stella, whose youthfulness belied a sharp mind, demonstrated her awareness of the community spirit among the women of Mackinac.

Stella was born to Lucy and Frank King in Gould, Michigan, in the Upper Peninsula. Late in my research for this book, two islanders approached me with their understanding that King was Anishinaabe. They were not sure of her specific band or of any other detail of this fact. Nonetheless, I paid attention and went to work. Cross-referencing the U.S. Census with the Wisconsin Census yielded discoveries. It emerges that Emerica Desjardins, the wife of Paul Aslin, was Stella's maternal great-grandmother. The census of 1880 reports that Emerica was "living with son Peter in Newton, Michigan. She was Indian." Though Emerica may have spent little time on Mackinac, many of her descendants did live or work there. There are recorded deaths and burials on the island of her maternal great-grandfather and grandfather, along with her grandmother.[11] The U.S. Census has an unclear account of Emerica, one that conflicts with earlier records in Mikana, Wisconsin (Barron County). The national Census states that Emerica was born in Quebec, and there is no mention of her as a Native person. It was commonplace for vague censuses in the 1800s to sometimes conflate a wife's birthplace with that of her husband. Joseph Asselin, Stella King's great-grandfather, was born in Quebec, and it is probable that the male-dominated census of the time simply wrote down Emerica's birthplace as Quebec if it was easiest to match it to that of her husband. The 1880 census in Wisconsin has Emerica listed in the Odawa community of Menaka as a sixteen-year-old girl when Joseph Asselin traveled there, most likely as a trapper. The records show that he married her when she was sixteen in the Catholic church in Menaka, a fully Odawa settlement. In all likelihood, Emerica was born in that Odawa community, and this explains the Wisconsin census affirming her Native identity. Additionally there is no mention of Emerica's parents in any census record, and sadly it was not unusual to omit documentation of Anishinaabe parentage.

Initial research indicated that the King family's first contact with Mackinac occurred when she was fifteen. However, further examination revealed that her island ties go back four generations. Although Stella King did not speak of her heritage when she was alive, it may be helpful to remember that she lived at a time (the twentieth century) when Native people were made to feel they could not speak of their past. Assimilation was fierce towards the end of the nineteenth century and did not abate until late in the twentieth.

The tiny hamlet of Gould was situated between Hiawatha Forest to the west and Sault Ste. Marie to the east.[12] Today, between 350 and 400 people live in Gould City, but the pioneer town had an even smaller population in 1905, the year of Stella's birth. It was a lumber town founded in the 1880s, and Frank King, Stella's father, may well have worked in the lumber industry along with his chief occupation as a fisherman. There was no port at Gould, but plenty of makeshift docks that provided access to Lake Michigan. The fishing industry in the Great Lakes was on the decline, but the King family survived as best they could. It must have been a great relief when he and Lucy moved the family to Mackinac. He was one of the last commercial fishermen on Mackinac, and though the business was struggling in the face of Mackinac becoming a tourist town, Frank was determined to make a go of it.

In her teens, Stella was immediately taken with island life; after growing up in rural Gould, it was a pleasant surprise to live in a bustling island community. The King family home sat at the edge of town on the corner of French Lane and Market Street.

Given the small population of Mackinac, Stella would have known a number of girls from island families. She attended classes at the Thomas Ferry school, also known as the Indian Dormitory, as it was built by Jane and Henry Schoolcraft, who envisioned the wood structure as a boarding house for Native people.[13] At school, she may have struck up a friendship with the children of Minnie Carson, who had taken "charge of the Mackinac Hotel" several decades earlier, or with the family of

Rose Webster.[14] Rose was the owner of the Island House hotel on the east end of town. It is also likely Stella was well acquainted with the May family and their candy store on Main Street. As a teen she became fast friends with Antoinette Early, whose family had the old Dousman farm at British Landing.[15]

In King's early years on Mackinac, the mixed-race population had shrunk, but the Ojibwe and French Canadians were still an essential island presence. After the decline of the fur trade, the Indigenous and French heritage people became the backbone of the fishing industry. Beginning in the 1840s, Mackinac merchants purchased the fishermen's catch, and one half of the market from Buffalo throughout the Great Lakes was centered on Mackinac.[16] In a thirty-year span, the trade increased "from 2,000 barrels to 250,000." A record in the early 1880s states that the fishermen "were all Indians and French men," but the history further reveals that this mixed-race group "lived in a state of barbarism and misery, and in some instances, quite slaves to the traders."[17] It is likely that by 1920, an independent fisherman like Stella's father, Frank, did not have to answer to those "bred to civilization," who went "beyond the restraint of laws. They were the worst class of men scattered among the most inoffensive and defenseless [the Native and French Canadian fishermen], and needless to say they let slip no opportunity of plundering them."[18] The traders boasted of taking fish from the barrels of Native people at night, on "a fishery where a dozen Indians were engaged," and when the plundered families were "reduced to starvation" the traders furnished them with credit, and "On these debts they [the fishermen] were frequently sold."[19]

It is probable that Stella King, as the daughter of a fisherman, had overheard something of this ruinous treatment and poor health of the earlier generation in her father's industry. Witnessing life on Mackinac, where the residents had few healthcare resources, was a driving force behind her desire to enter nursing school. That the King family had their own home on Market Street and finances that would permit them to send Stella off-island to nursing school indicates they were better off than the previous generation of fisherfolk. She and her colleague Antoinette became nurses about the same time, and of the two, only King stayed on as a nurse on Mackinac. Though she would leave for two winters to work for the Blodgetts in Washington, DC, it appears as if her plan had always been to remain on Mackinac for the better part of her career.

In the days when Stella was growing up, there were only itinerant doctors attending the island. With a small winter population, many physicians looked towards cities on the mainland for their year-round practices. When she first moved to Mackinac in the 1920s, the Post Hospital was occupied in the summer months by Dr. L. L. McArthur, but come winter it was nurse King in residence. By the 1930s, Dr. James H. Bogan became the island's physician. Islander Rosa Webb writes several letters worrying about Dr. Bogan's absence during the winter. Many like Dr. Bogan kept up a summer practice on the island and went elsewhere for more patients the rest of the year. When a doctor was on-island it was not always easy to get hold of him. We are told by Webb in a letter dated 1933 that when a doctor was needed, the patient had to alert Bailey's Drugstore, which then followed up on finding the necessary medical assistance.[20] Perhaps the drugstore in town had pony express types who rustled up both the doctor and Nurse King.

The Depression years saw a great many strong women living on Mackinac. Marie "Toots" McGulpin, with roots from early settlers on Mackinac, was born on the island in the early 1930s. Like the protagonist Anne, in the novel of the same title by Constance Fenimore Woolson set on Mackinac, Toots loved the outdoors and took every opportunity to go tobogganing and ice skating. She also traveled by dog sled, the family dogs sleeping in their burrowed dens outside in the snow. Yet she also grew up working hard at a number of chores in order to help her family survive the financial crisis that had affected the entire nation.[21] In winter, it was her job to go out on the frozen Lake Huron and cut up chunks of ice to be stored on the docks for use in summertime. In addition to ice harvesting, Toots had another regular job of cleaning the soot that caked the inside of her family home. This soot buildup was not unusual in a house that depended on heat from its coal stove. It was not a given that every resident's stove could be fired up all the time.[22] Irene Bunker Rickley is another Mackinac woman who recalls the relief she felt on the day coal was delivered. Irene knew the joy of those particular deliveries when once again she felt the warmth of the stove flood her family's house.[23]

Mackinac has made a name for itself making and selling fudge, and there were a number of women in that business who would have known Stella King and Daisy Blodgett during the Depression years. Emma Angell and Cora Phelps were a successful team whose candy store, Angell & Phelps, highlighted their "Spotless Kitchens" and "carefully packed" goods for mail orders. Their store, located on Main Street, was known for its professional appearance and mouth-watering pralines, fudge, and hand-dipped chocolates. They opened in 1914 and weathered the Great War and Depression years, keeping their shop open until 1941. After thirty-seven years in business, they sold their candy-making equipment to Gould and Verna Murdick, with the latter opening her "Verna Murdick's Candy Shop." Both Daisy and her daughter,

Helen, had a strong sweet tooth and were often customers in these downtown candy shops. King, as an owner of several buildings, would have been acquainted with the fudge proprietors as well. Stella and the Blodgetts also knew the Mays, another family of fudge makers on Mackinac. Ethel May handed down the skill of candy making to her granddaughter Tienne of May's Fudge in the later generation.[24] While many of the downtown shops were forced to close during those years, it is a testament to the women running these candy shops that they kept the sweet tooth alive on the island, while bolstering the overall economy.

By 1936, Rosa Webb recorded that Dr. Bogan had died, and afterwards the healthcare on the island became precarious.[25] He was succeeded by a number of doctors in a revolving door, but in the following years King was the only consistent healthcare practitioner on the island. Most of the temporary doctors were neither as skilled nor committed as Dr. Bogan. When Daisy's daughter, Helen, had a cut in her leg that would not heal, the druggist dispensed and administered medicine for her. The kicker was that he asked her not to tell the temporary doctor of his ministrations. It seems that both patient and druggist did not trust the current visiting physician.[26] As the population grew during the summer months, there was a greater need than ever for a medical center with up-to-date equipment and a staff to assist in emergencies and basic illnesses.

King was not only a nurse, but the forerunner of another hugely popular event. King and several friends, including Ling Horn, started the first Lilac Day parade on Mackinac, a phenomenon that has become a great draw for visitors on a state and national level. Mackinac is made up of mostly limestone soil, which is what these flowering bushes thrive in. A one-day spectacle with horse-drawn floats in its early years has grown into a nine-day annual festival. It is a worthy display for an island whose unusual quantity of lilacs turns its bluffs and downtown into a dazzling garden each June.

The initial event in 1948 did not exactly constitute a parade. A combination of ideas contributed to the present-day celebration. Stella had spent two winters working for Daisy Blodgett in Washington, DC, and after returning to life on Mackinac she retained a strong memory of the stunning cherry blossoms in the nation's capital and the festivals that celebrated them.[27] When King Beauty Salon on Mackinac was looking for a way to advertise their business, the nurse remembered the decorative cherry blossoms and realized that brilliant flowers had the capacity to draw attention.[28] She got hold of a friend's horse and wagon, decorated the buggy with lilacs, and drove it up and down Main Street with a sign to promote the hair salon. This incident was hardly a float in a parade, but it gave other businesses on the island a good idea. Suppose they created an annual parade where you could have a float that promoted your business. They asked Stella to help them with this plan, and she and Ling Horn were happy to oblige. King recommended that they set the date for the parade each year when the different strains of lilac were at the height of bloom. The first full-fledged parade in 1949 was so successful that it was repeated each year and has since grown into a festival with marching bands representing high schools from the state of Michigan and Canada, clowns and other acts, along with gorgeously decorated horse-pulled carriages.

The Lilac Parade is but one of King's many accomplishments. Her business sense was well-respected. Growing up, she and her family lived on French Lane in downtown Mackinac. Eventually her parents would move their modest house, setting the structure back from the street.[29] A female nurse's wages were low at this time, and as a single woman Stella was always looking for ways to supplement her income. After the death of her parents, she sold their house and became interested in a far larger home with a barn across the street. The house was owned by a family in mortgage arrears; the timing was right for Stella, and she bought the place for a low price. The nurse realized that her new barn and expansive garden were an ideal location for another business venture. She offered part of her yard to the independent carriage tours and taxi teams when they needed a place to hose down and water their horses.[30] A raised cement pavilion with a watering setup was arranged, to the mutual satisfaction of both parties.

Ever entrepreneurial, she turned part of her house into a rental property, which gave a home to shop owner Ruth Clark for several decades beginning in the 1940s. Stephanie Crane remembers spending half her summers with her "downtown grandma," Mrs. Clark, and the other half with her grandmother who lived in a large cottage on the West Bluff—another example of the ways in which the small island knit together its different social strata.[31] King also bought the building that housed Clarice McKeever Haynes's fine art studio on Main Street, and Dorothy's Zack's Picture Shop. Though she is best remembered as a nurse who handled every kind of medical emergency, her business acumen contributed to the economy of Mackinac during the Depression and in the following two decades. After Stella became the only nurse in Dr. Joe Solomon's practice in the 1950–1960s there were plenty of crises. One that stands out is the catastrophe of the *Cedarville*, an ore boat that collided with another ship. In that emergency, Stella King was on hand to treat the surviving crew members, who were suffering from hypothermia.[32]

King was a woman equally at home with hawking goods and with being a medical nurse. To Mackinac councilwoman Kathleen Hoppenrath, who worked for Stella at the Medical Center for three years, the nurse gave invaluable practical advice. "She took me in hand," offers Kay. "One bit of wisdom was: 'Never lay a hand on a patient.' Another was: 'Never tell a patient that it will be alright, because you don't know that for sure.'" From practical nurse to cookbook author, Stella could be found very early most mornings hauling a stack of her cookbooks in a red wagon to each and every store downtown in the hopes that they would sell a few publications for her.[33] In her multiple professions Stella King could be dour, she could be stern, but Mackinac's island nurse demanded of others the same high caliber of hard work that she exemplified.

Daisy Peck Blodgett

Born in Georgia, Daisy Peck was a mere infant in her family's home on the fashionable Peachtree Street in Atlanta when she and many others were evacuated in the Civil War.[34] After it had fallen, parts of the city were in flames. This was November 1864 during General William T. Sherman's famous "March to the Sea." The Peck family managed to reach safety in Augusta. Though Daisy grew up mostly in Atlanta, having returned there with her family immediately after the Civil War, she would eventually represent a unity of the North and the South. She married an abolitionist from Michigan, and though there is no way of knowing what her thoughts were about being raised in a slave-owning culture, it is likely—given her marriage to Delos A. Blodgett—she understood that our nation's greatest shame has been slavery, the most horrifying wrong inflicted on human beings.

In the decade after the war, she went with her father, Professor William Henry Peck, and lived at their home in the Bronx, New York. Peck was a well-known author of historical novels, including *The Flower Girl of London*, a forerunner of Eliza Dolittle in George Bernard Shaw's *Pygmalion*. Most of Peck's books and articles were published by the *New York Ledger*.[35] Following their years in New York, Daisy moved to Cocoa, Florida. The Peck family had been plunged into financial ruin, which prompted her to start up a boarding house along with her sisters. At age twenty-nine, she met Delos Blodgett, and married him a year later. She would spend much of the following fifty-odd years in Michigan, shuttling between Grand Rapids and Mackinac.

Delos was not only a successful lumberman, but had founded the Michigan towns of Hersey, Evart, and Baldwin, and contributed to the economic growth of Muskegon and Grand Rapids. He was one of the first men in Michigan to give women jobs in his lumber camps. He donated generously to the Catholic Church and often had pastors and church leaders from different denominations over to dinner. Delos was one to say: "I believe in one world at a time," meaning that he was an agnostic. It is likely he was friends with Frederick Douglass, as both were strong supporters of the women's movement (friends with Elizabeth Cady Stanton and Susan B. Anthony), and the two men were also members of the "Freethinkers," a nineteenth-century organization that rejected institutionalized religion. Douglass was close friends with the Freethinker leader Robert G. Ingersoll, as was Delos, who hosted Ingersoll twice to speak in his Grand Rapids home.[36] That Delos accepted Daisy's more religious turn of mind and encouraged church leaders to debate and speak their minds speaks to his open-mindedness.

As for Blodgett's support of the Women's Suffrage Movement, he met with Elizabeth Cady Stanton and Susan B. Anthony a number of times as their friendship grew. Anthony refers to him as "Dear Mr. Blodgett," and thanks him for his support when she spoke to a mostly unreceptive audience in Detroit in 1869, and in Traverse City ten years later.[37] Photos show him flanked by both historic women. Delos was an activist and donated ample funds to the cause. Eventually Michigan would be one of the first three states in the union to ratify the Nineteenth Amendment.

Daisy was proud to have married a man who believed in equal rights for women and African Americans. Delos is but one example, along with other husbands in this story of Great Lakes women, who believed in gender equality. Moreover, the intergenerational connections have a reach that extended from Boston to Mackinac, and from suffragists to businessmen. Elizabeth Cady Stanton attended Margaret Fuller's popular "Conversation" classes in Boston,[38] and years later the suffragist would pose for a photo at the Seneca Falls Convention with her good friend and supporter Delos Blodgett. Delos, who was married to Daisy Blodgett, had fallen in love with Mackinac Island just as Fuller had. As summer residents on the island, it is also likely the Blodgetts had read Fuller's *Summer on the Lakes*.

One trait that both Blodgetts shared was their strong inclination to give aid to those who had less than they. Yet it was not an easy transition when Daisy first moved to Michigan with her new husband. She had been a single woman until she was thirty, one who rowed for miles to get mail and groceries for her family in the often-roiling Indian River in Florida, ran the family boarding house, and was the chief caretaker of her father after her mother died.[39] Daisy Peck found her way to Mackinac Island in unusual circumstances. The widower Delos A. Blodgett, who had lived many years in Grand Rapids and built himself a fine home on Mackinac, lost his first wife, Jennie S. Wood, and fell into despair. After some time, and looking for a change of scenery, he traveled south to Florida. One afternoon while taking his daily constitutional along the Indian River near the town of Cocoa, he spotted a dramatic sight. It was a day of high winds and threatening clouds, but there was a young woman paddling alone in a canoe, battling whitecaps. Despite the waves, Daisy Peck was carrying an oar to a man who had lost his paddle in the middle of the river. Delos Blodgett claimed that she appeared to him quite like the heroine Grace Darling. Grace was a lighthouse keeper's daughter who became famous after performing daring sea rescues of many sailors off the Northumberland coast in England. The lumberman watched as Daisy delivered a paddle to the fair-haired young man capsized in the broad river. After the rescue, Delos came forward on the shore, complimenting her and introducing himself. When he learned about "The Peck House" for boarders, the lumberman wangled a room there as a paying guest.

In short order, he was completely smitten and felt compelled to find a way to keep seeing Miss Peck. He returned to Mackinac two weeks later, but the following year he was back in Florida proposing to Daisy. It is likely that the state of her family's finances contributed to her acceptance of marriage to a man more than twice her age. It is not known exactly what the cause was for the family's downturn in fortune, but memoirist Helen Blodgett Erwin, daughter of Daisy, was told that her grandfather William Henry Peck had turned to the bottle in his later years and mismanaged the orange grove business into which he had sunk a good deal of the family fortune. Additionally, there was a severe drought that nearly decimated the groves. Trying to recoup their losses, the family purchased a boarding house. Like Mark Twain, whose biographers point out the fabled writer's folly in a failed printing enterprise, Professor Peck should have stuck to his writing. His popular novels had been published serially by the well-known editor Robert E. Bonner, of the *New York Ledger* weekly newspaper.[40]

Daisy had always seen herself as a writer like her father, and while still in Atlanta she wrote and published a nonfiction piece in the *Atlanta Constitution* based on her experience surviving a hurricane. The disaster took down half the hotel in which she was staying on Sullivan's Island off the coast of South Carolina.

Henry Grady, the editor and founder of that venerable newspaper, had encouraged Daisy's writing and published several of her human-interest stories. Despite this promising start, Daisy's career as a professional writer did not flourish. It is known that her father discouraged another daughter, Myrtis, from an acting career, though she was said to have talent. It is possible he discouraged Daisy as well. Nonetheless, she maintained her prowess with the pen in the many speeches she wrote and delivered for the orphanage she started and the hospital she and Delos built for the Grand Rapids community.[41]

Daisy would oversee charitable causes in the service of cities or towns wherever she lived. Soon after the boarding house in Florida opened for business, she and her sisters came up with a plan to help the town of Cocoa Beach. As there were no sidewalks in the sand-ridden town, Daisy and her sisters conceived of a literary contest to raise funds for the walkways needed to get around. A year later, owing to the fundraiser, the sleepy Florida town saw its first sidewalks. That early community venture may well have been the start of her philanthropic and civic-minded career.

After Daisy and Delos were engaged, they began to discuss wedding plans. He was a Michigan man, and she wondered why he was so adamant that they marry in New York City, where he had spent little time. At last he spoke of what was behind this decision: "It is best if no one knows about the ceremony right now. My family and friends will learn that we are married soon enough." Further prodding from Daisy revealed a disturbing detail. "I am sure my children will come around," Delos said to her, "but I will tell you that when I wrote my son, John, of our nuptials he was extremely judgmental."[42]

Indeed he was. John had sent a telegram saying, "Father, I seriously hope you change your mind about this folly. At your age, you ought to be planning how you will be buried, not married."[43] Ignoring his son, Delos and Daisy were married at Grace Episcopal Church in New York on June 3, 1893. From their first days together, he often spoke of Mackinac Island, where he had built a house on the bluff above the Grand Hotel. Listening politely, Daisy had only an abstract sense of the place. Immediately following the wedding ceremony, the pair traveled in his private railroad car to his home in Grand Rapids. He hoped his two grown children would accept the marriage now that the deed was done. He felt certain they would fall in love with his bride's warmth and intelligence. But John and Susan refused to speak to her. Both were older than Daisy, and appalled that their father had gone through with the wedding to a woman almost forty years younger. In response, Delos addressed his finances. He made changes ensuring that his daughter would immediately receive one third of his fortune, his son another third, and he and Daisy the last third, which they would live on.[44] The children took the money but remained stone-faced where their new stepmother was concerned.

Grand Rapids was a conservative place in the Gilded Age, and with Susan and John influential in dictating social acceptance in the city, Daisy found that she was ostracized, not admitted to society in this northern setting. By nature a gregarious person who had engaged in community life wherever she lived, this was hard to bear. She turned to her horseback riding skills that had first been honed growing up in Atlanta. Every day she rode sidesaddle and took in her new surroundings in the city. What she learned in the upcoming months was that there was an untold number of underserved and homeless children in Grand Rapids. She and Delos had often spoken of building a large home for the needy children of the city. Members of society may not have invited her to their dinner parties, but they listened to Daisy's ideas for this first substantial orphanage, especially since those ideas were backed up by her pocketbook.

When not working on her new healthcare plans, she paid more attention than before to Delos's descriptions of Mackinac. Daisy's rejection from society encouraged her interest in this island in the Great Lakes. She was frankly eager to escape Grand Rapids for a while. Since the publication of books by Harriet Martineau, Margaret Fuller, and Constance Fenimore Woolson, along with the establishment of the Grand Hotel four years earlier in 1887, Mackinac was fast attracting tourists and well-off Americans to its shores. Travel by rail to the northern shores where one could climb on a ferry and cross the lake to Mackinac in forty minutes made it more accessible than before.

Once again she boarded her husband's private railroad car, but this time she and Delos traveled to northern Michigan. It was a fall day when summer lingered in the air, and Daisy was enchanted by the harbor, the little fort, and the town. Together the pair rode in his vis-à-vis carriage from the boat dock up past the Grand Hotel to the West Bluff. The Blodgett cottage, Isala Bella, had been designed with a barn-shaped roof, as dictated by Delos. He had been a farmer before his success in the lumbering business, and he favored an homage to that style. Unfortunately, Susan Blodgett Lowe, Delos's daughter, had been living in the house that summer, and when she saw Daisy at the front door she burst into tears. Her husband came forward and said to Delos, "If you take this cottage from Susan, you will break her heart."[45]

Realizing that the cottage held many memories for Susan, Daisy gently took her new husband by the arm and led him away from the magnificent home. "Dear, why don't we walk up the road a piece and see if we can find our own plot of land, a spot where we can build a cottage and let Susan stay at Isala Bella."[46] Her intrinsic kindness and diplomatic skills in the fore, she persuaded him to buy the place at the end of Pontiac's Trail. Their new property was a grand sweep of land with a small house on it, and ample ground behind it where they might eventually build a barn. Keeping the original kitchen area intact, they enlarged the cottage and named it Casa Verano. Once settled, Daisy's civic bent reared its head. She embraced the island, and with her keen curiosity she investigated its people and their needs.

Her summers on friendly Mackinac gave her courage to continue tackling crucial healthcare projects in Grand Rapids, and in years to come those on the island. Together she and Delos worked on the Grand Rapids orphanage project. He died before the planned orphanage was completed, but Daisy would see the project through and become the first president of the D. A. Blodgett Home for Children. The headline of the *Grand Rapids Herald* in 1908 read: "Mrs. D.A. Blodgett, new President of the Blodgett Children's Home, to be dedicated next Saturday." Daisy was pictured with her three children, and the article noted that "Mrs. Blodgett is a woman of great ability and unusual executive qualities. She doubtless will be a very strong and efficient president." The paper mentions that she is carrying out the work in which he "was so deeply interested."[47] She is also credited with being a star designer and interior decorator with the children in mind. It is an "old rose brick" with trimming of white terra cotta, and inside "close attention to harmony of color" and all furnishings. Even the dishes are chosen to be "pleasing to children."

The dedication ceremony of the D. A. Blodgett Children's Home published in the *Grand Rapids Herald* featured this headline: "The D.A. Blodgett Home Now Shelters the Little Waifs of Fortune." Flowery language aside, including references to the "nameless foundlings," a speech made at the time of the orphanage's opening reception highlights Daisy Blodgett's "untiring efforts."[48]

During the time she was the first president, the D. A. Blodgett Home for Children attracted national attention when it established a breastfeeding program. The infant feeding clinic was so successful that infant mortality was halved in the upcoming years.[49] When four outbreaks of scarlet fever arose in 1911, the orphanage board spent $100,000 in research to address the grave problem. It was lauded as the first study to be made of such an epidemic. Again, Daisy's leadership in these areas garnered attention on a national level. Though Blodgett had anticipated living a wholly quiet life on Mackinac after her busy involvement downstate, she would be drawn into community action that improved lives.

Daisy Day and the First Medical Center: Blodgett and King

How Blodgett joined forces with Stella King is a story unto itself. The professional connection between these two women was based on their mutual experience with healthcare and a keen desire to bring a medical center to Mackinac. To appreciate their connection—one between town and bluff, in many respects—it is helpful to look at the ambience of each setting. The life of Stella and other downtown residents has been discussed, but the summer cottagers, specifically Daisy, beg a short description. No better one can be offered than the words of one who lived in such a setting. In a letter to F. G. Hammit, Helen Blodgett Erwin describes the entertainment at a dinner party at her home, Casa Verano, where all the guests were handed a bundle of wood wrapped up in a ribbon. Each guest was to throw the tinder into the flames of the large fireplace and tell a short story while the wood burned. Also recounted was the manner in which "Mrs. [Daisy] Blodgett enjoyed parties which stimulated good conversation." Apparently this included competitions for telling ghost stories. At Casa Verano that evening, one Allyne Stocking won the prize for her "blood curdling" tale on August 12, 1894.[50]

Sitting atop the cliff walk of the West Bluff, the cottage belonging to Daisy and Delos boasts singular woodwork inside, both upstairs and down, and in its ten bedrooms. The long wraparound porch in front of the house gave Daisy and her family expansive views of little Round Island and the Straits of Mackinac.[51] Magnificent though it was, the surrounding grounds of this cottage and others in the Victorian Age often had a near rural look, indicating something of the rough-and-ready pioneer spirit behind the building of these homes. Unlike today's manicured look of the West Bluff, lawns were cut infrequently, and there is a photo of Delos Blodgett in 1898 with a scythe in hand and surrounded by tall grass in front of Casa Verano. Another shows a young Helen Blodgett on a horse in the same front lawn overlooking Lake Huron. She is happily oblivious to the high grass her horse stands in. From the cottage where the family lived, it was a pleasant walk or bike ride down the first hill past the Grand Hotel and onward into town.

Despite Helen Blodgett Erwin's documentation of the cottager life of the Blodgetts and a handful of newspaper articles mentioning Daisy Blodgett's work in Grand Rapids from 1893 to 1913, records of women's accomplishments in American communities were scant. Yet the institutions created by women speak for themselves: the library, the community center, and the medical center. Each of these were founded by, and labored on by women that include Stella King, Daisy

Blodgett, and Rosa Webb. While Webb and Blodgett lived through the Civil War years and the Victorian Age, their accomplishments on Mackinac came largely in the twentieth century. It was then that they assumed first glimmerings of equality that permitted them to move into action for Mackinac. Women may finally have gotten the vote in 1920, yet there were a multitude of other areas in which they were excluded. Until the early 1970s, for instance, they were often denied access to essentials as basic as credit cards.[52] No matter what station in society, women were the outsiders in multiple ways: they were second-class citizens and victims of discrimination. In the face of these ongoing disadvantages, many like Stella King and Daisy Blodgett applied innovative ways to secure civic landmarks. Their different economic status did not undermine their determination to work together as a philanthropic team.

On Mackinac, Daisy Blodgett was instrumental in her work for the library and for bringing to prominence a key element of horse culture, but she is best remembered for her ability to raise money for the establishment of a medical center. Her initiative and hard work was noted over the years, especially in the Mackinac papers. One reporter, Katherine Doyle, called attention to "The Daisy Day Charity" being named for Daisy, and going strong some fifty years after it was begun.[53] Blodgett ran the charity for more than five years on her own.

It was an emergency that brought Daisy and Stella together and signaled their eventual teamwork for the much needed healthcare. In the 1930s not everyone on Mackinac had a phone, and serious medical alerts on Mackinac were sent through Bailey's Drug Store. On the morning of September 10, 1936, Daisy Blodgett put through a call to the store, and Stella King and Antoinette Early were sent for immediately.

We can picture the two nurses rushing out of Bailey's, barely stepping outside when Jimmy Brady, the gregarious coachman for the Blodgett family, called out:

Miss King. Miss Early! Over here, the Vis-à-vis.[54]

Their professional status was easily recognizable. They wore white uniforms with high collars as starched and stiff as those worn by clergy. As reported by Daisy, Stella often pinned on a small brooch at the top of her long buttoned dress.

Antoinette's cap stood upright, while Stella's sat back on top of her luxurious chestnut hair, which was in a knot under her hat. The pair had been friends for years.

Several horse-drawn taxis and tour buggies lined up past the drug store, a sign that business had improved once the worst of the Depression years had passed. People were desperate for work, and Jimmy Brady was grateful for his new position as coachman at the Blodgetts'. The elegant carriage, a victoria (vis-à-vis) with two seats facing one another, stood out among the hackneys and gigs like a Cadillac among Corollas. When the two young women climbed in, Jimmy, who sat up front, would have craned his head around to make sure they were safely seated. According to Helen, the coachman was not one to ever slap his lines on the horse's back. He spoke softly to his horse, lifting his lines slightly to get the animal moving. As one keyed into humane treatment of animals and people alike, Stella may have noted that the whip remained in its socket as the carriage trotted along Market Street, heading out of town.

The friendly Brady spoke at once of the emergency to Stella and Antoinette. The news that the doctor had already been to see Mrs. Matthews would be conveyed, and perhaps Mrs. Blodgett's concern as to how long the newest physician on the island would last. It would not be surprising if Brady had expressed his appreciation of the pair of nurses in his carriage. Nursing in America had only begun to earn the respect it deserved during and after World War I.

It is likely that the quiet Stella King kept her eyes glued on the cow pasture to the right that the carriage was passing as it climbed the steep bluff hill and headed towards the Grand Hotel. Even if she was determined not to speak to this fellow, her outspoken friend, Antoinette Early, had other ideas: "What happened to Mrs. Matthews? Is she about to die or something?"[55]

No doubt Brady knew enough to stop speaking of the situation. It was up to Mrs. Blodgett to give the details about her sister. The horse trotted past the long porch of the hotel. It is unlikely the pair of nurses came this way often. The carriage passed eight huge Victorian homes and rounded the corner at Pontiac's Trail. Beyond that short first hill, three picturesque stables immediately came into view, each one on the right belonging to the cottages to the left on the cliff walk. The coachman was closely associated with all three, and if asked could have cheerily offered up information such as "That red barn is oldest, and it's used by visitors at White Birches, the guest house for Mrs. Blodgett. The next stable belongs to Cragmere, the home owned by Helen Erwin, Mrs. Blodgett's daughter. The last one here is our barn, and Mrs.

Blodgett saw to it that it was built back in the last century. She's been part of some 'barn committee' on the island. She loves her horses, I'll say that!"[56]

When they pulled up to Casa Verano, King may have braced herself for meeting Daisy Blodgett in her own home. The two had sat on some of the same island committees, but Stella had scarcely held a conversation with her, and she may well have assumed Mrs. Blodgett was a lady often on her high horse, quite literally. If Stella had seen her on horseback, Daisy was sidesaddle, wearing a black riding habit, top hat, and long skirts swooped over on one side of the horn. Given the outward trappings of privilege, it would not be surprising if King figured that here was a woman without a care in the world.

When the nurses knocked at the front door, the butler on duty would have approached from within, the light from the mullioned windowpanes catching the lapels of his coat and making them shine. Tucker had worked for Daisy nearly two decades and was married to Ollie, the pantry maid. He had a haughty demeanor and may well have stared briefly before speaking. Though service people came to the back pantry entrance, he would have quickly discerned that these were the nurses Mrs. Blodgett had called for. Tucker dressed in a morning suit every day of the year. His shirt cuffs showed approximately two inches beyond his jacket sleeves and he wore a high collar. Ella, the laundress, starched both collar and cuffs for him, and each morning he put on his long dress coat over the white shirt and black pressed pants. This man appeared tall even though he was not quite five foot ten.[57]

The great room Tucker led people into had extraordinary woodwork. Spiral-and-fan-designed carpentry adorned the spacious stairway. Brass and Tiffany lamps hung on the walls. If King wondered what would happen next, she had no cause to worry. Daisy Blodgett would have appeared shortly. She was an older woman with an ample figure and a warm and open face. On this occasion, her clear gray eyes most certainly registered grief. Hardly the woman Stella would have seen whisking through the woods on her tall horse.

Perhaps there was a sodden, embroidered handkerchief balled in one hand as Daisy explained that Myrtis, her sister and faithful companion, had suffered a stroke. Supporting Daisy at this time was Helen, who had closed up Cragmere, the cottage next door, and come to stay with her mother. If she had come downstairs, she may have stood politely, the play of light on the fretted woodwork as Daisy introduced her to Stella and Antoinette. Given the family emergency, Helen's morning ride was probably postponed but not canceled. She was no sidesaddle rider, and crop in hand, she liked to dress in wide, pleated jodhpurs and to ride astride. She was tall and sturdy with intelligent brown eyes. It's possible her mother was let down that Helen was riding at a time like this, but with a wan smile, she would have led King and Early in to see Myrtis.

Myrtis Peck had survived the Civil War and the downturn of her family's fortune. When she married Charles Matthews, a cotton broker from Charleston in 1886, she believed her fortune had improved. Yet after his death from consumption two years later, she discovered steep debts accrued by Mr. Matthews. She struggled alone for a number of years, making occasional visits to Daisy on Mackinac and in Grand Rapids. At the death of her husband, Myrtis became financially dependent on the Blodgetts. After the death of Delos in 1908, she came to live permanently with Daisy. Though she had occasional bouts of depression and wrote movingly in her journal of missing Charles for the rest of her life, Myrtis was gamely active most of the time. She lived at Daisy's stately residence in the Dupont Circle section of Washington and at Casa Verano when the family went to Mackinac for the summer season. A volume titled *Colonial Families* describes her as Daisy's "companion and assistant in all her social, philanthropic and patriotic undertakings." Further, it states that both sisters are said to be "indefatigable workers in the uplift of humanity." Daisy is noted further for her patriotic duty during World War I, working the canteens. She is praised for equestrian expertise, her illustrious husband, and three lovely children. Her participation in the League of American Pen Women is duly noted. If Myrtis was mostly left in the dust in this account and felt slighted, she is careful not to show it, even in her daykeeper journal.[58]

Daisy was an independent woman, a widow for over twenty years when King came to work for the Blodgetts, caring for Myrtis full time in 1936. Both Blodgett and King had emerged post–World War I and during World War II as action women in their communities. During the Second World War, Blodgett turned her home in Washington, DC, into a care center for wounded soldiers. As a dedicated air warden, Blodgett was awarded a red insignia at a ceremony in the Capitol.[59] As for Stella King, she was the indispensable nurse for Myrtis for two years in Washington, and later, on Mackinac, she became the health practitioner everyone depended on.

Women had gained more freedoms in this pre- and postwar era, but there was still inequality, especially between the monied class and those without. Looking at the journals of Myrtis Peck Matthews and Helen Blodgett Erwin exactly one year before Myrtis suffered a major stroke, we can see this distinction. Of note is Helen's casual, privileged take on life as opposed to Myrtis, who is concerned with domestic and monetary matters.

Sisters Myrtis and Daisy had known years of financial worries. Though Daisy Peck eventually married into money, her early personal experience had taken her from a life of comfort living with the Peck family in Atlanta, to a position of great financial uncertainty in Cocoa Beach, Florida. The boarding house she owned and ran with her sisters was not doing well when Delos Blodgett appeared in her life. She was strongly encouraged by her sisters to accept the offer of marriage by lumber baron Delos. Still, she was a hard worker and it wasn't easy to give up her independence, even when confronted with her family's financial uncertainty. After their union, she supported a number of her relatives for the rest of their lives. Delos himself had been a pioneer, both as an explorer in Michigan territory, a farmer, and a lumberman. He grew up in a modest cabin in Vermont with a father who was an itinerant farmer. His family moved often and finally settled in the Chicago area.

In contrast, Delos and Daisy's oldest daughter, Helen, was a child of the Gilded Age and never experienced her parents' hardship. She went to Mackinac the first time in 1895, the year she was born, and in 1921 she and her husband, Henry Parsons Erwin, bought the cottage next door to her mother on the West Bluff. Helen was a poet whose published work appeared in *Vanity Fair* magazine and numerous publications in Virginia, where she lived for the last twenty years of her life. She was also a memoirist who wrote much about her life on Mackinac. Her journal entries give a social history of Mackinac from the point of view of well-off cottagers, including Daisy Blodgett, during the Depression. During the 1930s, the Blodgett family retained enough assets to hold on to their wealth. Nonetheless, Helen's Aunt Myrtis remembered what it was like to have very little. The diary of the two women on Mackinac in 1935 elucidates the disparity between Helen's perspective and that of her aunt.

Day by Day Journal, 1935
Myrtis Peck Matthews
June 26—

Left Washington at 6:00 P.M. for Mackinac Island with Tucker, the butler, Ollie—pantry maid, Hattie—cook, and Mattie, the parlor maid. Very hot in

Washington and was so tired and lonely when I got on train and said good bye to dearest Daisy. Hated to leave her when she has so much to do.

Daykeeper Journal, 1935
Helen Blodgett Erwin
July 1—

> Left at 11:45 for Mackinac. Mother and I, and two maids, Butts and Katie

Servants in the upper classes were often addressed by their last names by employers. Butts was the family's sewing maid. The first names of Tucker, the butler, and Butts, the sewing maid, have not been found.

Helen traveled that year from Detroit to Mackinac with her young children and Daisy on the steamer *Octorara*. The young ones, Eileen, Hope, and Hal, enjoyed a ventriloquist show on board, and the entire family participated in bingo and a deck-golf tournament.[60]

July 1—Myrtis

> Very busy getting everything to look fine for Daisy's arrival tomorrow. Mona and I took a nice walk and gathered flowers. We had Mrs. Orton and Mrs. Butler to dine with us tonight. I am feeling so well and am sleeping splendidly.

West Bluff cottager Ruth Orton Camp lived in a Victorian home with a view of the Straits of Mackinac. Camp is notable as the dear friend of Daisy's daughter and the future editor and publisher of the *Island News*, a forerunner of the longstanding Mackinac newspaper the *Town Crier*.

July 2—Helen

> Arrived in Detroit at 7:30. Left for Mackinaw at 8:05. Hot long trip, and then the Algomah left us! Came over at 10, on a yacht.

Here is Myrtis's observation the same evening:

July 2—Myrtis

> We expected Lee, the new coachman and all the servants, horses, dogs, and Polly, but they did not arrive 'til 7 o'clock, and we were quite disappointed that Daisy and Helen failed to catch the boat, however they came over at ten on a private yacht.

Note Myrtis's qualification of this ride to the island: the "private" yacht. She is always aware of wealth in her surroundings, whereas Helen, born into it, is not.

July 3—Helen
Lovely ride. Sorel is full of beans! I like him.

July 3—Myrtis
Helen riding her fine $1000 horse, Sorel, for the first time. And driving her new horse, too.

It was early in the following September of 1936 that Myrtis had a major stroke. Helen writes about the fall emergency, including descriptions of Stella King and Antoinette Early coming to nurse the patient. Some occasions were more exciting than others. Helen documents one: "I took care not to go too far into the woods alone as a bear had been seen on the island. This was a most unusual occurrence. In fact, no one remembered quite when a bear had been there before, but it was thought the animal had crossed over from the mainland on the ice and had hidden on the island.

One night when the doctor was driving Nurse King up for her evening shift, a bear rose suddenly out of the bushes at the side of the road on one of the streets leading from the village to the cottages. The horse bolted, only being restrained with great difficulty from a runaway. After that, the horse would never go down that street again. Also, garbage cans had been found turned over and trash strewn near that area. Everyone knew that the bear had been there."[61]

Yet nothing—not even a bear—deterred King's sense of medical responsibility. For a month she dutifully attended her patient on Mackinac. The medical emergency of Myrtis's stroke was enough of a major incident on the island that the *Republican-News and St. Ignace Enterprise* wrote about her departure from Mackinac with her sister, Daisy, and Stella King and Antoinette Early:

October 15, 1936
One of the state ferries made a special trip to the Island early Monday morning to convey Mrs. Myrtis Matthews and relatives to Mackinaw City. Mrs. Matthews suffered a paralytic stroke a month ago at the summer home of her sister, Mrs. Daisy Blodgett, and was in a critical condition at the time of her departure. Accompanying

Mrs. Matthews to her home in Washington, D.C. were her sister, Mrs. Blodgett, a niece, Mrs. Henry P. Erwin [Helen], and two nurses, Misses Stella King and Antoinette Early, who have been attending Mrs. Matthews since she became ill.

It was a chilly October day when Daisy and Stella, with Myrtis in tow, boarded the ferry at British Landing. Antoinette Early was not with them, although stated as such in the newspaper. As for Stella King, she had accepted Blodgett's offer to be the full-time nurse for Myrtis, and to the spend the winter in Washington, DC, at Daisy's home on 16th and P Streets.

King had spent five weeks at the cottage on the West Bluff and was surprised by the approachable Mrs. Blodgett. She saw much evidence of the good works the older woman had been up to for most of her career, especially on Mackinac. Mrs. Blodgett had worked on the Community House and the first library with Rosa Webb. Most interesting to Stella was her employer's annual charity, Daisy Day: the charity event aimed at garnering enough funds for a much-needed medical center on the island. Given Stella's knowledge that no such building and equipment to house doctors, nurses, and patients existed, she was thrilled to hear that such a project was afoot. During this period, between her nursing and Daisy's worry over her sister in the next two years, the pair did not sit down often and discuss the future of this hopeful medical center.

Towards the end of King's second winter in Washington, her charge suffered a massive stroke and died. Daisy assured Stella that a fleet of doctors could not have taken better care of Myrtis. A month later, King returned to duties as a nurse on Mackinac.

Late in the summer of 1939, Daisy and Stella had an important meeting. They had connected regularly downtown on the Library Committee, rummage sale, and Community House business with Rosa Truscott Webb and other island women. This was different, though it is possible Stella had mixed feelings about returning to Casa Verano—too many memories of poor Myrtis Peck Matthews crowding her brain. At that meeting, no stately butler opened the door as when King first came to the cottage. It was simply Daisy, all smiles. Daisy, no longer her employer but a friend who cared deeply about the community of Mackinac. They sat in the sunroom at Casa Verano, a sweeping view of Lake Huron before them. The Mackinac Bridge would not fill this picture window until 1956. Perhaps Ollie wheeled in a trolley for tea, and the two compatriots enjoyed some of Hattie, the cook's fine nut bread with cream cheese and cucumber tea sandwiches. What is known is that Daisy spoke of her worries regarding the state of her annual event, Daisy Day. It had gotten off the ground and yet did not raise the monies expected. She described the catchy slogans she'd used to attract public interest in her charitable causes in Washington and for the orphanage and hospital in Grand Rapids. She spoke of how Helen came up with the idea of using her own name as a moniker: Daisy Day. They had decided that the participants could wear a chain of daisies on the day of the event, and Daisy created a few stations with ladies in charge at tables out front, hoping people would stop to buy daisies. Helen had worked at the boat docks, and Mrs. Webb and Mrs. Schermerhorn at a couple of hotels, with the latter overseeing the funds.[62] Nonetheless, interest in the fundraiser for the medical center was tepid and not enough money had been raised.

Stella had spoken up immediately. She had two ideas. First, she vetoed the plan of simply asking people on Daisy Day to buy daisies, stating that there was no money in it. The nurse suggested that instead they gather and clean metal cans, the kinds filled with beans and other fruits and vegetables. They would decorate them with daisies and then appeal to children from Mackinac to carry the cans downtown and walk around asking for donations. Third, together Daisy and Stella decided to expand the one-day fundraiser, figuring that a three-day event would be far more effective for raising money. Islanders and tourists alike could not miss it.

The event that had started with Blodgett at the helm and Webb and Schermerhorn over at the Astor House grew into an annual three-day event that became a major fundraiser on Mackinac. Soon enough, Blodgett would devise a plan to have her grandchildren Eileen, Hope, and Hal, along with other island children, give pony cart rides to those who donated to the cause. Jocko, the Croghan family pony, was hitched to a two-wheel wicker governess cart stationed at the edge of Marquette Park right across from the grocery store. The children, along with adults in charge, were assigned different posts, either at the headquarters based at the Chippewa Hotel or in front of other establishments such as the Murray, Windermere, Island House, or Iroquois hotels. No matter that they had to dress up in their Sunday best. This writer remembers wearing a frock, a straw hat with a band, and white gloves when driving the pony cart full of tourists from Doud's Market to the end of the yacht dock. It was a short cart ride, but donations poured in from the passengers.

The plan to involve children in the cause worked. From its inception, many adult islanders were involved in Daisy Day as well, including "Mrs. Keith Lines, and Miss Elizabeth Flanagan. At the Grand Hotel, Mrs. W.S. Woodfill; Mrs. Armin Rickel," and many others at the downtown hotels, with "Mrs. Rosa Webb" stationed at "old

Fort Mackinac" and "Mrs. Henry Erwin at the docks." Consciousness was raised and enough money in the upcoming years to build a medical center and facilities for year-round healthcare.[63] Helen Erwin records one of those early days in her daykeeper on August 21, 1936. She mentions those on her team: "Daisy Day: Rose and I sold daisies all day on the State Dock and smaller docks. Had long chats with Helen Puttkammer and Helen Porter."

Ironically, the event of the major stroke suffered by Myrtis that brought Stella King and Daisy Blodgett together had been yet one more healthcare emergency on Mackinac where no medical center was available. Yet memorably, these two women from different classes in the Depression years put their heads together to create positive community change. "Daisy Day" became a more viable fundraiser than it had been previously, one that resulted in Mackinac's first medical center. The expanded fundraiser grew into a popular island tradition that continues today.

Mackinac Horse Culture

A horse culture generally refers to a group of people whose close connection with horses involves breeding or herding. Horse culture on Mackinac means something altogether different. On this island, there is continued use of horsepower to do the work of the community that in most parts of the world has been given over to mechanization. In keeping with communities that forge a daily working relationship with horses, Mackinac society depends on horses for a livelihood.

Businesses sell the experience of riding a rental horse, driving a buggy, or being driven around in a horse-drawn taxi or carriage tour. The entertainment value is high for tourists. Equally popular, though not for monetary gain, is the privately owned horse for pleasure riding.

It wasn't until the sixteenth and seventeenth centuries, when the Spanish conquistadors introduced horses to the Native Americans, that they began to ride. The animals were used for trading and hunting, and very quickly they also became a spiritual symbol for many tribes. Horses were first ridden north of the Detroit area when Antoine de la Mothe Cadillac brought three horses there in 1704. In short order they were used to pull up stumps and were harnessed for the lumber business and rented out to others who needed horsepower. Some twelve thousand horses were on the streets of Detroit, along with more than eighty stables by 1894.[64]

As for the horse culture on Mackinac in the Victorian era and early twentieth century, no discussion would be complete without attention paid to Anishinaabe riders. For over a thousand years, and well before Europeans discovered Mackinac, Indigenous people lived on the island and revered it as a holy place. Though they did not have horses in their early days there, the noble steed would eventually become a significant part of their lives. Harrisonville, or the village, as it is commonly known, has had a population of Anishinaabe who have their own horses. Today they ride Western or English, and like many growing up on the island, whether living in the village, the town, or on a bluff, there are those who enjoy cantering bareback and taking their horses into the lake for a swim. The Bazinaw family had horses, both for pleasure riding and for business. Milt Bazinaw owned a successful dray line for a decade and was a familiar sight driving his team and delivering groceries, hay, and other goods. Another Native resident, Don Andress, who grew up in the 1930s, came to be known as "Chief Mackinac" and rode his horse Babe in the Lilac Parade each year.[65]

Those in the village who were not Anishinaabe loved their horses as well. The extensive Cowell family rode daily and made a team of horses the heart of their livelihood. Like Milt Bazinaw, the Cowells owned and drove a dray line. The elder Mr. Fuller Cowell, living on Mackinac in the 1920s and 1930s, was a farrier as well. With his traveling anvil and mobile forge, he shod horses downtown and on the bluffs. Eventually he passed on his business of the service dray company to his son, Reuben. Whether it was Reuben Cowell or Milt Bazinaw delivering goods the island over, the connection of horses and their service was felt from the bluffs to town, from Daisy Blodgett to Stella King. In using her yard as a base to water teams of horses, King became familiar with independent taxi drivers and the Chambers family, whose carriage horses made ample use of her water trough. The Chambers own and run a successful taxi and carriage-tour company today.

The ban on cars that has resulted in the horse-and-carriage transportation on Mackinac has long been a draw to visitors. This unique feature would not have occurred if not for dedicated horse lovers. Prominent among equestrians on the West Bluff at the turn of the century was Daisy Blodgett. Long before motorized vehicles were officially banned on the island, Daisy nurtured a pleasure-riding horse culture on the island. An expert rider, she believed—along with most islanders—that Mackinac was too small to sustain cars racing down its streets and that the tradition of horse and carriage should be made law. To get around, visitors and residents alike could easily walk, ride bikes, or rent a horse-drawn taxi. If they were equestrians, they could lease, rent, or buy a horse as well.

Needing a stable for their horses, summer residents Delos Blodgett, Alexander Hannah, and John Cudahy wrote a letter in 1889 to the quartermaster general in Washington, DC, requesting a lease to build on the back lots of their properties on Mackinac.[66] The barn for Delos's family cottage was built within the year, primarily with the view of housing a driving horse or two. After he and Daisy were married in 1893, she put forward the plan for another stable behind the new cottage where they lived. Delos was no horseback rider, but Daisy rode sidesaddle and drove her own phaeton and other carriages. This avid equestrian fostered a riding committee that encouraged the idea of leisure riding and enjoyment on the island. Once the Mackinac Island State Park was formed (three years after Casa Verano was built) the park encompassed a large part of the island and there was great potential for riding trails. In the succeeding years, Blodgett pushed for these trails to be made. Acquainted with Keith Lines, who owned the Grand Hotel Livery Stables, she suggested that he open a riding-instruction business. Under his able tutelage, many island children became young equestrians.[67] Daisy's own grandchildren Hal, Eileen, and Hope Erwin took lessons from him as well. With Mr. Lines as the major trail master, the Blodgett grandchildren created woodland paths on Mackinac, including Blodgett Trail east of British Landing Road.

Remarkable to many was the sight of Daisy riding sidesaddle on her seventeen-hand Morgan. She rode this way, both legs decorously hidden under long skirts and together on one side of the horse's flanks, in Atlanta, Grand Rapids, on Constitution Ave. in Washington, DC, and of course, on Mackinac. She could be seen on her horse Dan even in the last years of her life. Women had been riding astride since the early part of the twentieth century, but not Daisy. She rode determinedly sidesaddle as late as 1945. It was testament to her skill and stubbornness that she stuck with a tradition she'd practiced since 1875, when she first began to ride as a young woman. It is no overstatement to say that uninitiated visitors to Mackinac were thrilled to see a lady in the 1940s sail by in full riding habit, cantering in the ostensibly precarious sidesaddle fashion. The Blodgetts loved their horses and the island trails. They drove a variety of carriages to church, downtown to shop, and to the shore for picnics. Family rides were a daily event. Daisy, her daughter Helen, and even granddaughter Eileen never missed their morning rides. A way of life long past for most in this world. Yet this family and others on Mackinac shaped the culture of horses and riding, which have become a large part of the island's appeal and present-day tourist economy.

It was not easy for women to find a venue for community participation in the nineteenth and early twentieth centuries. Though the Daughters of the American Revolution (DAR) has not had an unblemished past, it became a service organization in 1890 that permitted women to assist in historic preservation and in the fine arts.[68] On Mackinac, Daisy Blodgett and two other members of the organization helped fund the creation of the first library on the island, named "The D.A.R. Library." A monument in Marquette Park also stands as testament to the work of this organization. An article in the *Island News* states: "Island Chosen by the DAR as 'Michigan's Most Beautiful Spot' and Commemorated by a Monument Honoring the DAR."[69]

Blodgett and King demonstrated initiative and ingenuity in their island community. They were blessed with enormous energy and steely determination; the ever-ambitious Daisy even learned how to swim when she was seventy years old, and in the icy Lake Huron to boot. It is not known whether Stella took up that gauntlet, but surely she was capable. King was known to be a hard worker and not one who took time off to kick up her heels. She is revered by islanders who appreciate that the right way is not always the easy way forward. This pair of leaders spearheaded committees to promote civic action on Mackinac. Whether working on ways to bring about a first library or the medical center, Daisy and Stella recognized the power of relationships to bring about constructive change.

Conclusion

The biographies in this study reveal thirteen women who laid the foundation of society on Mackinac. From their leadership roles in the fur trade to the areas of education, healthcare, and culture, these women were at the helm of organizing and safeguarding this island community in Great Lakes country. Beyond the scope of this work, there are numerous other women who have shaped the civic growth and welfare of Mackinac. Brief references to some deserve a mention here.

In addition to fur traders, philanthropists, writers, and healthcare advocates, there were also the outstanding hoteliers of the nineteenth century. Along with Rose Webster, proprietor of the Island House Hotel for forty-six years,[1] there was Maria Chapman, who owned the Lakeview Hotel for about twenty years.[2] The attractive building with an open wood-columned porch was built in 1858. Just two years later, Maria's husband Reuben died, and she assumed full management.[3] In the twentieth century, Jeanette Doud owned and operated the Windermere Hotel at the western end of Main Street. After Jeanette's death, her daughter, Margaret, became the manager. Notably, Margaret Doud has been mayor of Mackinac since 1975. Not far from the Windermere is the Iroquois Hotel on the waterfront. Margaret McIntyre took over ownership of the Iroquois after her husband, Sam, died. She had the good luck of having three daughters also involved in running the hotel until it sold in 2020.[4]

Ironically, it took the death or disablement of their partners for many of the Mackinac women to own and operate their businesses.

Regarding early hospitality industries on the island, recent scholarship reveals that black entrepreneurs Jeanette and Jean Bonga owned a hotel in the 1780s. The Bonga Tavern was situated on Main Street, and it was not the only African American enterprise on Mackinac. Approximately one hundred years later, Emma Ford and her husband, Joseph, managed a successful restaurant in the 1890s. This, too, was on Main Street.

Emma Ford's advocacy for civil rights and fight against discrimination toward women is well-documented. Yet her connection to Mackinac is a new discovery, one which director of Fort Mackinac, Steve Brisson, describes as "an incredible discovery." The Mackinac Island State Park has in its archives the only photos of Emma Ford. A negative of a portrait of her was found, along with a photograph of Ford holding her horse, which is hitched to a carriage outside her restaurant. The location on Mackinac has been identified; Ford's restaurant stood in the place of the present-day Chippewa Hotel.[5] She operated her restaurant on Mackinac, challenged Jim Crow laws in Michigan, and was president of the Phyllis Wheatley Club in 1907. No doubt Ford had read much of Wheatley, the brilliant African American poet.[6]

Ford was born Emma S. Warren in the year 1863, in Windsor, Ontario, and would later live in Grand Rapids and on Mackinac Island. In 1881, she married Joseph Ford, and in the years to come, she became the mother of two children. Joseph supported his wife's life work, and he belonged to an organization that fostered the belief in women's suffrage. In 1892, Ford was appointed as the superintendent of the Work Among Colored People in Grand Rapids.[7] It is likely that she knew abolitionist Delos A. Blodgett, along with healthcare advocate Daisy Blodgett, both residents of Grand Rapids at the time. Emma Ford emerges as a key activist, educator, and business woman on Mackinac and throughout the state.

Following the popularity of Constance Fenimore Woolson's *Anne* came *The Loon Feather*, a novel written in 1940 about the conflict of Native people and white traders on Mackinac. While Woolson made the island itself an alluring character in *Anne* and other work, Iola Goodspeed's vague depictions of the landforms and woods reveal that unlike Woolson she did not live on Mackinac or have accurate knowledge of its setting. Nevertheless, like *Anne*, this book became a national public success and raised awareness of Native contributions on the island.[8]

The 1940s also saw the first newspaper on the island published by a woman.[9] Newspaperwoman Ruth Orton Camp lived in a cottage on the West Bluff that looked out over the Straits of Mackinac. Her house and barn were on a stretch of road just beyond the cottages on the cliff walk. She lived around the corner from her good friend Helen Blodgett Erwin, daughter of Daisy Blodgett. Ruth and Helen rode together for decades, beginning in the 1920s. Both were married, and both were writers—Helen, a poet and diarist, and Ruth, a reporter. The two dearly loved a good story. While Ruth stayed busy at the island paper, Helen was a well-known raconteur on the island, no doubt keeping her good friend apprised of the news. Camp gave the local paper a lively character with articles that demonstrated an interest in history not seen in its earlier iterations. She inherited the *Mackinac Island News* from Roger Andrews, who started the paper in 1932. She had labored as a reporter there in the 1930s and was not often given credit for her articles.[10]

When Camp took over the *Island News*, it was ten cents a copy and published in Cheboygan, Michigan. She was its editor, publisher, and chief reporter. In her section on history, she made a point of recalling how the DAR assisted in discovering the burial place of Madeline Laframboise. By the 1940s when Camp and the DAR called attention to Laframboise, her very name had disappeared from public knowledge. Camp made a point of discussing how "Madam La Framboise who upon her husband's death, entered the fur trading business and shoulder to shoulder with the men of the times dealt with the old John Jacob Astor trading post."

Another Mackinac writer, Edith Hamilton, became an international success with her book *Mythology*, along with other landmark publications. Born in 1867, Hamilton's family built their cottage on Mackinac's East Bluff in 1888.[11] Edith and her sister, Alice, spent summers there when growing up. After attending Miss Porter's School in Connecticut and Bryn Mawr College, Edith became an educator at the latter. Her second career as an author came after retirement when she was sixty-two years old. In 1930, she published her first book, *The Greek Way*. With her successive publications, most notably *Mythology*, she became a household name and gained renown among those interested in the Golden Age of Greek history. She was a Book of the Month Club author; her clear and invigorating prose made the history and myths of ancient Greece and Rome accessible to readers.[12]

Edith was not the only genius in her family, for her sister, Dr. Alice Hamilton, was the first woman on the faculty at Harvard University. Industrial toxicology became her field of expertise, and she investigated the toxicology of specific chemical compounds and the high-risk effects of industrial metals. From their cottage porch, the Hamilton sisters must have appreciated the colorful sailboats and impressive freighters passing through the Straits of Mackinac. Such an expansive view might well have expanded their own sensibilities, contributing to this pair's gifts to the world.

The Hamiltons' connection to Mackinac reflects a long history of sisters who supported one another. Therese Marcot Schindler and Madeline Marcot Laframboise were certainly the most remarkable pair from the same family in the nineteenth century. Despite racism and general discrimination against women, these two rose to dazzling success. Margaret Fuller noted that although Native women on Mackinac carried "heavy burthens" in life, they also had the background experience to be self-sustaining, unlike many white women of the era.[13] From the nineteenth century through the first quarter of the twenty-first century, the connection of women with each other has been truly intergenerational. Laframboise and Therese were Anishinaabe and also sisters, as are present-day residents Brenda and Trisha Bunker. Like their historic forbears, the Bunker sisters consider community responsibilities to be an essential way of life. They possess a high bar of professional excellence in their given careers. Brenda, as manager of the island bank, and Trisha, as a co-owner with her son, Michael Gamble, of Gamble Construction, are descendants of a long line of Ojibwe men and women in the Great Lakes region.[14]

Caregiving connections abound as well. Nurse Stella King was the only health-care provider on Mackinac for many years and she delivered both Brenda and Trisha Bunker on Mackinac. Owing to King's expertise, Trisha survived a dangerous breech birth. She is a member of the Sault Ste. Marie Tribe of Indians and attends powwows with her daughter Madison on the mainland of Mackinaw City. Trisha's memories growing up on Mackinac include making woven baskets of sweetgrass and preparing deer hides to be used for leather moccasins and clothing.

It is an understatement to say that the women of Mackinac are multitaskers. There are those who sit on or head up institutions such as the Community Foundation, City Council, Medical Center, State Park, or Arts Council while parenting or working full-time jobs and engaging in outreach programs.[15] While there are many who dedicate themselves to the common good, my focus in these chapters has been on the women who paved the way, those who created the Mackinac community that we take for granted today. Our leaders of the past often braved the unknown in their effort to better themselves and those within their compass. They must be remembered.

Afterword

I grew up summers in a house that once belonged to Daisy Peck Blodgett, one of the women who figures in this book. That house, "White Birches," was my family home, but before I was born, it was Daisy's guest cottage. Daisy was also my great-grandmother, and it is fair to say that the Blodgett name and our six generations on the island have been etched into my psyche.

If a sense of place can be a guiding force, then certainly my lifetime familiarity with the island has served me well. Yet in my youth I trod the heights of Robinson's Folly, never realizing how Constance Fenimore Woolson gorgeously describes that setting in her book that became a national bestseller. I lollygagged along the shore road in front of Madeline Laframboise's home without a glimmering that she was a famous fur trader in the Straits region. As a girl, I participated each year in Daisy Day on Mackinac to raise funds for the medical center. I had no idea that it was Daisy Blodgett who established this annual community event and that she and nurse Stella King worked hard to make that first healthcare center a reality. When I was a college student working one summer as a tour guide at Fort Mackinac, I had not heard of Jane Schoolcraft, who lived on Mackinac for nine years. Yet she was the first Indigenous poet in America to write her verse in Odawa and then create English translations. This includes the original of the poem "Hiawatha."

If my script for giving tours in those days did not highlight Jane Schoolcraft, and my schooling did not include the achievements of Madeline Laframboise, we can be glad that today Laframboise has been inducted into the Michigan Women's Hall of Fame along with another great woman, Agatha Biddle. Yet their full histories on Mackinac, along with those of other island women had not been written. How my commitment to their stories arose stems from an unusual convergence of ancestor and accident.

By accident I mean a serious physical fall that put me in the hospital for twenty-two days. By ancestor, I mean Daisy Blodgett. Let me explain. Since receiving my PhD in 1992, I had recognized the dearth of written history on Mackinac women. I flirted with a plan to sit down and write a book about them, but like many ideas in the face of busy life, this one slid away from me. Then one August morning in 2015, I went for a ride down Blodgett Trail on Mackinac. After taking a jump, the gelding I was on reared, and I flew out of the saddle. The last thing I saw was the treetops. As I was lying unable to move on the hard ground with the horse tramping dangerously near my head, I hoped for rescue to the island's medical center. This was the institution that came into being owing to the hard work of Daisy Blodgett, and later Daisy and Stella King together. That realization (pondered more fully later) became the wake-up call to write this book, and never mind the irony of the name of the trail where I lay smashed and wondering if I'd walk again.

Thankfully, a couple of bicyclists discovered me and I was delivered to the medical center in town, where the doctor's x-ray machine found multiple fractures in the spine and news that my sacrum resembled a bag of crushed potato chips. I had broken my back. Put on a gurney, I was pushed through the packed downtown streets to the boat dock. I traveled on the ferry across Lake Huron to the mainland, where an ambulance was waiting to take me to a hospital in Petoskey, Michigan. After a seven-hour surgery and long months of rehab, I became committed to the valiant women whose courage I have striven to reveal.

Acknowledgments

This book would not have come into being without the support of Mackinac community groups and my longtime island peers. Every bit as essential to the life of this project are the historians I depended on. Their work provided me with the springboard to explore lives that mattered. First on that list is Edwin O. Wood, editor of *Historic Mackinac*, whose volumes I and II were given to me in 1972. As a young person, I was entranced with Wood's inclusion of such luminaries as Margaret Fuller, Constance Fenimore Woolson, Anna Jameson, Harriet Martineau, and Juliette Kinzie, all of whom left valuable records of their time on Mackinac in the nineteenth century. It would be decades before I went forward to make use of their essays, novels, and social histories, but their words had taken root.

Megan Marshall's remarkable biography of Margaret Fuller, and Ann Boyd Rioux's compassionate history of Constance Fenimore Woolson were key sources that led to my research into the dramatic roles of these women on Mackinac. Articles by Dave Armour on the early history of Mackinac were indispensable to me. I give thanks to Grace Armour, who put into my hands a strong essay on David and Elizabeth Mitchell, a Scotsman and Odawa woman who represent the diverse citizenship of Mackinac when it was a bustling fur-trading center.

In writing a history about the Indigenous and white women who established the island community, I have many experts whom I relied on. For the outstanding scholarship by Indigenous writers in the state of Michigan and the Great Lakes region, I thank Staci Drouillard, Margaret Nooris, Susan Sleeper-Smith, and Theresa Weller.

I am indebted to the Mackinac Public Library for inviting me in 2002 to give a lecture on the Blodgetts and their philanthropic action on the island. That talk for the authors series set me on the path to examine overlooked women of Mackinac and the Great Lakes. I would not have gotten far in my research were it not for the rigor of five years training at the University of Pennsylvania many years ago. Hours in the stacks and rare book room at Van Pelt Library gave me the research tools of patience and thoroughness. Scholars Peter Conn, Daniel Hoffman, and Elaine Scarry came to my rescue more times than they realize.

I thank Sue Allen, Lisa Craig Brisson, Judith Goodman, Mary Maurer, Anneke Myers, and Cordie Puttkammer for trooping over to my house one fall morning in 2015 to hear about my plan to have an exhibit and write about the Mackinac women who were early leaders. They offered immediate support and shared terrific ideas for my project. Also sharing their belief in this book are Stephanie Fortino and Stephanie McGreevy. A large thank-you goes to Kim and Stephanie Crane for sharing family photographs and memories of their island ancestors.

Once I began writing, Mackinac stories emerged. I appreciate the honesty and courage of my Anishinaabe island friends, whether surviving the Holy Childhood boarding school in Petoskey, or working hard today to support a family and contribute to the economy of Mackinac. They include Nancy Bazinaw Pfeiffelman, Ben Horn, Kathy Andress, Trisha Bunker, Michael Gamble, Brenda and Craig Bunker.

With great admiration, I extend a hand to George Goodman, former president of the Mackinac Island Community Foundation. Along with the Mackinac Arts Council, he sponsored my early work on the unsung stories of women. To Philip Rice, director of the Arts Council, I say, "You represent the open mind and heart, and the music you composed for Jane Schoolcraft's poems will not be forgotten." I am grateful for the counsel of Nicki Croghan and Pam Chamberlain, who urged me not to dash off a quick book on the intrepid women of my study. With that in mind, I began to dive deep, and found the perfect home for my project at Michigan State University Press. I received beneficial critiques from Keith Widder, who read much of my earliest draft. Anthea Croghan edited every chapter in the next iterations; her recommendations throughout were invaluable. Both Heather and Rob Kalmbach stepped in towards the end of my five-year rescue of the overlooked women of Mackinac. I am grateful for Heather's excellent and timely suggestions on the early chapters, and many thanks go to Rob and Tim Murray for assisting with the photographs. In the depth of a freezing winter day on Mackinac, one more photographer came to my rescue. Sara Wright rode her snowmobile across the island and took pictures in my house of two key nineteenth-century Anishinaabe women in the book.

I was fortunate indeed to have Julie Loehr as my first editor. She was an early advocate who shared her joy that this story is being told. Since her retirement, editor Catherine Cocks has guided me in context and content, and her clearsighted overview and critical nudges have overall strengthened my book. She has been patient and open-minded throughout the process. I give great thanks to her for championing my work. As for the post-editing stage, I am deeply appreciative of the production and marketing teams at MSU Press, including Anastasia Wraight, Bonnie Cobb, Nicole Utter, Elise Jajuga, and Kristine Blakeslee. Additionally, it was my pleasure to work on the maps with Ellen White, whose direct style is a joy to behold.

I thank the archivists who assisted me in tracking down letters, daguerreotypes, and other images: Caroline Schroeder and Carolyn Cruthirds at the Museum of Fine Arts, Boston; Page Harrington and Janine Napierkowski at Girl Scouts USA; Wenxian Zhang, Special Collections at Rollins College; and Christopher Coutlee from the Toronto Public Library. At the University of Michigan, I received able assistance from project archivist Caitlin Moriarty. Caitlin directed me to the only known image of Bamewawagezhikaquay, also known as Jane Schoolcraft, and to a stunning portrait of Ozhaguscodaywayquay.

For clarifying the public domain of Jane Schoolcraft's writings, I am grateful to Patrick Kerwin, manuscript reference librarian at the Library of Congress. Washington, DC, can be a damp and chilly place in winter, but not so in the Reading Room at the LOC, where I spent time and wish to thank manuscript librarians Edith Sandler and Lara Syzpszak for their counsel regarding the Henry Schoolcraft Papers. Trekking north, I visited Jane Schoolcraft's early home in Sault Ste. Marie, Michigan, and received an education from Bernard Arbic at the Chippewa County Historical Society. I appreciate his knowledge of the vivid portrait of Jane Schoolcraft's father, so carefully restored at the Detroit Institute of Arts.

On Mackinac, I give special thanks to Betty Bedour and the Mackinac Island Medical Center, which has been generous in allowing the images of Stella King to be shared. The Mackinac Island Public Library is ever gracious in lending the image of Rosa Webb for this biographical record. Island librarian Ann St. Onge gave able assistance, guiding me to the collection of early island newspapers and correspondence from the family of Rosa Truscott Webb late in her life. I thank Phil Porter for directing me to a collection of Webb's letters at the Petersen Center, and in getting involved in the detection work of finding where on earth Woolson lived on the island. At the Petersen Center, Brian Jaeschke, registrar of Mackinac State

Historic Parks, worked patiently with me to find the best possible photographs of the Mackinac houses belonging to Elizabeth Mitchell and Agatha Biddle, and he delivered photos and permissions of Mackinac women to me in record time. I value the ongoing support of the director of Mackinac State Historic Parks, Steve Brisson, especially his honesty and humor regarding the long process of my project.

A helpful early surprise in my research was Bethany Fleming's chapter "Mediating Mackinac" from *Gender, Race and Religion in the Colonization of the Americas* (ed. Nora Jaffary). I have also appreciated the many articles and goodwill of Mackinac's historian for the *Town Crier*, Frank Straus. Both Frank and Bethany have cheered me on when I most needed words of encouragement.

I am grateful to Eric Hemenway for introducing me to Regina Gasco-Bentley, the chairperson of the Little Traverse Bay Bands of Odawa Indians. We sat down together for several hours at the government council building not far from Mackinac, where I gained insights into the nuances of gender division of labor in Odawa history. Our conversation ranged from the travesty of the past to the striving for positive lives today, including tribal attention to violence towards women and the history of assimilation of Indigenous people. I am honored to have spent time with Gina and her assistant, Rebecca Fisher, who shared the beauty of the Firekeeper's Lodge with me.

I am grateful to my son, Rob, and my two daughters, Anthea and Heather. They, along with Tim Murray, my supportive husband, have stood by me on this journey. Their presence in my life means everything.

Notes

Introduction

1. Madame Madeline Laframboise may have learned to read but not write in the later years of her life. See chapter 1 for the brief history of her life.

2. The term *Indigenous people* refers to a First Nation, first people. Anishinaabe is the Indigenous name for their people in Canada and northeastern America. The different nations of Anishinaabe include the People of the Fire: the Odawa, Ojibwe, and Potawatomi.

3. Elizabeth Therese Baird, *O-De-Jit-Wa-Wing; or Contes du Temps Passe: The Memoirs of Elizabeth T. Baird* (Green Bay, WI: Heritage Hill Foundation, 1998).

4. A short description of Biddle may be found in the Michigan Women's Hall of Fame listing, and a more concerted discussion of her merit by Eric Hemenway of the Department of Repatriation, Archives and Records at the Little Traverse Bay Bands of Odawa Indians.

5. Margaret Fuller, *Summer on the Lakes* (Boston: Freeman and Bolles, 1844), 201.

6. Constance Fenimore Woolson, *Anne* (New York: Harper & Brothers, 1882).

7. Dwight Bazinaw and the sisters Brenda and Trisha Bunker are three Native residents on Mackinac today whom Stella King delivered. Mr. Bazinaw and I had phone interviews during February and March of 2019, and meetings on Mackinac Island in the summer and fall of 2020. I had helpful conversations with Trisha and Brenda Bunker in the summer and fall of 2020.

8. This information on Stella King sent me back to the drawing board (and the census records going back several generations in her life) to verify her hidden history of being Odawa. I thank islanders Kay Hoppenrath, Trish Martin, and Sue Allen for giving me a heads-up to

research the matter.

9. Michael A. McDonnell, *Masters of Empire* (New York: Hill and Wang, 2015); Keith R. Widder, *Beyond Pontiac's Shadow: Michilimackinac and the Anglo-Indian War of 1763* (East Lansing: Michigan State University Press, 2013). Both McDonnell and Widder make extensive study of the Native alliances that benefited them, particularly in war and battle strategy.

10. David A. Armour, "David and Elizabeth: The Mitchell Family of the Straits of Mackinac," *Michigan History* 64, no. 4 (1980): 17–29.

11. Kees-Jan Waterman and Jan Noel, "Not Confined to the Village Clearings: Indian Women in the Fur Trade in Colonial New York, 1695–1732," *New York History* 94, no. 1–2 (2013): 40. Although this observation references New York as opposed to the Mackinac region, there is every likelihood that women were hunting in the Great Lakes as well.

12. Madeline Laframboise, Last Will, March 2, 1846, Probate Court Records, book 1, Mackinac County Court, St. Ignace, Michigan. Also "Mackinac Register," Collections of the State Historical Society of Wisconsin, 20 vols. (Madison: State Historical Society of Wisconsin, 1855–1931), 12:162–63; American Fur Company Store Records, Mackinac Island State Park Commission, Mackinac Island, Michigan.

13. *Putnam's Magazine* ran in three linking iterations over a time span from 1853 to 1908. Its focus was American literature, science, art, and politics.

14. Woolson was close to her nephew Samuel Mather, to whom she wrote about her love of Mackinac. Chapter 7 in this study reveals her multiple communications and publications about the island. Sam and his sister, Kate Mather, would create a memorial to their aunt on the East Bluff, a beauty spot visited by many today.

15. Many of her communications reside in the Rosa Webb Collection of letters at the Mackinac Public Library, and the collection at the Keith Widder Library in the Petersen Center, Mackinaw City, Michigan.

16. John McDowell's article "Therese Schindler of Mackinac: Upward Mobility" mentions women traders other than Laframboise, including key players Susan Johnston in Sault Ste. Marie and Catharine Cadotte; *Wisconsin Magazine of History* 61, no. 2 (1977): 270–85.

17. Karen L. Marrero, *Detroit's Hidden Channels: The Power of French-Indigenous Families in the Eighteenth Century* (East Lansing: Michigan State University Press, 2020), xxi.

18. Marrero, *Detroit's Hidden Channels*, xxi.

19. Madeline Laframboise, Last Will, March 2, 1846; and American Fur Company Store Records, Mackinac Island State Park Commission.

20. A useful discussion of Native languages, including Athapascan, Uto-Aztecan, Chinookan, Siouan, and Algonquin, may be found in *The Norton Anthology of American Literature*, 5th

ed., vol. 1, ed. Nina Baym (New York: W.W. Norton, 1998), 7.

21. I have received valuable advice from members of the Anishinaabek Odawa Little Traverse Bay Bands, and closer to home (on Mackinac) oral interviews with those from the Sault Ste. Marie Tribe of Chippewa Indians, including Mike Gamble and his mother, Trisha Bunker; Brenda and her son, Craig Bunker. Also other Native friends and interviews on Mackinac with Jamie Andress, Kathy and Don (Chief Mackinac) Andress, and Dwight Lapine.

22. Margaret Fuller, *Woman in the Nineteenth Century* (Boston: John P. Jewett & Co., 1855), see p. 1590.

23. See Abby Slater's reference to this quote in her study *In Search of Margaret Fuller* (New York: Delacorte Press, 1978), 4.

24. Fuller, *Summer on the Lakes*, 250.

25. Anna Brownell Jameson, *Winter Studies and Summer Rambles in Canada* (London: Saunders and Otley, 1838); and Jameson, *Winter Studies and Summer Rambles in Canada*, ed. Paul A.W. Wallace(Toronto: McClelland & Stewart, 1923). Both editions were used for this study.

26. My chapter 5 provides a close study of how Anna Jameson became a witness of Schoolcraft's genius.

Chapter One. Elizabeth Bertrand Mitchell (1761–1827)

1. This quotation bringing Elizabeth to life with pertinent details of the event is mine.

2. Elizabeth Therese Baird, *O-De-Jit-Wa-Wing; or Contes du Temps Passe: The Memoirs of Elizabeth T. Baird* (Green Bay, WI: Heritage Hill Foundation, 1998), 17.

3. David A. Armour, "David and Elizabeth: The Mitchell Family of the Straits of Mackinac," *Michigan History* 64, no. 4 (1980): 17–29.

4. Ibid.

5. Ibid.

6. Susan Sleeper-Smith, *Indian Women and French Men: Rethinking Cultural Encounter in the Western Great Lakes* (Amherst: University of Massachusetts Press, 2001).

7. Fort Michilimackinac is a historic fort built in the eighteenth century by the French and later occupied by the English. It sits at the northernmost point of the Lower Peninsula of Michigan.

8. Armour, "David and Elizabeth."

9. Baird, *O-De-Jit-Wa-Wing*, 19–20.

10. Métis refers to an Indigenous group, the term coming into practical usage in the nineteenth century when many male fur traders married mixed-race women. Under debate is whether it refers to all mixed-race people who are the progeny of Native Americans and Europeans. See discussions of the etymology and use of the word in Jacqueline Peterson's "Prelude to Red River: A Social Portrait of the Great Lakes Métis," *Ethnohistory* 25, no. 1 (Winter 1978): 50; also in Richard White's *The Middle Ground: Indians, Empires, and Republics in the Great Lakes Region, 1650–1815* (Cambridge: Cambridge University Press, 1991), 230–31; Peter S. Schmautz's *The Ojibwa of Southern Ontario* (Toronto: University of Toronto Press, 1991), 48–49; W. J. Eccles, *Essays on New France* (Oxford: Oxford University Press, 1987), 50–54; and Keith Widder's *Battle for the Soul: Métis Children Encounter Evangelical Protestants at Mackinaw Mission, 1823–1837* (East Lansing: Michigan State University Press, 1999), 3.

11. Baird, *O-De-Jit-Wa-Wing*, 16–23. E. T. Baird takes great pains to describe the elaborate dress of the Native women at weddings on the island at the time.

12. David A. Armour, "Mitchell, David," in *Dictionary of Canadian Biography*, vol. 6 (Toronto: University of Toronto, 2003), 590.

13. Baird, *O-De-Jit-Wa-Wing*, 16.

14. Ibid.

15. Baird, *O-De-Jit-Wa-Wing*, 16. Though E. T. Baird states twice that Elizabeth liked to drive herself in a calash, it is likely that it was a somewhat different carriage than the one spoken of in the memoir. The standard calash was a two- or four-wheeled carriage that had facing passenger seats with the coachman or driver sitting up front.

16. Ibid.

17. Ibid.

18. Armour, "David and Elizabeth." These early Protestant missionaries would be followed by others, the most influential being Amanda and William Ferry. Reverend and Amanda Ferry established a mission and early school on Mackinac that ran for eleven years, 1823–1834. The Mission Church and school that the couple built are standing today.

19. While Elizabeth and David Mitchell's other sons left the island to pursue various careers, Daniel stayed on Mackinac to assist his mother with the day-to-day fur-trade business.

20. Baird, *O-De-Jit-Wa-Wing*, 17.

21. Armour, "David and Elizabeth."

22. Ibid.

23. Ibid.

24. Widder, *Battle for the Soul*, 57.

25. Henry Rowe Schoolcraft, *A Register of His Papers in the Library of Congress*, prep. Edwin A. Thomson and others, revised edition, ed. Harry G. Heiss (Washington, DC: Manuscript Division, Library Division, Library of Congress, 1999), box 2. David Armour notes in his article "David and Elizabeth" that Elizabeth Mitchell's son stayed on Mackinac as her assistant. Apparently, his assistance did not last. The papers of Henry Schoolcraft at the Library of Congress, "Indian Agent" on Mackinac, 1833–1841, reveal that Elizabeth's son William did not want to do "violence to his conscience" in the matter of giving alcohol to the Native American traders, and resigned from his mother's fur-trade business. William also spent considerable time helping George Johnston, the brother of poet Jane Schoolcraft, to get sober, yet another connection to the intertwined women on Mackinac.

26. Armour, "David and Elizabeth." It is not known which island church, Ste. Anne's or Mission Church.

27. Ibid.

28. John J. Bigsby, *The Shoe and the Canoe*, vol. 2 (London: Chapman and Hall, 1817), 147.

29. Dave Armour alludes to this possibility in "David and Elizabeth." For greater detail on smuggling in the Great Lakes from colonial times forward, see Edward Butts's premise in *Outlaws of the Lakes* (Michigan: Thunder Bay Press, 2004) that smugglers assisted in the victory of the British in the War of 1812.

30. Bigsby, *The Shoe and the Canoe*, 147.

31. Her grave on Mackinac has not been found.

Chapter Two. A Dynamic Family on Mackinac: Therese Marcot Schindler (1775–1855), Madeline Marcot Laframboise (1780–1846), and Elizabeth Therese Baird (1810–1890)

1. John E. McDowell, "Therese Schindler of Mackinac: Upward Mobility in the Great Lakes Fur Trade," *Wisconsin Magazine of History* 61, no. 2 (1977): 125–43.

2. Bethany Fleming, "Mediating Mackinac: Métis Women's Cultural Persistence in the Upper Great Lakes," in *Gender, Race and Religion in the Colonization of the Americas*, ed. Nora E. Jaffary (Surrey, England: Ashgate Publishing, 2007), 131.

3. Elizabeth Therese Baird, *O-De-Jit-Wa-Win-Ning; or Contes du Temps Passe: The Memoirs of Elizabeth T. Baird* (Green Bay, WI: Heritage Hill Foundation, 1998), 3. The memoirist Elizabeth T. Baird is particularly qualified to write about Laframboise. She spent a good deal of her youth in her great-aunt's home on the island and claims to have been

particularly petted and spoiled by Laframboise. Baird was a sharp observer of society and the postwar era on Mackinac.

4. Gurdon S. Hubbard, *The Autobiography of Gurdon Saltonstall Hubbard* (Chicago: R.R. Donnelly & Sons, 1911), 22.

5. In his article "Therese Schindler of Mackinac: Upward Mobility," John McDowell examines the success of both sisters, Therese and Madeline, and also cites other women traders, including key players Susan Johnston in Sault Ste. Marie and Catharine Cadotte. Regarding Madeline Laframboise's annual profits, see Collection 264, Grand Rapids Public Library, Grand Rapids, Michigan.

6. *Bruce M. White, "The Woman Who Married a Beaver: Trade Patterns and Gender Roles in the Ojibwe Fur Trade," Ethnohistory 46, no. 1 (1999): 109–47.*

7. Juliette Kinzie, *Wau-Bun: The Early Day in the Northwest* (Wisconsin: Menashba Publisher, The National Society of Colonial Dames, 1948), 9.

8. Editor Edwin O. Wood references the historian, Francis Parkman, and his discussion of Pontiac's conflict with Michilimackinac. Francis Parkman, *The Conspiracy of Pontiac and the Indian War after the Conquest of Canada* (New York: Macmillan, 1918), 723.

9. In the 1830s Jane Schoolcraft, the Ojibwe poet, certainly lived in a house on Mackinac; however it was the Indian Agency house, and she and her husband, Henry, did not own their home, as did Laframboise.

10. McDowell, "Therese Schindler of Mackinac," 270–85.

11. Fleming, "Mediating Mackinac," 131.

12. Anna Brownell Jameson, *Winter Studies and Summer Rambles in Canada* (London: Longman, Brown, Green, and Longmans, 1852), 26.

13. See Bruce M. White's article *"The Woman Who Married a Beaver" for a discussion of Anishinaabe women's work during the fur-trade era.*

14. Fleming, "Mediating Mackinac," 133.

15. Richard Perry, "The Fur Trade and the Status of Women in the Western Subarctic," *Ethnohistory* 26, no. 4 (1979): 363–75, 368.

16. Writing in the last decades of the twentieth century, Perry appears unaware that the word "Chippewa" was the European term for the Ojibwe.

17. White, *"The Woman Who Married a Beaver,"* 109–47.

18. Keith Widder, *Battle for the Soul: Métis Children Encounter Evangelical Protestants at Mackinaw Mission, 1823–1837* (East Lansing: Michigan State University Press, 1999), 11; Fleming, "Mediating Mackinac, 125–34.

19. *Mackinac Register*, Collections of the State Historical Society of Wisconsin, 20 vols. (Madison: State Historical Society of Wisconsin, 1855–1931), 12:162–63; American

Fur Company Store Records, Mackinac Island State Park Commission, Mackinac Island, Michigan.

20. See McDowell's article "Therese Schindler: Upward Mobility" and David A. Armour's "Marcot, Margueritte-Magdlaine (La Framboise)," *Dictionary of Canadian Biography*, vol. 7 (Toronto: University of Toronto Press, 1988), 582–83.

21. Widder, *Battle for the Soul*, 3.

22. McDowell, "Madame Framboise," *Michigan History* 56 (1972): 271–86.

23. Baird, *O-De-Jit-Wa-Win-Ning*, 19.

24. Ibid., 20.

25. Author's conversation with Regina Gasco-Bentley, chairwoman of the Little Traverse Bay Bands of Odawa Indians, 12:00–2:00 P.M., September 8, 2021, Government Tribal Center, Harbor Springs, Michigan.

26. Armour, "Marcot, Margueritte-Magdlaine," 582–83.

27. In her study of Agatha Biddle and other Métis women, Bethany Fleming discusses the quill work and extensive handiwork that the Native women carried forward into the culture even as they lived under the new American regime. Bethany Fleming, "Mediating Mackinac: Métis Women's Cultural Persistence in the Upper Great Lakes," in *Gender, Race and Religion in the Colonization of the Americas*, ed. Nora E. Jaffary (Surrey, England: Ashgate Publishing. 2007), 133. Juliette Kinzie echoes and amplifies these descriptions in *Wau-Bun*, 7–8.

28. Jameson, Anna Brownell. *Winter Studies and Summer Rambles in Canada*, London: Longman, Brown, Green, and Longmans, 1852. pp. 262.

29. Ibid., 313.

30. Author interview with Regina Gasco-Bently, September 8, 2021, Government Tribal Center, Harbor Springs, Michigan.

31. See McDowell's essays on Therese Schindler and Madame Laframboise referenced in this chapter: "Therese Schindler of Mackinac" and "Madame Laframboise."

32. Baird, *O-De-Jit-Wa-Win-Ning*, 19.

33. A sound description and history of the North West and Hudson's Bay fur-trading companies can be found in Ida A. Johnson's *The Michigan Fur Trade* (Grand Rapids: Michigan Historical Commission, 1919), 90–98; this study was reprinted in 1971.

34. Ibid.

35. Kinzie, *Wau-Bun*, 9.

36. Widder, *Battle for the Soul*, 9.

37. Hubbard, *Autobiography*, 22.

38. McDowell, "Therese Schindler," 270–85.

39. Ibid.

40. Fleming, "Mediating Mackinac," 130.

41. Baird, *O-De-Jit-Wa-Win-Ning*, 19.

42. Widder, *Battle for the Soul*, 6.

43. Edwin O. Wood, ed., *Historic Mackinac* (New York: Macmillan Company, 1918), vol. 1, *Churches on Mackinac*, 405.

44. Wood, *Historic Mackinac*, vol. 1, chap. 9, "Sketches from Schoolcraft's Diary at Mackinac—1835–1841," 228.

45. Keith Widder, "Magdelaine Laframboise: The First Lady of Mackinac Island," *Mackinac History* 6 (2007): 7.

46. Ibid.

47. Baird, *O-De-Jit-Wa-Win-Ning*, 19–20.

48. Widder, "Magdelaine Laframboise," 6, with first publication in "Historic Women of Michigan: A Sesquicentennial Celebration," Michigan Women's Historical Center and Hall of Fame.

49. Widder, *Battle for the Soul*, 62–66.

50. Ibid.

51. Margaret Fuller, *Summer on the Lakes in 1843* (Boston: Charles C. Little and James Brown, 1844), 250.

52. "Donation of Indian Chiefs to Madelon Laframboise," April 28, 1823, Henry S. Baird Papers, State Historical Society of Wisconsin.

53. In *Winter Studies and Summer Rambles*, social historian Anna Jameson gives numerous examples of Indigenous people on Mackinac and in Sault Ste. Marie who have converted to the Presbyterian or Catholic faith but still honor their Native beliefs. See expanded discussion of, in chapter 5 of this study.

54. Fleming, "Mediating Mackinac," 130.

55. Fuller, *Summer on the Lakes*, 250.

56. McDowell, "Therese Schindler."

57. Susan Sleeper-Smith, "Women, Kin, and Catholicism: New Perspectives on the Fur Trade," *Ethnohistory* 47, no. 2 (2000): 423–52.

58. Mary C. Wright, "Economic Development and Native American Women in the Early 19th Century," *American Quarterly* 33, no. 5 (1981): 525–36.

59. The business of furs has been replaced by the tourist trade, with upward of 7,000 people—cottagers, seasonal workers, and visitors—in the summer season.

60. McDowell, "Therese Schindler."

61. John Jackson, *Children of the Fur Trade: The Forgotten Métis of the Pacific Northwest* (Corvallis: Oregon State University Press, 2007). Though Jackson writes about Native

women beyond the Great Lakes, his study rings true for many Indigenous people in the nation.

62. In Karen Marrero's *Detroit's Hidden Channels: The Power of French-Indigenous Families in the Eighteenth Century*, she analyzes the plight of Marie Magdelene, whose ethnicity was erased from record, and gives useful revelations on Indigenous marriages ([East Lansing: Michigan State University Press, 2020], xxi–xv).

63. Theresa L. Weller, *The Founding Mothers of Mackinac Island: The Agatha Biddle Band of 1870* (East Lansing: Michigan State University Press, 2021).

64. Author's conversation with Regina Gasco-Bentley, chairperson of the Little Traverse Bay Bands of Odawa Indians, September 8, 2021.

65. Baird, *O-De-Jit-Wa-Win-Ning*, 22–23.

66. Ibid.

67. Ibid., 5.

68. Records are inconsistent regarding the exact date of George Schindler's death, but it is thought to be circa 1825. He was stepfather to Therese Schindler's only child, Marianne Fisher, and he and Therese adopted Lucy and Martha Tanner. He was described as incapacitated some years after his marriage to Therese, and she took over and grew their fur trade and initiated a maple sugar business on Bois Blanc Island.

69. McDowell, "Therese Schindler."

70. Baird, *O-De-Jit-Wa-Win-Ning*.

71. McDowell, "Therese Schindler."

72. Baird, *O-De-Jit-Wa-Win-Ning*, 10.

73. Ibid., 12.

74. Ibid., 13, 34.

75. Ibid., 37.

76. Ibid., 73.

77. Ibid., introduction.

78. The following chapter on Agatha Biddle in this study takes up the dramatic cultural war experienced by her daughter, Sophia, during this religious tussle on Mackinac.

79. Baird, *O-De-Jit-Wa-Win-Ning*, 39.

80. Ibid., 1.

81. Ibid.

82. Ibid., 139.

83. Ibid., 26.

84. The Selkirk or Red River Colony was set up by Thomas Douglas, 5th Earl of Selkirk in Scotland. This was a Hudson Bay colony.

85. Weller, *Founding Mothers*, 106.

86. Baird, *O-De-Jit-Wa-Win-Ning*, 29.

87. Ibid., 31.

88. Weller, *Founding Mothers*, 107.

89. Henry and Elizabeth Therese Baird Papers, 1798–1937, Wisconsin Historical Society, Wisconsin, Mss. 5, box 1, folder 9.

90. Baird, *O-De-Jit-Wa-Win-Ning*, 31.

91. Wood, *Historic Mackinac*, 2:237–38.

92. Pontiac's War refers to the attack on the British that occurred in June 1763 when the Ojibwe found a way to enter Fort Michilimackinac, through the game of *baaga'adowe*, an early form of today's lacrosse.

93. Madaline Laframboise, Last Will, March 2, 1846, Probate Court Records, book 1, Mackinac County Court, St. Ignace, Michigan, 23–25.

Chapter Three. Agatha Biddle (1797–1873)

1. Lynn Armitage, "Mackinac Island Finally Telling Native Side of History," https://indiancountrytoday.com/archive/mackinac-island-finally-telling-native-side-history.

2. Armitage, "Mackinac Island Finally Telling Native Side."

3. Bethany Fleming, "Mediating Mackinac: Métis Women's Cultural Persistence in the Upper Great Lakes," in *Gender, Race and Religion in the Colonization of the Americas*, ed. Nora E. Jaffary (Surrey, England: Ashgate Publishing, 2007), 131, 133.

4. Records of the Bureau of Indian Affairs, Record Group 75, Special File #156: Biddle, Agatha, testimonial for Samuel Abbott, Michilimackinac, October 19, 1837, National Archives of Canada, preliminary draft transcription.

5. Elizabeth Therese Baird, *O-De-Jit-Wa-Win-Ning; or Contes du Temps Passe: The Memoirs of Elizabeth T. Baird* (Green Bay, WI: Heritage Hill Foundation, 1998), 22.

6. Fleming, "Mediating Mackinac," 132.

7. Baird, *O-De-Jit-Wa-Win-Ning*, 22.

8. Keith Widder, *Battle for the Soul: Métis Children Encounter Evangelical Protestants at Mackinaw Mission, 1823–1837* (East Lansing: Michigan State University Press, 1999), 63.

9. Baird, *O-De-Jit-Wa-Win-Ning*, 24; Widder, *Battle for the Soul*, 16.

10. Fleming, "Mediating Mackinac," 125.

11. Keith Widder, in *Battle for the Soul*, emphasizes that Métis like Josette Pierce, who married an American officer, would have been "the exception rather than the rule" in the "rigid

social circle of Fort Mackinac" (63).

12. Nathaniel Philbrick, *Mayflower* (New York: Viking, 2006), chaps. 7 and 9.

13. Darren R. Préfontaine's well-researched history of the Great Lakes Métis takes us through the eighteenth century, and while the Métis population increased in the nineteenth century, the same problems of not fitting into the Euro-American culture prevailed. Darren R. Préfontaine, *Metis Legacy: A Metis Historiography and Annotated Bibliography* (Saskatoon, Canada: Gabriel Dumont Institute of Metis Studies and Applied Research, Pemmican Publications, 2001).

14. Baird, *O-De-Jit-Wa-Win-Ning*, 22.

15. Frank Straus, "A Look at History: Agatha Biddle's House Will Become Native American Museum," August 8, 2015; also Straus's article "Mackinac Island Finally Telling Native Side of History," March 30, 2017. Both pieces in *(Mackinac Island) Town Crier*.

16. Richard White, *The Middle Ground: Indians, Empires, and Republics in the Great Lakes Region, 1650–1815* (Cambridge: Cambridge University Press, 1991).

17. Susan Sleeper-Smith, *Indian Women and French Men: Rethinking Cultural Encounter in the Western Great Lakes* (Amherst: University of Massachusetts Press, 2001); Fleming, "Mediating Mackinac," 126, 133.

18. Widder, *Battle for the Soul*, 54.

19. Karen Marrero, *Detroit's Hidden Channels: The Power of French-Indigenous Families in the Eighteenth Century* (East Lansing: Michigan State University Press, 2020).

20. Author interview with Regina Gasco-Bentley, chairwoman of the Little Traverse Bay Bands of Odawa Indians, 12:00–2:00 P.M., September 8, 2021, Government Tribal Center, Harbor Springs, Michigan, at the Government Council Building of Little Traverse Bay Bands of Odawa Indians.

21. See chapter 5 in this book for an in-depth understanding of Jane Schoolcraft's trials in life and her remarkable contribution to American culture and literature.

22. David A. Armour, "David and Elizabeth: The Mitchell Family of the Straits of Mackinac," *Michigan History* 64, no. 4 (1980): 17–29. See Myra Peter's letter in 1824 to her sister, in Keith Widder's *Battle for the Soul*, 49.

23. Widder, *Battle for the Soul*, 53.

24. Baird, *O-De-Jit-Wa-Win-Ning*, 4.

25. Records of the Bureau of Indian Affairs, Special File #156 (Washington, DC: National Archives, 1818–1837).

26. Widder, *Battle for the Soul*, 201. A sworn statement by one John Beaubien in 1837 declares that Agatha was a full-blood Native woman, while Powell A. Moore stated in the Indiana Historical Bureau (vol. 1 1959, as cited in Widder, *Battle for the Soul*) that Agatha was

one-half Native. Widder makes the valid point that no matter which historical version is correct, Agatha maintained a loyalty to her cultural Native roots throughout her life.

27. Baird, *O-De-Jit-Wa-Win-Ning*, 22–23.

28. Ibid.

29. Armour, "David and Elizabeth," 10–11.

30. Baird, *O-De-Jit-Wa-Win-Ning*, 15–16. Elizabeth T. Baird both admired and, it is fair to say, stood in mild shock before Mitchell's larger-than-life personality.

31. Biography of John Johnston, of Sault Ste. Marie, in *Rose-Belford's Canadian Monthly and National Review*, ed. Wm. Kingsford (1872; Nabu Press, 2012), 7:1–8.

32. Edwin O. Wood, ed., *Historic Mackinac* (New York: Macmillan, 1918). In chap. 9, "Pontiac," Wood reprints a handwritten conversation that historian Francis Parkman had with Edward Biddle regarding Biddle's opinion of Henry "mangling" and "fabricating" Indian history. Excerpt from Francis Parkman's *The Conspiracy of Pontiac and the Indian War after the Conquest of Canada* (New York: Macmillan, 1918), 167–68. See further dissection of Henry Schoolcraft in connection with the Anishinaabe and his wife, Jane, in the chapter in this book on Jane Schoolcraft.

33. Straus, "A Look at History."

34. Widder, *Battle for the Soul*, 51–52. Cornelia Fonda's name was given to her by the missionaries; her birth name is unknown. See records of the Girls School for the Protestant Mackinaw Mission in 1827, which notes that Cornelia was fourteen when she matriculated at the boarding school. The year was 1824. These documents were compiled in appendices by the American Board of Commissioners for Foreign Missions records, April 5, 1833.

35. Fleming, "Mediating Mackinac," 133.

36. Baird, *O-De-Jit-Wa-Win-Ning*, 23. Elizabeth Therese Fisher Baird was nine years old when she attended Agatha's wedding service and reception. No doubt her close observations of dress and other behavior at the special occasion (the vain Mr. Bailly, noisier than ever) was elaborated on and much discussed by her grandmother Therese Schindler and great-aunt Madeline Laframboise at a later date, adding weight to Baird's remarkable memoir.

37. Straus, "A Look at History."

38. Katie Cedarholm, former curator of education at MSHP (Mackinac State Historic Parks), interviewed in an article by Sasha Zidar, "Biddle House Restoration Set to Be Completed in 2019," *(Mackinac Island) Town Crier*, 2017.

39. See further details in this study's chapter on Laframboise.

40. Fleming, "Mediating Mackinac," 133.

41. Baird, *O-De-Jit-Wa-Win-Ning*, 22–23.

42. Elizabeth T. Baird writes of the battle for the souls of islanders by the Presbyterians and

Catholics that was relieved only when "the Military stepped in and called an Episcopal Minister to serve as chaplain. Mackinac once more settled into a state of peace and was again a pleasant place to live in and to visit" (*O-De-Jit-Wa-Win-Ning*, 24).

43. For a comprehensive study of the battle between the Protestants and Catholics on Mackinac Island, see Keith Widder's *Battle for the Soul*.

44. See Theresa L. Weller's *The Founding Mothers of Mackinac Island: The Agatha Biddle Band of 1870* (East Lansing: Michigan State University Press, 2021); and also Straus, "A Look at History."

45. Records of the Bureau of Indian Affairs, Special File #156 and Special File #144 (Washington, DC: National Archives, 1818–1837).

Chapter Four. Juliette Magill Kinzie (1806–1870)

1. Brief interpretation of the meeting between Madeline Laframboise and Juliette Kinzie by Melissa Croghan. This encounter is based on Juliette Kinzie's book *Wau-Bun: The Early Day in the Northwest* (New York: Derby & Jackson Publisher, 1856).

2. Among relatives on Mackinac, Madeline Laframboise counted her son and daughter, Joseph and Josette, along with Madeline's sister, Therese Schindler, and her family. Madeline's grandniece, Elizabeth T. Baird, had married and moved away from the island in 1824, but made a number of visits home in the subsequent years. There is a record of Therese Schindler giving an oral history to the Indian agent Henry Schoolcraft in 1838.

3. To reinforce Agatha Biddle's relationship with her mentor Madeline Laframboise, and to offer a useful example of the connection between Native islanders, I give this example.

4. This is where my vignette ends.

5. Edwin O. Wood, ed., *Historic Mackinac*, vol. 2, chap. 6, "Mrs. Kinzie Visits Mackinac" (New York: Macmillan, 1918), 161.

6. Kinzie, *Wau-Bun*.

7. Ibid., 9.

8. Ibid., 6–8.

9. Ibid., 8–9.

10. Ibid., xvi–xx.

11. Ibid.; in the 1948 edition the editor, Louise Kellogg, adds a note describing Kinzie's uncle (1790–1830) as a former Indian agent in Chicago, in addition to having been a doctor (xvi–xx and 2).

12. Dr. Beaumont's exploration of the open cavity in the stomach of Alexis St. Martin for

weeks while he was conscious has been recognized as exploitation of patient rights. Further, there was a large class distinction between the officer Beaumont, part of the elite society on Mackinac, and treatment and attitudes toward the French Canadian voyageurs. Beaumont, while making medical discoveries regarding the digestive system, was also taking advantage of his patient. See Reginald Horsman, *Frontier Doctor: William Beaumont, America's First Great Medical Scientist* (Columbia: University of Missouri Press, 1996); Robert Helms, "Alexis St. Martin (1794–1880), the Intrepid Guinea Pig of the Great Lakes," *Guinea Pig Zero: Journal for Human Research Subjects*, no. 6 (1998).

13. Kinzie, *Wau-Bun*, xvi. Also see *Wisconsin Historical Collection*, vol. 20 (Madison: State Historical Society of Wisconsin, 1911); the entry on John H. Kinzie's life is a valuable contribution in respect to his connection to the women of the Great Lakes region, as is Elizabeth T. Baird's recollections of the John Kinzie family when as a child she knew his parents in Fort Dearborn. See pp. 6–8 in Baird's *O-De-Jit-Wa-Win-Ning*. See too the introduction to Kinzie, *Wau-Bun*, the 1948 edition, for further description.

14. Kinzie, *Wau-Bun*, xviii.

15. Ibid., chap. 7, 52–58.

16. Ibid., 5. Shawneeawkee was the name given to all Kinzie family members. Its translation was "Silver Man," as John H. Kinzie's father was a silversmith who made and repaired silver for Native Americans. Juliette would become as empathetic as her husband to the plight of the native people.

17. Ibid., 6.

18. Ibid., 6–8.

19. Nina Baym, Introduction to *Wau-Bun: The Early Day in the Northwest*, by Juliette Kinzie (Chicago: University of Illinois Press, 1992).

20. Ibid.

21. Ibid.

22. Ibid.

23. Kinzie, *Wau-Bun*, 1–3, and chap. 16.

24. Ibid., chaps. 18 and 19, pp. 157–94.

25. Ibid., 8.

26. Ibid., 3, 6.

27. Ibid.

28. Wood, *Historic Mackinac*, 1:408.

29. Kinzie, *Wau-Bun*, 11.

30. Juliette Kinzie would not be on Mackinac long enough to see the full emotional and religious fallout between the Catholics and Presbyterians on Mackinac in the 1830s. For

a comprehensive understanding of that strife, see Keith R. Widder's *Battle for the Soul: Métis Children Encounter Evangelical Protestants at Mackinaw Mission, 1823–1837* (East Lansing: Michigan State University Press, 1999).

31. Kinzie, *Wau-Bun*, 7.

32. Ibid.

33. Ibid., 9–10.

34. Ibid., 9.

35. Ibid., 9. See Keith Widder's comment that in her memoir, *Contes du Temps Passe*, Elizabeth T. Baird indicates that Laframboise learned to read when she was in her forties. "Magdelaine Laframboise: The First Lady of Mackinac Island," in *Mackinac History* (Mackinac Island State Park Commission, 2007), vol. 6, leaflet no. 1.

36. Kinzie, *Wau-Bun*.

37. Ibid.

38. Of the significance of being a woman writer, author Toni Morrison wrote about her belief that being female and being black enlarged her perceptions of life in a way that other people could not begin to touch. Kinzie was not African American, but as a female writer she would have appreciated Morrison's perspective. "Tony Morrison, in Her New Novel, Defends Women," interview, *New York Times*, August 26, 1987. More recently Karen Marrero highlights a history of women in the female kinship networks and of the Desauniers sisters, who in 1727 "established a powerful economic empire" in the Illinois Great Lakes region. She elaborates on the overall strength and influence of women of French-Indigenous family networks. Karen Marrero, *Detroit's Hidden Channels: The Power of French-Indigenous Families in the Eighteenth Century* (East Lansing: Michigan State University Press, 2020), xiii, 91.

39. Kinzie, *Wau-Bun*, vii.

40. Ibid., 11.

Chapter Five. Literary Leaders: Jane Johnston Schoolcraft (1800–1842) and Anna Brownell Jameson (1794–1860)

1. Anna Brownell Jameson, *Winter Studies and Summer Rambles in Canada*, ed. Paul A. W. Wallace (Toronto: McClelland and Stewart, 1923). Also see the letter dated March 18, 1839, in which Anna Jameson writes to Henry Schoolcraft that she has published "legends which Mrs. Schoolcraft gave me, and they have excited very general interest." Henry R. Schoolcraft, *Personal Memoirs of a Residence of Thirty Years with the Indian Tribes on the*

American Frontiers (Philadelphia: Lippincott, Grambo and Co., 1851).

2. Jameson, *Winter Studies*, 258–420. Jameson devotes sixty pages in *Winter Studies* to her connection with Jane Schoolcraft's family, the poet receiving the lion's share of her attention, but her social history and travel book also includes Jane's brothers William and George, along with her sister Charlotte, the Reverend MacMurray (married to Charlotte), Jane's and Charlotte's uncle Wayishky, and the poet and her sister's mother, Ozhaguscodaywayquay. Jameson stayed on Mackinac approximately two weeks and then traveled by canoe with Schoolcraft to Sault Ste. Marie, where she stayed several weeks more and then traveled with the family in the Great Lakes.

3. Jameson's book *Winter Studies and Summer Rambles in Canada* was first published in 1838 by Saunders and Otley in London. The later McClelland edition includes all three volumes, unlike other editions after the book was first published. Also in the unabridged McClelland edition is an essay with documentation of Jameson's time in the Great Lakes region, in addition to the inclusion of the author's notes throughout this text.

4. Ibid.

5. Ibid., 353.

6. Ibid.; and see a contemporary view by Melinda Gates, whose global foundation has saved the lives of many women. She writes: "To me, feminism is just making sure that every single woman has her full voice and her full decision-making authority. If that's the definition of feminism, I really don't know a woman—or a man—who wouldn't sign up for it. We do need men in this." Article by Gates in "Help Women Help the World," *Delta Sky Magazine*, September 2019 issue.

7. Judith Johnston, *Anna Jameson* (New York: Routledge Publishing, 1997), 123.

8. Ibid., 123; and see also the biography of Jameson, *Memoirs of the Life of Anna Jameson* (Boston, 1878), written by her niece, Geraldine Bate.

9. Johnston, *Anna Jameson*.

10. Jameson, *Winter Studies*, 17.

11. Ibid., 31–33.

12. Ibid., 266–67.

13. Ibid.

14. Ibid., 355–56.

15. Ibid., 381.

16. Ibid.; and see editor commentary on "God and the Red Man," and appreciation of Jameson's inclusive vision of spirituality (p. 7).

17. Robert Dale Parker, ed., *The Sound the Stars Make Rushing through the Sky: The Writings of Jane Johnston Schoolcraft* (Philadelphia: University of Pennsylvania Press, 2007), 77.

18. Richard G. Bremer, *Indian Agent and Wilderness Scholar: The Life of Henry Rowe Schoolcraft* (Mount Pleasant, MI: Clarke Historical Library Press, Central Michigan University, 1987), 197–200. See accusations of corruption leveled against Henry by Edward Biddle; William Johnston, a brother of Jane Schoolcraft; and Michael Dousman, a well-known Mackinac trader (197–200). Further, see records of such accusations in Biddle's, Dousman's, and Johnston's letters in *Letters Received*, Michigan Superintendency and Office of Indian Affairs. Edward Biddle, husband to Agatha, had written to Commissioner Crawford in Washington regarding the matter. Records of the Michigan Superintendency of Indian Affairs, letters received and sent, 1814–1851. U.S. Bureau of Indian Affairs, Washington, DC, Record of National Archives and Records Service, 1963.

19. Parker, *Sound the Stars Make*, 58–59.

20. Library of Congress, #64. The number given is the container number in which documents on Henry and Jane Schoolcraft are held. Separately, also regarding Schoolcraft's pen names, see Parker, *Sound the Stars Make*, 33–35.

21. Jameson, *Winter Studies*, 366–68.

22. There is reasonable belief that the homestead of Jane Schoolcraft is one of the older buildings in the town of Sault Ste. Marie, Michigan; E. J. Sundstrom, "Oldest Building in Sault Ste. Marie?" *(Sault Ste. Marie) Evening News*, May 19, 1966, 5.

23. "Biography of John Johnston, of Sault Ste. Marie," in *Rose-Belford's Canadian Monthly and National Review*, ed. Wm. Kingsford (Toronto: Rose-Belford Publishing Co., 1881), 7:7–8.

24. Ibid.

25. Edwin O. Wood, ed. *Historic Mackinac*, vol. 2, Eliza Steele quoted: "A Summer Journey in the West, 1841" (New York: Macmillan Co., 1918), 596.

26. See Robert Dale Parker's literary analysis of Schoolcraft's work, particularly her poetry, in *Sound the Stars Make*.

27. Jameson, *Winter Studies*, 368.

28. Ibid., 259–60.

29. Keith Widder, *Battle for the Soul: Métis Children Encounter Evangelical Protestants at Mackinaw Mission, 1823–1837* (East Lansing: Michigan State University Press, 1999).

30. Jameson, *Winter Studies*, 259–60.

31. Ibid., 265.

32. Ibid., 265.

33. Ibid., 347.

34. Ibid., 372.

35. Parker, *Sound the Stars Make*, 13.

36. Wood, *Historic Mackinac*, 169.

37. Henry Rowe Schoolcraft, *Algic Researches, Comprising Inquiries Respecting the Mental Characteristics of the North American Indians*, First Series: *Indian Tales and Legends*, 2 vols. (New York: Harper and Brothers, 1839).

38. Parker, *Sound the Stars Make*, 70, 72.

39. Library of Congress, #7,2.

40. Library of Congress, #15.

41. Jameson, *Winter Studies*, 369, 283.

42. Parker, *Sound the Stars Make*, 59.

43. Jameson, *Winter Studies*, 366.

44. Robert E. Bieder, "Sault Ste. Marie and the War of 1812: A World Turned Upside Down in the Old Northwest," *Indiana Magazine of History* 95 (March 1999).

45. See Susan Sleeper-Smith's extensive study on the subject in her *Indian Women and French Men: Rethinking Cultural Encounter in the Western Great Lakes* (Amherst: University of Massachusetts Press, 2001).

46. Jameson, *Winter Studies*, 363–64.

47. H. R. Schoolcraft, *Algic Researches*.

48. *Rose-Belford's Canadian Monthly and National Review*, ed. Wm. Kingsford, 7:7–8.

49. Parker, *Sound the Stars Make*, 12 and 28.

50. H. R. Schoolcraft, in his *Algic Researches*; see Henry's "Notes intended to be used to draw up a biographical notice, or memoir of Mrs. Henry Rowe Schoolcraft." It is significant that Anna Jameson communicated with Henry regarding this project, urging him forward and realizing the historical import of such a memoir of her friend, Jane Schoolcraft. Henry's memoir of his wife was not to be completed or published.

51. *Rose-Belford's Canadian Monthly and National Review*, ed. Wm. Kingsford, 7:7–8; and also Parker, *Sound the Stars Make*, 77.

52. Parker, *Sound the Stars Make*, 26.

53. Henry Schoolcraft published widely, including *The Red Race of America* (1847); *Outlines of the Life and Character of Gen. Lewis Cass* (Albany, 1848); *American Indians, their History, Condition, and Prospects* (Auburn, 1850); and *Plan for Investigating American Ethnology* (1846).

54. In addition to *Lord Jim*, Joseph Conrad's short story "Heart of Darkness" is much anthologized and addresses the imperialistic character Kurtz and his corrupt action in the Congo.

55. Parker, *Sound the Stars Make*, 29–30.

56. Library of Congress, #45. This letter from Jane on Mackinac was written in 1840.

57. Library of Congress, #70.

58. Parker, *Sound the Stars Make*, 222. This observation set forth by Robert Parker is possible, while his wishful notion of a happy union between Henry and Jane is unlikely. As for Henry's career, the government eventually fired him for misuse of funds as an Indian agent. See also Bremer, *Indian Agent*, 197–200.

59. Library of Congress, #45.

60. Library of Congress, #37.

61. Jameson, *Winter Studies*, 283.

62. Ibid.

63. Library of Congress, #36.

64. Parker, *Sound the Stars Make*, 35.

65. Jameson, *Winter Studies*, 266.

66. See Brian Dunnigan's *A Picturesque Situation: Mackinac before Photography, 1650–1860* (Detroit: Wayne State University Press, 2008), 209, fig. 6.6 for Anna Jameson's drawing of Jane Schoolcraft's home in "Island of Mackinaw—Lake Huron, Indians' Village." It is a popular drawing included in several books on Mackinac and is part of the Toronto Public Library collection.

67. The exact location of the "Old Agency House" on Mackinac has been provided to me by Mackinac State Historic Parks (MSHP), with thanks to former director Phil Porter, email, April 1, 2020. The Agency House was Jane and Henry Schoolcraft's home on Mackinac.

68. Jameson, *Winter Studies*, 266.

69. Though there is not a precise comparison between Jane Schoolcraft's torn position and that of any one of the Cherokees sent on the infamous "Trail of Tears," the general tenor of abuse, of land theft by the U.S. government, and wrong treatment of the Native Americans throughout the nation cannot be glossed over. Regarding the "Trail of Tears," there was a treaty signed by Andrew Jackson that promised the Cherokees food and care on the long journey west and full protection of their new lands there. Both promises were broken. Soldiers forced the Indians off their land with no provisions for the full journey on foot, and soon enough their "new" territory was stolen.

70. Library of Congress, #62.

71. Michael A. McDonnell, *Masters of Empire: Great Lakes Indians and the Making of America* (New York: Hill and Wang, 2015), 3–7.

72. Doug Kiel, "American Expansion Turns to Official Indian Removal," in series *Erosion of the Middle Ground: Native Peoples of the Great Lakes after 1815*, National Park Service, https://www.nps.gov/articles/american-expansion-turns-to-indian-removal.htm.

73. Jameson, *Winter Studies*, 321.

74. Ibid., 321–22; and see Anna Jameson, *Legends of the Madonna as Represented in the Fine Arts* (Boston: Ticknor & Fields, 1861).

75. Jameson, *Winter Studies*, 323.

76. Henry Schoolcraft to Lucius Lyon, January 18, 1837, Michigan Historical Collections, Lyon Papers, University of Michigan, Ann Arbor.

77. Bremer, *Indian Agent*, 191.

78. Charles Robbins Gilman, *Life on the Lakes*, vol. 1. His text is presented in epistolary form, with details on Mackinac in Letters 10–20. His collection was published in New York, 1836, by an unidentified press. See Edwin O. Wood's *Historic Mackinac*, 1:409 for the editor's description of a theatrical troupe and entertainment, the removal of the pulpit, and a rough stage erected at Mission Church on Mackinac.

79. Wood, *Historic Mackinac*, vol. 1:409.

80. Parker, *Sound the Stars Make*, 44 and 111. See Jane's comment that she believes she should stay out of politics as this is the sphere of men, and yet she equivocates on this stance, inferring that northern Michigan will bounce back after the years of war and contest for control of the Great Lakes. Note that Robert Parker's analysis of Jane's poem "Pensive Hours" includes a probable reference to the War of 1812 (*Sound the Stars Make*).

81. Keith R. Widder, "The Missionaries of the Mackinaw Mission, 1823–1937: Presbyterians and Congregationalists on the American Frontier," *Presbyterian Historical Society* 67, no. 4 (Winter 1989): 273–81.

82. Wood, *Historic Mackinac*, 408.

83. Widder, *Battle for the Soul*, 134. This reference is restricted to the "Americanization" that caused the demise of the mission, including the closure of the fur trade on the island.

84. Wood, *Historic Mackinac*, vol. 1, see chapter on "Churches of Mackinac Island," 405.

85. Ibid.

86. Library of Congress, #45, July 2, 1840.

87. Jameson, *Winter Studies*, 274–75.

88. Library of Congress, #13, May 10, 1836. See letters written by Jane to Henry and to William MacMurray, husband of her sister Charlotte, asking for more laudanum.

89. See https://kleurrijkbrontesisters.blogspot.com/2014/02/laudanum-called-aspirin-of-nineteenth.html, regarding use of laudanum among nineteenth-century writers. Mrs. Gaskell's trenchant political writing about the plight of factory workers in Manchester, England, includes her protagonist in the novel *Mary Barton*, who falls prey to laudanum.

90. Jameson, *Winter Studies*, 332.

91. Ibid., 331.

92. H. R. Schoolcraft, *Personal Memoirs*, August 5, 1836.

93. Jameson, *Winter Studies*, 332.

94. Ibid., 335.

95. Ibid.

96. Ibid., 138 and 289.

97. See the discussion later in this chapter referencing Schoolcraft's poem "To the Pine Tree."

98. Library of Congress, #72.

99. Jameson, *Winter Studies*, 335.

100. Ibid.

101. Ibid., 333.

102. Ibid., 348.

103. Ibid., 349.

104. Ibid., 265.

105. Parker, *Sound the Stars Make*, 70–71, 43.

106. John Ball, *Autobiography of John Ball* (Glendale, CA: Arthur H. Clarke, 1925), 146–47.

107. Jameson, *Winter Studies*, 280.

108. Ibid., 263–64.

109. Ibid., 271.

110. Ibid., 331.

111. Ibid., 256–57.

112. Ibid., 320.

113. Ibid., 268–69.

114. Ibid.

115. Ibid., 284.

116. Ibid., 288; and oral interview, August 2019, by author with Ojibwe Jim Francis on Mackinac, speaking of the history of Native women chiefs on numerous islands north of Mackinac.

117. Jameson, *Winter Studies*, 283.

118. Ibid., 276.

119. Ibid., 99–100.

120. Ibid., 276–77.

121. Ibid., 338.

122. Ibid.

123. Ibid., 291, 289, 277.

124. Ibid., 280.

125. Parker, *Sound the Stars Make*, 50–52. Also see Margaret Nooris's "Bicultural before There Was a Word for It" for a discussion of Schoolcraft's translations of her poems into Ojibwe. In *Women's Review of Books*, December 12, 2008 (Wellesley, MA: Wellesley Centers for Women). Further, see Parker, *Sound the Stars Make*, 90, regarding Henry's notes on a memoir of Jane Schoolcraft sent in a letter to Anna Jameson. After her trip with Jane, Jameson hopes to have more news of her friend. It is likely that the only way this occurs is through the notes that Henry sends her of Jane's life.

126. Jane Schoolcraft, speaking of Anna Jameson, says "she is indeed a woman in a thousand." Wood, *Historic Mackinac*, vol. 2, "Sketches from [Henry] Schoolcraft's Diary, entry August 5, 1837 (223–24).

127. Jameson, *Winter Studies*, 327.

128. Ibid., 271.

129. Ibid., 319.

130. Ibid., 320.

131. Ibid., 368–72.

132. Ibid.

133. Ibid., 371.

134. Henry Schoolcraft was "a hot-tempered go-getter with a concern for his image," according to Jean Delisle, who wrote about a victim of Schoolcraft, John Tanner. Tanner, an interpreter, was the pawn in a war of egos between the Baptists and the Presbyterians, with Henry allegedly ordering the wife and child of Tanner to be kidnapped. See John T. Fierst's "Return to Civilization: John Tanner's Troubled Years at Sault Ste. Marie," *Minnesota History Magazine* 50, no. 1 (Spring 1986): 26; and Delisle's account in "Through the Lens of History," *Language Update* 8, no. 3 (2011), https://www.noslangues-ourlanguages.gc.ca/en/favourite-articles/through-the-lens-of-history-john-tanner-a-white-indian-between-a-rock-and-a-hard-place-ii.

135. Jameson, *Winter Studies*, 273.

136. Elizabeth T. Baird, *O-De-Jit-Wa-Win-Ning; or Contes du Temps Passe: The Memoirs of Elizabeth T. Baird* (Green Bay, WI: Heritage Hill Foundation), 29.

137. Jameson, *Winter Studies*, 329.

138. Ibid., 382.

139. Ibid.

140. Bremer, *Indian Agent*, 195–200.

141. Jameson, *Winter Studies*, 294–311.

142. Library of Congress, #37, 24–35.

143. Nooris, "Bicultural."

144. The author's personal communications with Native friends on Mackinac Island who were sent to such boarding schools attest to this abuse. Eric Hemenway, an Odawa from Cross Village, Michigan, also spoke of the widespread abuse, on Interlochen Public Radio, November 8, 2017. The school was begun by a local tribe in conjunction with the Catholic Church.

145. Jane's son, John, was sent to the Round Hill School in Philadelphia. The nine-year-old child did not do well and was stricken with sadness over the separation from his mother.

146. Henry Schoolcraft lost his job in 1841, just one year before Jane's death. Bremer, *Indian Agent*, 197, 229.

147. Parker, *Sound the Stars Make*, 70.

148. Library of Congress, #88, Memorandum: *Abstract of Monies Received for Investment*. Also see Bremer, *Indian Agent*, 221–22, where he relates that Reverend MacMurray and his wife, Charlotte, left the Sault, and he became the rector at an Anglican church in Dundas, Ontario. Jane Schoolcraft had visited the MacMurrays whenever she could, along with her mother—all of whom lived in the Sault for most of the poet's life. It follows that the sister whom Jane visited in Ontario when she died would have been the rector's wife, Charlotte.

149. Bremer, *Indian Agent*, 255–56.

150. Nooris, "Bicultural."

151. Library of Congress, #64.

152. Library of Congress, #64.

153. Library of Congress, #62.

154. Wood, *Historic Mackinac*, chap. 9, p. 227; from Henry Schoolcraft's *Personal Memoirs* and Letters.

155. Ibid., p. 224; from Henry Schoolcraft's *Personal Memoirs* and Letters.

156. Given Henry Schoolcraft's verbal and literary abuse of Jane, it is entirely possible that he isolated his wife (kept Jameson's communications from her), as controlling men often do.

Chapter Six. Margaret Fuller (1810–1850)

1. William H. Gilman, ed., *The Journals and Miscellaneous Notebooks of Ralph Waldo Emerson*, 16 vols. (Cambridge, MA: Harvard University Press, 1960–1982), 16:22.

2. Harriet Martineau, *Society in America* (London: Saunders and Otley, 1837); reissued by

Cambridge University Press in 2009; Anna Brownell Jameson, *Winter Studies and Summer Rambles in Canada* (London: Saunders and Otley, 1838).

3. Megan Marshall, *Margaret Fuller: A New American Life* (New York: Houghton Mifflin Harcourt, 2013), 202.

4. Margaret Fuller, *Summer on the Lakes* (Boston: Freeman and Bolles, 1844).

5. Robert N. Hudspeth, ed., *The Letters of Margaret Fuller*, 6 vols. (Ithaca, NY: Cornell University Press, 1983–1994), 3:147.

6. Fuller, *Summer*, 237.

7. Hudspeth, *The Letters of Margaret Fuller*, 1:95. Marshall, *Margaret Fuller*, 9.

8. *Memoirs of Margaret Fuller Ossoli*, 2 vols., ed. R. W. Emerson, J. F. Clarke, and W. H. Channing (Boston: Phillips, Sampson, 1852), 28.

9. See Megan Marshall's fine study, *The Peabody Sisters: Three Women Who Ignited American Romanticism* (New York: Houghton Mifflin Harcourt, 2005).

10. *Our Famous Women*, anthology, chap. 13, "Kate Sanborn" (Hartford, CT: Hartford Publishing Co., 1888), 300.

11. Marshall, *Margaret Fuller*, 135.

12. Margaret Fuller, *Woman in the Nineteenth Century* (New York: Greeley and McElrath, 1845).

13. Ibid., 25.

14. Ibid. Also helpful is the essay "Civil Wars" by Dorothy Wickenden on Frances A. Seward, who was married to Senator William H. Seward. This piece examines the struggles of women and the abolitionist movement during the time Margaret Fuller also fought for women's rights. Frances and her husband are an example of greater parity in marriage than many in the years 1830–1860, and yet she suffered under her inferior position, watching as the Married Women's Property Act was voted down in 1841. When it was finally passed by the legislature, Frances was able to become "legal owner of her father's property" after his death. This translated into a sensibility of independence for her, one that was apparent in her work for Harriet Tubman and the Underground Railroad. *New Yorker*, January 25, 2021, 16–25.

15. Joan Von Mehren, *Minerva and the Muse: A Life of Margaret Fuller* (Amherst: University of Massachusetts Press, 1994), 225.

16. Marshall, *Margaret Fuller*, 204.

17. Fuller, *Summer*. See Fuller's several discussions of Catlin, 30–31 and 196.

18. Brian Dunnigan, *A Picturesque Situation: Mackinac before Photography*, 1650–1860 (Detroit: Wayne State University Press, 2008).

19. Fuller was not the only paying guest at Laframboise's house to remark on "the widow of a Frenchman." Amanda Ferry, a Presbyterian missionary to the island, wrote in 1825 of her stay at the home that Capt. Pierce, brother to the future U.S. president, had built for the fur trader in 1820, though Ferry announced that the house was "a small incommodious building." Fuller's focus was on the trader herself, not the house that was both a school for children and lodgings for others. "Frontier Mackinac, 1823–1834," letters, ed. Charles A. Anderson, *Journal of the Presbyterian Historical Society* 26, no. 3 (September 1948): 182–91.

20. Fuller, *Summer*.

21. Ibid., 251.

22. Ibid., 250.

23. Elizabeth Therese Baird, *O-De-Jit-Wa-Win-Ning; or Contes du Temps Passe: The Memoirs of Elizabeth T. Baird*. Though E. T. Baird published her memoir in the latter part of the century, she reaches backward to the time when she lived on Mackinac, 1810–1824, and to her many visits home after moving to Green Bay, Wisconsin.

24. Fuller, *Summer*, 201.

25. Ibid., 200. George Johnston was a Native man of mixed race, the same as his sister Jane Johnston Schoolcraft.

26. Ibid., 179, 200–201, 175.

27. Marshall, *Margaret Fuller*, 135.

28. Fuller, *Summer*, 250, 252.

29. Marshall, *Margaret Fuller*, 213, 204.

30. Fuller, *Summer*, 251.

31. Marshall, *Margaret Fuller*, 270–71, 284–85.

32. Bernard Rosenthal, Introduction to *Woman in the Nineteenth Century* (New York: Norton and Co., 1971).

33. Hudspeth, *The Letters of Margaret Fuller*, 1:53, 261, 182.

34. Marshall, *Margaret Fuller*, 381–83.

35. See Joan Von Mehren's *Minerva and the Muse: A Life of Margaret Fuller* (Amherst: University of Massachusetts Press, 1994). Elaine Showalter has written a strong biography of Julia Ward Howe: *The Civil Wars of Julia Ward Howe* (New York: Simon and Schuster, 2016).

36. Marshall, *Margaret Fuller*, 393.

37. Fuller, *Summer*, 196.

38. Ibid., 205.

39. Ibid., 19.

40. Ibid., 201.

Chapter Seven. Constance Fenimore Woolson (1840–1894)

1. David A. Armour, *100 Years at Mackinac* (Mackinac State Historic Parks [MSHP], January 1996). Dr. Armour writes that Samuel L. Mather and his sister, Katherine Mather, established the memorial to honor their aunt, Constance Fenimore Woolson, in 1916. William Ordway Partridge was the statuary artist responsible for the stone monument. In *Historic Mackinac*, vol. 1 (New York: Macmillan Co., 1918), 606, editor Edwin O. Wood states that the bronze tablet was erected in 1916 by her nephews. This is a misperception as it was not a pair of nephews but the brother and sister who were dear to Fenimore Woolson. See references to the content of shared letters between them in this chapter on Woolson.

2. There is a monument in tribute to a generic group of women in the DAR (Daughters of the American Revolution) for their contributions to Mackinac. That monument is a stone edifice on the west side of Marquette Park. Also, as of the publication of this book, a statuary head study of Agatha Biddle has been erected in the Native American exhibit, part of the MSHP historic sites on Mackinac.

3. Constance Fenimore Woolson, *Anne* (New York: Harpers and Brothers, 1882). By 1903, the book would be republished, both in New York and London.

4. Anne Boyd Rioux, *Constance Fenimore Woolson: Portrait of a Lady Novelist* (New York: W.W. Norton and Co., 2016), 151. This incisive biography is revealing on a number of levels, especially its focus on the courage and ambitions of Woolson, her discipline, and her drive in the face of many obstacles. See also valuable discussions of her family members and her relationship with Henry James.

5. Woolson's words etched in stone in the memorial to Constance Fenimore Woolson in Sinclair Grove on the East Bluff of Mackinac Island, Michigan. Though arranged as if they are a poem, they originate in the prose sections of chapter 5 in *Anne*, with the first five lines on p. 40 and the second four from p. 39. It is likely that Samuel and Katherine Mather, Woolson's nephew and niece, culled the chosen lines to be engraved.

6. Rioux, *Constance Fenimore Woolson*, 3.

7. James Fenimore Cooper was a prolific American author whose work is considered to be part of the Romantic literary movement. He was most famous for his five "Leatherstocking

Tales" (novels), including *The Pioneers*, published in 1823; *The Last of the Mohicans* (1826), set during the Seven Years War; and *The Deerslayer* (1841). An indication perhaps of Cooper's own romantic inclinations is that the protagonist, Hawkeye, in the first book written in the series, is an old man. In the following novels featuring Hawkeye, aka Natty Bumppo or Deerslayer, our hero appears successively younger (as opposed to older) in each new iteration.

8. In *Portrait of a Lady Novelist*, Anne Rioux refers twice to the Woolsons' summer cottage, commenting on how eventually the family had to give it up (26–27). There was no cottage, but Woolson never forgot the charms of the place her family rented, along with the Hurlbuts, at the large United States Indian Agency House.

9. Phil Porter, *View from the Veranda* (Michigan Reports in Mackinac History and Archaeology, No. 8, 1981), 64.

10. An article in the *(Cheboygan, Michigan) Northern Tribune* published in 1882 discusses Woolson's summers at the old Agency House with her "invalid" father. It is likely her other family members also summered in the large building. It had become a boarding house in the years after Indian agents such as Henry Schoolcraft and his wife, the poet Jane Johnston Schoolcraft, resided there.

11. Rioux, *Constance Fenimore Woolson*, 27.

12. Ibid., 78.

13. Woolson to Henry James, in a letter dated August 30, 1882. *The Complete Letters of Constance Fenimore Woolson*, ed. Sharon L. Dean (Gainesville: University Press of Florida, 2012), 535.

14. Rioux, *Constance Fenimore Woolson*, 55.

15. Ibid., 73–74.

16. Constance Fenimore Woolson, "Fairy Island," *Putnam's Magazine* (New York: G.P. Putnam, 1870), 62–69.

17. Rioux, *Constance Fenimore Woolson*, 63.

18. Ibid., 47.

19. Woolson, *Anne*, 17.

20. Woolson ruminated about her engagement to Zeph Spalding in a letter to her nephew, Samuel Mather, the year before she died. *The Complete Letters of Constance Fenimore Woolson*, 535.

21. Rioux, *Constance Fenimore Woolson*, 66. The 400 referred to the exclusive group invited to Caroline Astor's annual ball at her home in New York City. See also the story of the Astors and Vanderbilts in the Gilded Age, with discussions of Mrs. Astor and women of wealth

who were shut out of the male world of industrial empire building and coped by engaging in the dubious art of conspicuous consumption. Terrence Gavan, *The Barons of Newport* (Newport, RI: Pineapple Publications, 1998); and Sean Cashman's *America in the Gilded Age* (New York: New York University Press, 1984).

22. Constance Fenimore Woolson, "Gotham," *Daily Cleveland Herald*, January 14, 1871.

23. Rioux, *Constance Fenimore Woolson*, 52.

24. See Margot Livesey's analysis of relationship woes in a number of Woolson's stories. Constance Fenimore Woolson, *Castle Nowhere: Lake Country Sketches*, introduction by Margot Livesey (Ann Arbor: University of Michigan Press, 2004).

25. Woolson to Sam Mather, one of her closest confidants, December 10, 1893, *Complete Letters of Constance Fenimore Woolson*.

26. Woolson to Sam Mather, February 24, 1977, *Complete Letters of Constance Fenimore Woolson*, 89.

27. Rioux, *Constance Fenimore Woolson*, 53–54.

28. Ibid., 178.

29. *Constance Fenimore Woolson: Collected Stories*, ed. Anne Boyd Rioux (New York: Library of America, 2017).

30. R. W. B Lewis, *The Jameses: A Family Narrative* (New York: Farrar, Straus and Giroux, 1991), 423.

31. Lewis, *The Jameses*, 401.

32. Ibid., 396.

33. Rioux, *Constance Fenimore Woolson*, 219–20.

34. Ibid., 129.

35. Woolson to Henry James, August 30, 1882, *Complete Letters of Constance Fenimore Woolson*, 211.

36. Rioux, *Constance Fenimore Woolson*, 151–52.

37. Woolson to her editor, Henry Alden, January 17, 1890, *Complete Letters of Constance Fenimore Woolson*, 396.

38. Woolson, "Fairy Island," 62–69.

39. *Harper's Magazine*, "The Wishing Springs" (New York: Harper's Magazine, 1872). See also an excerpt of it in Wood, *Historic Mackinac*, 1:577–78.

40. First published as Constance Fenimore Woolson, *Castle Nowhere: Lake Country Sketches* (New York: Harper & and Brothers, 1875).

41. Porter, *View from the Veranda*. See appendix with dates of the construction of cottages on the East and West Bluffs, the first one built in 1885 (pp. 64–65).

42. Woolson, "Fairy Island," 62–69.

43. Ibid.

44. Ibid.

45. Ibid.

46. Porter, *View from the Veranda*, 4–6. Mackinac Island would become a national park for two decades, after which it became Michigan's first state park.

47. Ibid.

48. *Constance Fenimore Woolson: Collected Stories*, ed. Anne Boyd Rioux, 176–207.

49. Phil Porter, director, MSHP, email communication, April 1, 2020.

50. Woolson, *Castle Nowhere*, 176–207.

51. Ibid.

52. In *Battle for the Soul: Métis Children Encounter Evangelical Protestants at Mackinaw Mission, 1823–1837* (East Lansing: Michigan State University Press, 1999), Keith Widder speaks of how unlikely it was that Madeline Laframboise would be included in the soirees held at the fort and other elite gatherings (62–63).

53. Woolson, *Anne*, 9.

54. Woolson, *Castle Nowhere*, 176–207.

55. Ibid.

56. The *Hartford Courant* newspaper declares that the protagonist was based on a young woman other than Woolson who resided in the Old Agency House; however too many autobiographical features in the book argue against that line of thought. Among them are Anne's and Woolson's tendencies towards opera-singing in the forest, love of nature and books, and unhappy experience at boarding school. Finally, as in most novels, the creation of character is both an assimilation of life observations and an act of the imagination.

57. Woolson, *Anne*, 27.

58. Ibid., 3–12.

59. Ibid., 89.

60. Ibid., 3–17.

61. Rioux, *Constance Fenimore Woolson*, 115–16.

62. Ibid.

63. Ibid., 173–74.

64. See Anne Rioux's discussion in *Portrait of a Lady Novelist* of Samuel and Katherine (Sam and Kate), "her closest family to the end of her life" (30).

65. Wood, *Historic Mackinac*, 1:579.

66. Constance Fenimore Woolson, "The Wishing Springs," *Harper's Magazine*, September 1872.

67. In her piece "The Wishing Springs," she describes a once well-known spring near Devil's Kitchen on Mackinac.

68. Constance Fenimore Woolson, "Miss Grief," first published in May 1880 issue of *Lippincott's Monthly Magazine* (Philadelphia: J.B. Lippincott).

69. Amy Gentry, "'Constance Fenimore Woolson' Gives 19th Century Novelist Second Look," *Chicago Tribune*, February 25, 2016.

70. Brenda Wineapple, review, "'Miss Grief' and Other Stories," ed. Anne Boyd Rioux with introduction by Colm Toibin, *New York Times Sunday Book Review*, February 29, 2016.

71. Charles Dudley Warner, "Editor's Study," *Harper's Magazine*, no. 88 (New York: Harper and Brothers, 1894), 967.

72. Woolson, *Castle Nowhere*, intro. Margot Livesey.

73. Armour, *100 Years at Mackinac*, which shows the Mackinac Island State Park Commission minute book with directions by Kate and Sam Mather as to the creation and care of the grounds at Woolson's Mackinac memorial.

Chapter Eight. Rosa Truscott Webb (1853–1942)

1. John W. Hannen, "John Jacob Astor House Was Trading Center in Early History of Mackinac," *Lansing State Journal*, July 27, 1941.

2. Rosa Truscott Webb, from the collection of her letters to Wilfred Puttkammer, who sat on the Board of the historic Beaumont Memorial Hospital. Rosa Webb Papers, donation from Emerson Dufina. The Peterson Center, Keith R. Widder Library, Archive Collection, Mackinaw City, Michigan.

3. Collection, History: Rosa Webb, the Rosa Webb Room, Mackinac Island Public Library.

4. This letter is dated 1931; Rosa Webb Papers, Petersen Center, Keith R. Widder Library, Mackinac State Historic Parks (MSHP).

5. For ninety years, beginning in 1867, the Thomas W. Ferry School operated in the Indian Dormitory in Marquette Park. The old dormitory has been converted into the Manoogian Art Museum. A brick school was built for children on the west shore road in 1960.

6. Rosa Truscott Webb Papers, Petersen Center, Keith R. Widder Library.

7. See biographical notes on Rosa Webb in the Petersen Center and in the Rosa Truscott Webb Papers at the Mackinac Public Library.

8. Phil Porter, *The Soldiers of Fort Mackinac: An Illustrated History* (East Lansing: Michigan State University Press, 2018), 109.

9. https://www.hotelnewsresource.com/article89670.html.

10. Ibid.

11. Webb Papers, Keith R. Widder Library.

12. Ibid.

13. Ibid.

14. Ibid.

15. Webb Papers, Keith R. Widder Library. All following quotations from Webb's letters to Wilfred Puttkammer are from this collection at the Keith R. Widder Library, MSHP.

16. *Lansing State Journal*, July 27, 1941.

17. Ruth Orton Camp, "Mackinac's Shoestring Library Helps Itself," *Island News*, June 30, 1949.

18. Webb, letter to Wilfred Puttkammer, March 4, 1935.

19. Ibid.

20. Ibid.

21. The seven highly ranked colleges on the East Coast include Wellesley, Smith, Bryn Mawr, Radcliffe, Barnard, Vassar, and Mount Holyoke. The linked schools were women's colleges, though most have gradually become coed.

22. The *Flint Journal*, March 16, 1939, describes Rosa Webb as "the first Girl Scout Leader in the state." The article features a photo of Girl Scouts honoring her for that first troop in Michigan.

23. "Honor Library Founder," *Detroit News*, September 1, 1936. With photograph of Daisy P. Blodgett presenting a large bronze tablet at "the old Astor House, Mackinac Island," to Mrs. Rosa S. Webb. Unlike most newspaper citations of women in the 1930s, this one identifies Webb with her first name.

24. Rosa Webb in sleigh with horse on iced-over Lake Huron, Photo Collection, Mackinac Island Public Library. The photo is undated, but she appears to be about eighty years old.

25. Rosa Webb, journal notes, Keith R. Widder Library Archives, Collection MSHP, most likely written in 1942, as Marcia Webb relates that these passages were written shortly before her mother's death.

26. See letters written regarding her life in Flint, in the Mackinac Island collection of Rosa Webb Papers, and also her late-life memories recorded in the Widder Library Archives, Collection MSHP.

27. Collection, Mackinac Public Library.

28. Ibid.

29. In her last years on Mackinac, she became chairman of the Board of Trustees for the Community Association and remained active at the D.A.R. Library.

Chapter Nine. Daisy Peck Blodgett (1863–1947)
and Stella King (1905–1984)

1. Dwight Lapine, lifelong resident of Mackinac Island, Michigan, oral history interview with author. Several interviews, fall 2018 and summer 2020.

2. Frank Straus, "A Look at History: Nurse Stella King was Instrumental in Island Health Service," *Mackinac Town Crier*, July 8, 2006.

3. Stella King came to Mackinac in 1920, and but for two years spent working in Washington, DC, she lived on the island until her death in 1984. Helen Blodgett Erwin Papers, 1910–1965 [hereafter HBE], author's collection, 1961; Dwight Lapine, oral history interview with author, 2018.

4. Delos A. Blodgett's activism in the cause of abolitionism is noted in the discussion of how he was "from the essence of his nature, an Abolitionist in the days when that sentiment was far from general or popular." *The Cyclopedia of Michigan: Historical Biographical Synopsis of General History of the State* (Detroit: Western Publishing and Engraving Company, 1890), 92–94. Blodgett's support of the suffragist movement and friendship with Elizabeth Cady Stanton and Susan B. Anthony has been documented in writings by Anthony and in other source material. See "One of Michigan's Foremost Citizens for Many Years," *Grand Rapids Herald*, November 2, 1908.

5. *Michigan Natural Resources* magazine, "Special Straits Issue" (May–June 1981–1982): 33–34 and 60. Also see Phil Porter's *View from the Veranda*, Reports in Mackinac History and Archaeology, no. 8 (Mackinaw City, MI: Mackinac State Historic Parks, 1981), 2–4.

6. Samuel Clemens and Charles Dudley Warner, *The Gilded Age* (Hartford, CT: American Publishing Co., 1874).

7. Porter, *View from the Veranda*, 22–23, discusses the barn the Blodgetts built, and chap. 4, "Cottage Life," 31–35, gives an excellent description of Daisy and Delos's life as Victorian cottagers on Mackinac, including a photo of Daisy sidesaddle on her horse in front of Casa Verano, her island home. See also p. 54.

8. HBE Papers.

9. Dwight Lapine, oral history interview with author, March 15, 2019.

10. Patricia Martin, lifelong resident of Mackinac, oral history interview with author, August 2019.

11. There is a veritable feast of King family relatives residing in Saint Ann's Cemetery on Mackinac. Were it not for the discovery late in the process writing this book, of Stella King's likely Native heritage (hidden by her during her lifetime), I would not have

happened upon the census from 1849 of Stella's grandmother's birth on the island, July 29, 1849, and her burial at Saint Ann's, February 7, 1917. Previous research placed King on the island and her father and mother there for the first time in 1920. While this is accurate, she had many ancestors who lived, worked, and died on Mackinac. Though her great-grandfather Joseph Louis Asselin, married to Emerica, was born in Quebec, he was buried on Mackinac. This suggests the likelihood that Emerica, Stella's Native great-grandmother, may well have visited or spent time on the island too.

12. Lapine, oral history interview, June 20, 2020.

13. In 1962, the Indian Dormitory was no longer the island school. The newer brick school sits on the west end of the island near the end of the boardwalk. See the news section "Looking Back 50 Years" in the *St. Ignace (MI) News*, September 15, 2011.

14. A. T. Andreas, ed., *History of the Upper Peninsula of Michigan, Mackinac County* (Chicago: Western Historical Co., 1883), 22.

15. HBE Papers.

16. Andreas, *History of the Upper Peninsula of Michigan*, 21.

17. Ibid.

18. Ibid., 22.

19. Ibid.

20. See chap. 8 for islander Rosa Webb's full discussion of Mackinac's healthcare in the 1930s.

21. The French Colonial–style McGulpin House with its steep pitched roof is one of the oldest houses in the state of Michigan. William McGulpin owned a bakery on the island in 1820.

22. Obituary of Marie "Toots" McGulpin Weak, *Mackinac Town Crier*, June 25, 2020.

23. Irene Bunker Rickel's conversations with author, summer 2021, and online in February 2022.

24. Phil Porter, *Fudge, Mackinac's Sweet Souvenir* (Mackinaw City, MI: Mackinac State Historic Parks, 2001), 18–23.

25. Rosa Truscott Webb Papers, Keith Widder Library, Petersen Center, Mackinaw City, Mackinac State Historic Parks.

26. HBE Papers.

27. *Island News*, ed. and pub. Ruth Orton Camp, Mackinac Island, Michigan, June 20, 1948.

28. There is no known connection between Stella King and the King Beauty Salon, though one suspects it could have been a relative who owned the business.

29. Lapine, oral history interviews, summer 2020.

30. Ibid.

31. Email and oral history interviews with Stephanie Crane, June and August 2020.

32. The shipwreck of the *Cedarville*, an ore boat that collided with a Norwegian vessel in 1965, occurred 3.5 miles southeast of the Mackinaw Bridge.

33. Oral interview with Mackinac councilwoman Kathleen Hoppenrath, August 31, 2020. Also of interest is Hoppenrath's personal history on the island. Her mother, Cecilia Flanagan, worked on the Library Committee in the 1940s.

34. Daisy Peck was born in Greenville, Georgia, in 1863. Her family also had homes in Atlanta and New York City. They were living in their main domicile, a spacious home on the fashionable Peachtree Street in Atlanta when General William T. Sherman destroyed most of the city, burning what was in his path on the "March to the Sea."

35. Bernice McCullar, "Professor Writes Novels with Amazing Success," *Atlanta Journal Constitution*, September 19, 1966. McCullar notes that Professor Peck was a learned man, having graduated from Harvard University in 1757. He was paid $5,000 for a story, a phenomenal sum in the post–Civil War years of the nation. Most likely, the fee was for a serialized book-length story in the *New York Ledger*, the newspaper that published his weekly chapters.

36. Obituary, Delos Abiel Blodgett, *Grand Rapids Herald*, November 2, 1908. Also see the *Cyclopedia of Michigan*, 92–94.

37. One citation of Anthony's connection to Delos Abiel Blodgett may be seen in her 1904 inscription to a farmer, Grace Bartholomew, in the classic two-volume biography *Life and Work of Susan B. Anthony*, where she writes of "dear Mr. D.A. Blodgett" who is "purchasing so many Histories of Woman Suffrage to give to his friends." The books were not inexpensive items, having gilt titles and a gilt medallion on the front panels of each volume. Delos did his best to educate everyone he knew about the need for women to have equal rights.

38. Megan Marshall, *Margaret Fuller: A New American Life* (Boston: Houghton Mifflin Harcourt, 2013), 216, 237.

39. HBE Papers.

40. For an additional understanding of Southerner professor William Henry Peck, see his novel *The Stonecutter of Lisbon*, published by Robert E. Bonner at the *New York Ledger* in 1870. The book is fascinating for a number of reasons. It was written on the heels of the Civil War by a Georgian resident and a former slave owner. Daisy Peck Blodgett's father was a prolific author of some sixty historical novels, said to be very carefully and authentically researched. The book is a deeply sympathetic look at the oppressed stonecutters of Portugal, who were treated like slaves, according to Peck. The novel appears

to be written by a man of the South who finally understands the horror of slavery.

41. In addition to written documentation of Daisy Blodgett in the Grand Rapids and Washington, DC, newspapers, and in a study of "Colonial Families," her most valuable history has been preserved in descriptions of her life on Mackinac in the Bentley Historical Library (University of Michigan) and given by her daughter as documented in Porter, *View from the Veranda*, and most significantly in the papers of Helen Blodgett Erwin and Myrtis Peck Matthews. Blodgett also kept a number of personal journals and was a prolific letter writer. Those journals and the letters she received were stored in ten cooper barrels at The Rocks, the home of Daisy's daughter Mona Gaillard in Rock Creek Park. Regrettably for scholars, all the cooper barrels were tossed out when the estate was sold to John D. Rockefeller IV.

42. HBE Papers.

43. Ibid.

44. *Springville (Vermont) News*, November 17, 1892. The article discusses its native son, Blodgett, and the $7,200,000 that he divides equally among his two children and himself.

45. HBE Papers. This memoir was related to Helen verbatim by her own mother, Daisy Blodgett.

46. Ibid.

47. The D. A. Blodgett name in affiliation with the orphanage that he and Daisy Blodgett built has been expanded to a number of locations in Grand Rapids with group homes that provide safe haven for abused or neglected children.

48. *Grand Rapids Herald*, November 1908. As was customary in the days when only the husband, not the wife, received credit for major civic accomplishments, the large orphanage in Grand Rapids was called the D. A. Blodgett Home for Children. Years later, the term "orphanage" fell out of favor, and yet institutions with the updated term "group home" for children continue today, with some of the needy being sent to foster homes. Helen Blodgett Erwin writes in 1957 that she and her sister, Mona Gaillard, eventually donated the D. A. Blodgett Home run by their mother to the "Mary Free Bed" Recovery Home. Today this is a drug rehabilitation facility, and there are a number of D. A. Blodgett–affiliated group homes in the Grand Rapids area. Daisy would be heartened to know that this building and others connected to her work and that of Delos are still used to aid those in need.

49. See articles on this breakthrough accomplishment at the D. A. Blodgett Home for Children, including http://www.migenweb.org/kent/histories/dablodgett.html. Also under Daisy Blodgett's leadership in 1910, the orphanage conceived the idea of temporary

foster care and began to implement the plan.

50. Porter, *View from the Veranda*, 17 and 34. The letters written by Helen Erwin to F. G. Hammit are housed at the Bentley Historical Library, University of Michigan.

51. This cottage, Casa Verano, built by Daisy and Delos Blodgett and lived in by Daisy for fifty-five years, has a strong family legacy. Except for eight years, the home has been kept in the Blodgett family nearly 130 years, and since the early 1960s owned by the Goodwin family. Bruce, Lydia, and McDonald Goodwin, the present-day owners, are the great-grandchildren of Daisy.

52. Rose Eveleth, "Forty Years Ago Women Had a Hard Time Getting Credits Cards," *Smithsonian Magazine*, January 8, 2014. See documentation of women and minorities pushing for civil rights and how at long last in 1974, the Equal Credit Opportunity Act was passed, making it impossible for banks to continue denying credit on the basis of sex, religion, and race.

53. Katherine Doyle, "East Bluff, West Bluff, All Around the Town," *(Mackinac Island) Town Crier*, June 8, 1986.

54. Conveyed to HBE Papers and shared with author, 1975.

55. Ibid.

56. In order to bring the atmosphere and individuals alive, I have included dialogue snippets consistent with the tone and facts set forth in Helen Erwin's interviews with the author, and in her "daykeeper" logs. This inclusion points to Blodgett's contribution to horse culture.

57. Facts from HBE Papers.

58. Ruth Lawrence, ed., *Colonial Families of America* (New York: Colonial Dames of America and the National Americana Society of New York, 1920), 218.

59. HBE Papers.

60. *Daykeeper*, the journal kept by Helen Blodgett Erwin, 1934–1936.

61. HBE Papers.

62. Ibid.

63. The early days of the charity Daisy Day were written up in the *Island News*, with the headline "Wear a Daisy," August 12, 1934.

64. Bill Loomis, "Before the Motor City, the Horse Age in Detroit," *Detroit News*, November 30, 2014.

65. Brandon Patterson, "Mackinac Island Icon, Don (the Duck) Andress Dies at 82," *Detroit Free Press*, April 24, 2018.

66. Porter, *View from the Veranda*, 22.

67. HBE Papers.

68. The DAR rightly came under fire in 1939 when the organization refused to have the African American opera singer Marian Anderson sing at D.A.R. Constitution Hall. Since that deplorable racist act, the organization has striven to rectify its past. The DAR has honored a number of outstanding women in recent history, including Mary Hemmings Bell, who was the slave of Thomas Jefferson. They have striven to give posthumous tributes to Native American women and those of all creeds and colors.

69. *Island News*, September 8, 1949.

Conclusion

1. From 1892 to 1938, Rose Webster owned and ran the Island House Hotel. Under her watch, this hotel with a spectacular view of the marina added a ballroom orchestra, high tea, and two large wings.

2. For the original marker and sign affiliated with the hotel, along with online history, see "Historical Marker—L982A—Lake View Hotel (Marker ID#L982A)," Michigan Department of Natural Resources, https://www2.dnr.state.mi.us/Publications/PDFS/ArcGISOnline/StoryMaps/mhc_historical_markers/pdfs/MHC491982012.pdf.

3. When Reuben and Maria built the hotel, it was first known as The Lake View House. Following Maria's ownership of the hotel, her daughter and son-in-law, Jeannie and Claude Cable, became the proprietors in 1880, changing the name to The Lakeview.

4. Along with Margaret McIntyre, owner of Hotel Iroquois, her three daughters who have been managers there for decades are Rebecca, Mary K., and Marti McIntyre.

5. Editor Stephanie Fortino of Mackinac Island's *Town Crier* writes that the historic photographs were found in the William H. Gardiner Collection on Mackinac, and that it was "State Park Commissioner Phillip Pierce, who suggested the state park expand its research in Black history at Mackinac Island." Fortino, "Black Entrepreneurs Started Island's Hospitality Industry," *(Mackinac Island) Town Crier*, June 18, 2022.

6. Christine Byron of Grand Rapids shared this information with Stephanie Fortino. "Black Entrepreneurs Started Island's Hospitality Industry," *(Mackinac Island) Town Crier*, June 18–24, 2022. For a biography of the fascinating, intellectual Phyllis Wheatley, whose work has been much anthologized, see "Phyllis Wheatley," Poetry Foundation, https://www.poetryfoundation.org/poets/phillis-wheatley.

7. Fortino, "Black Entrepreneurs Started Island's Hospitality Industry," June 18–24, 2022.

8. Iola Fuller Goodspeed, *The Loon Feather* (New York: Harcourt, Brace & World, 1940). A number of readers and critics have taken offense at her characterization of Native people.

Woolson's *Anne* fares better in terms of presenting a mixed-race family without bias.

9. Ruth Orton Camp began publishing about Mackinac in the *Island News*, July 5, 1947. It was published during the months of June–September and available to readers in the Straits region.

10. Ruth Camp had been a writer for many years and gained attention for her piece about Hull House, a settlement in Chicago that fostered childcare and gave donations to the needy. In 1943, the *New York Times* wrote of Camp taking on the duty of acting director of Hull House, and she is quoted as saying that she hoped "to aid in childcare problems of mothers in war works." Here is one more "Great Woman" finding a way to contribute to society during wartime.

11. Porter, *View from the Veranda*, 64.

12. Edith Hamilton, *Mythology* (New York: Little, Brown & Co., 1942).

13. Margaret Fuller, *Summer on the Lakes, in 1843* (Boston: Little, Brown, 1844), 179.

14. In another connection, Brenda and Trisha's grandfather, Darcy Bunker, was a talented Mackinac horseman who lived in Washington, DC, for fifteen winters when working for Helen Erwin, daughter of another "Great Woman," Daisy Blodgett. Oral interview with Leanne Brodeur, July 2012.

15. Positions of note at these institutions include Stephanie McGreevy, executive director at the Community Foundation; councilwomen Anneke Myers and Kay Hoppenrath on the City Council; Mayor Margaret Doud at the Medical Center; Marlee Brown at the Mackinac Island State Park Commission; and Rebecca MacIntyre, founder of the Mackinac Arts Council.

Index